Michael Kuhn | Shujiro Yazawa (eds.)

Theories about and Strategies against Hegemonic Social Sciences

BEYOND THE SOCIAL SCIENCES

Edited by Michael Kuhn, Hebe Vessuri, Shujiro Yazawa

ISSN 2364-8775

1   *Michael Kuhn,* Shujiro Yazawa *(eds.)*
    Theories about and Strategies against Hegemonic Social Sciences
    ISBN 978-3-8382-0586-1

Michael Kuhn | Shujiro Yazawa (eds.)

THEORIES ABOUT AND STRATEGIES AGAINST HEGEMONIC SOCIAL SCIENCES

ibidem-Verlag
Stuttgart

Bibliografische Information der Deutschen Nationalbibliothek
Die Deutsche Nationalbibliothek verzeichnet diese Publikation in der Deutschen Nationalbibliografie; detaillierte bibliografische Daten sind im Internet über http://dnb.d-nb.de abrufbar.

Bibliographic information published by the Deutsche Nationalbibliothek
Die Deutsche Nationalbibliothek lists this publication in the Deutsche Nationalbibliografie; detailed bibliographic data are available in the Internet at http://dnb.d-nb.de.

This book was initially published by the Center for Glocal Studies (CGS), Seijo University, Japan. Permission for this republication was kindly given by the CGS.

∞

Gedruckt auf alterungsbeständigem, säurefreien Papier
Printed on acid-free paper

ISSN 2364-8775

ISBN-13: 978-3-8382-0586-1

© *ibidem*-Verlag
Stuttgart 2015

Alle Rechte vorbehalten

Das Werk einschließlich aller seiner Teile ist urheberrechtlich geschützt. Jede Verwertung außerhalb der engen Grenzen des Urheberrechtsgesetzes ist ohne Zustimmung des Verlages unzulässig und strafbar. Dies gilt insbesondere für Vervielfältigungen, Übersetzungen, Mikroverfilmungen und elektronische Speicherformen sowie die Einspeicherung und Verarbeitung in elektronischen Systemen.

All rights reserved. No part of this publication may be reproduced, stored in or introduced into a retrieval system, or transmitted, in any form, or by any means (electronic, mechanical, photocopying, recording or otherwise) without the prior written permission of the publisher. Any person who does any unauthorized act in relation to this publication may be liable to criminal prosecution and civil claims for damages.

Printed in the EU

BEYOND THE SOCIAL SCIENCES

The social sciences, what do they let us know about the world's social, a place of war, of poverty, *and* of wealth? Certainly, one cannot make them responsible for what is going on in the world. Is there any spot on the globe that is not somehow involved in a war? Is there any place in the world, where the growth of wealth does not exist next to the growth of poverty? Certainly, war, wealth, and poverty are the major essentials of "modernity" and they have been in the forefront of social concern for more than 200 years. The social sciences have been researching the social world with a multitude of professional thinkers also for over two centuries. Has the knowledge they gained helped to make anything better, or at least helped to reduce wars and poverty? Obviously not. Or is even the opposite is the case? Again, one cannot accuse the social sciences for this, knowledge is knowledge, but what is their impact upon the world? Not much, one must conclude, considering the fact that we still live in a world of war, wealth, and poverty. Hence, we have to raise the question what social thought under the regime of the social sciences is all about then.

The book series "Beyond the Social Sciences" publishes social thought and invites readers and writers to reflect on the social sciences and their approach to social thought, the theories they contribute to understand the social world, and how to go beyond the social sciences' way of thinking about the world.

It particularly invites contributions that critically reflect upon:

- the disciplinary structure of social sciences
- key theories founding global social science theorizing
- epistemological and methodological issues of global social sciences
- institutional aspects of global social sciences
- international collaboration practices
- the global social science structure
- international discourse practices
- international science policies
- alternative approaches to social thought

Series editors are:

Michael Kuhn, World Social Sciences and Humanities Network (World SSHNet), Achim

Hebe Vessuri, Universidad Nacional Autónoma de México (UNAM), Mexico City

Shujiro Yazawa, Seijo University, Tokyo

Foreword

From the beginning of the 1990s onwards, irrespective of individual terminological preferences, we have been living in a new age of the world, namely "The Era of Globalization." Whether we take it positively or negatively, we have to acknowledge that the overwhelming wave of globalization in the fields of economics, politics, society, culture or whatever arena we take into consideration has been connecting every corner of the world and shrinking the globe.

At the same time, we also recognize that globalization has more often than not brought about and strengthened the power imbalance between "the center," i.e. Euro-American developed countries, and "the peripheral," i.e. mostly non-Euro-American developing countries. That is why some opponents of globalization criticize it for being nothing more than "Americanization" or "McDonaldization." The field of social sciences is no exception to this criticism in that its theories, methods, presumptions, objectives, scopes have long been based on, (re)produced within, and dominated by Euro-American traditions.

Accordingly, those social scientists who are sensitive to undesirable situations in the present globalized world are strenuously addressing the issues of Euro-American-centric hegemonic social sciences. The World Social Sciences and Humanities Network (World SSH Net) is one of the most active networks of social scientists problematizing the hegemonic social sciences in the era of globalization. According to the mission statement articulated on its website (http://www.worldsshnet.org/home), the World SSH Net 1) aims to develop a world social sciences and humanities community, beyond the hegemonic patterns of Western science, 2) reflects on social phenomena worldwide, beyond the theoretical frameworks of nationally confined societies, and 3) promotes dialogue and cooperation between scholars from the social sciences and the humanities, beyond the boundaries of disciplines.

This book, Theories about and Strategies against Hegemonic Social Sciences, represents one of the recent results of the World SSH Net's endeavors to materialize its mission. On 12/13 May 2012, the World SSH Network held a "thinkshop," entitled "Theories about and Strategies against Hegemonic Social Sciences," in Tokyo, which was co-sponsored by the Center for Glocal Studies, Seijo University, Japan, and the Calouste Gulbenkian Foundation, Portugal. The papers presented at the thinkshop were elaborated afterwards by their respective contributors by incorporating the outcomes of the discussion and published in this book.

The Center for Glocal Studies (CGS) is a research center established just four years ago at Seijo University for 1) formulating and establishing a new research field, "glocal studies," and 2) promoting this new field. Refining the concept of "glocalization," which was introduced by the British sociologist Roland Robertson in the middle of the 1990s, the center has tried to formulate "glocal studies" in order to shed light on hitherto inadequately examined socio-cultural dynamics within myriad "contact zones" between the "global and local," the "central and peripheral," and the "external and internal" realities of various different groupings and/or communities. In conducting glocal studies, the CGS focuses on developments that symmetrize what is thought of as an asymmetrical socio-cultural power balance between Euro-American and non-Euro-American nations. In this sense, the Center for Glocal Studies shares the same interests as the World SSH Net and the contributors to this book.

Since its establishment, the CGS has organized and held many symposiums, workshops and lectures on glocalization. Meanwhile, one of our colleagues, Prof. Shujiro Yazawa, and the president of the World SSH Net, Dr. Michael Kuhn, suggested to us that the center would be a co-sponsor of a thinkshop focusing on changing scientific concepts and paradigms in the era of globalization. As we share the same interests and views, the center wholeheartedly agreed and decided to co-sponsor the thinkshop as part of our research endeavors.

At the subsequently held thinkshop, 17 social scientists from Europe, Africa, South/East/Southeast Asia and Central America came together and presented their expertise and discussed theories about and the strategies against the hegemonic social sciences. At the thinkshop, I, as one of its participants sometimes witnessed heated debate over sensitive issues, such as the concept of human rights. The debate sometimes became so hot that short cooling-off breaks were needed. As a whole, however, the thinkshop effectively functioned as a "platform" for revealing less visible reflections on the world social science system.

I am confident that the accomplishments published in this present book represent a small but invaluable step forward for every social scientist willing to face up to one of the most irresolvable challenges in the era of globalization; developing theories about and strategies against the hegemonic social sciences.

Professor Tomiyuki Uesugi
Director
Center for Glocal Studies (CGS)
Seijo University

Table of Contents

Foreword   5
Tomiyuki Uesugi

Preface   13
Michael Kuhn, Shujiro Yazawa, Kazumi Okamoto

Theories about "Globalization" and "Hegemonic Sciences"?   19

Philosophies and Ideologies of Globalization: Postmodernism, Postcolonialism and How to Go Beyond Them   21
Léon-Marie Nkolo Ndjodo

"Hegemonic Science": Critique Strands, Counterstrategies, and Their Paradigmatic Premises   61
Michael Kuhn

What is Hegemonic Science? Power in Scientific Activities in Social Sciences in International Contexts   103
Kazumi Okamoto

Counter Strategies? **135**

The Emergence of Hegemonic Social Sciences
and Strategies of Non (counter) Hegemonic Social Sciences 137
Kwang-Yeong Shin

The Transcendental Dimension
in the Construction of the Universal Social Sciences 165
Shujiro Yazawa

Three Decades of Chinese Indigenous Psychology: A Contribution
to Overcoming the Hegemonic Structures of International Science? 183
Doris Weidemann

Towards Internationalism:
Beyond Colonial and Nationalist Sociologies 207
Sujata Patel

Who is the Social Scientist in the Twenty-First Century?
Commentaries from Academic and Applied Contexts
in the Mainstream and the Periphery 231
Hebe Vessuri

Making Social Knowledge One-Step Outside Modern Science:
Some Cases of Social Knowledge-
Making Strategies from Peripheries 267
Kumaran Rajagopal

Alternative Theories? **297**

A Universal but "Nonhegemonic" Approach to Human Rights in
International Politics: A Cosmopolitan Exploration for China 299
Sang-Jin Han, Guimei Bai, Lei Tang

Individualization and Community Networks in East Asia:
How to Deal with Global Difference in Social Science Theories? 333
Young-Hee Shim, Sang-Jin Han

Notes on the Contributors 363

Preface

This book is a publication of the project "Social Sciences in the Era of Globalization," conducted by KNOWWHY GLOBAL RESEARCH in collaboration with the World SSH Net, funded by the Calouste Gulbenkian Foundation. The aim of this project is to engage a group of international and interdisciplinary scholars about the challenges the social sciences are facing in the era of globalization.

Since the publication of the Wallerstein Report in 1996, substantial changes in world conditions have dramatically altered the social sciences and the way social scientists view their discipline. These have affected the social sciences more than any paradigmatic shift of theories within a given approach to science ever could do. To mention only a few:

First, the transformation of the only real alternative society system, the project of socialism in the Soviet Union, later followed by China, into globally acting market economies, the very society model the Soviet Union, China, and their allies around the world had opposed for almost a century.

Second, together with the dissolution of this alterative society model, the abolishment of an alternative science system and of an alternative approach to social science thinking has transformed Historical Materialism, the set of theories fundamentally opposing the science model of capitalism and their representative democracies and its scientific interpretations of the world, into a mere variation of the multiplicity of relativized theories within the Western science system.

This, the transformation of the whole world into an arena for the competition for power between nation-states and using the growth of global capital to exploit this growth for their global political power, called "globalization," has shifted the battle between antagonistic science approaches into a competition about theories within the Western model of science reflecting about a widely unified world—and into a "battle of cultures" with a newly emerging opposition. Overcoming the threat of a war between the two world society systems and the unification of the world under the regime of global capitalism has replaced the threat of a 'hot' war between the two world powers by a world of wars.

Thirdly, probably based on the same Western model of science, the emergence of new science universes, have eroded the global scientific monopoly and theories, so far mainly created in Europe and the United States. It is evident that significant and powerful science arenas are emerging in countries like China, India, Brazil, South Africa, Korea, and Mexico. Namely, both the sciences in China and India are growing rapidly and have the potential to become global scientific superpowers.

Fourthly, and less visible than the changing scientific world power architecture, but certainly more significant in effect, are changes related to scientific concepts and paradigms that guide social thoughts. While Euro-American sciences have, to a great extent, set the global scientific standards for the social and human science knowledge productions during the last century, the era of globalization created a space for developing new approaches to social science thinking, which question the monopoly of European paradigms and concepts. Academics in the former colonies of Europe, as well as in other newly created states, have started expressing their grievances about their work as being victims of "Western" scientific colonization that still colonizes their forms of thoughts and reflections. Social scientists that have had little or no colonial experience, likewise, complain about imposed knowledge concepts and agendas, and claim a new role in the globalizing scientific practices and discourses. Some Asian scholars entirely refuse to accept the Western knowledge concepts any longer, and propose "Islamic" or "Hindu" social sciences based on their indigenous religious-cultural backgrounds, incorporating an explicit opposition to Western knowledge paradigms. Academics in Africa experience a similar shift, divided between those who defend a catching-up strategy aiming at a deeper inclusion inside the existing science world and those who reject collaborations with Western-dominated sciences and defend a refuge into indigenist and nativist alternatives. Latin American scholars, who have had a longer history of defending a genuine "Latin-American" thinking, combine local knowledge with radical rereadings of Western scholarship to challenge the Western intellectual knowledge monopoly.

Aspiring for a nonhegemonic science world, the group of scholars gathered in this project, together with other invited colleagues who have participated in a series of three international thinkshops, reflect on the effects these changes in the world have on the world's social science system and its ways of theorizing.

The first thinkshop took place in Tokyo in May 2012 under the title "Theories about and Strategies against Hegemonic Sciences." The second thinkshop will take place in Mexico City in February 2013 and focuses on "Multiple Epistemologies: Science and Space—Science and Culture—Science and Society." The third thinkshop will take place in Zwickau, Germany, in September 2014 and will focus on "The Global social science world : Beyond the 'Western' universalism."

The outcomes of these reflections on all thinkshops will be published in a report with the working title "Social Sciences in the Era of Globalization."

This book with the title "Theories about and Strategies Against Hegemonic Social Sciences" is the first publication of the project group. It publishes the outcomes of the first thinkshop hold in Tokyo at the Seijo University, Center for Glocal Studies.

This book presents its findings in three sections. Section 1 offers thoughts about "Theories about Globalization" and "Hegemonic Sciences." With contributions from scholars from Europe, Africa, and East Asia, it discusses whether the existing theories of hegemonic sciences allow us to understand how they were and are constructed and if the strategies implied in these theories are appropriate for building a nonhegemonic science world. Section 2, "Counter Strategies," presents thoughts from colleagues from East

Asia (Korea and Japan), Europe, India, and Latin America. These deepen the debate from section 1 with alternative ideas about the challenges and ways of transforming the universalization of the Western model of science into nonhegemonic sciences. Section 3 contains two chapters, jointly written by colleagues from in East Asia (China and Korea), that invite the readers to consider alternatives ways of theorizing about the issues of human rights and individualization.

On behalf of the project group and all other thinkshop participants the editors of this book want to express their gratitude to Seijo University and the Calouste Gulbenkian Foundation. Saying this is not just a matter of politeness. International science collaborations are, last but not least, also very costly. Without the engaged support of such innovative and creative foundations and universities, social science thinking would more and more drown in the circular reproduction of mainstream theorizing. We also want to thank Helen Jardine and Jack Rummel for editing the chapters, all written by nonnative English speakers, into proper American English.

Editors: Michael Kuhn and Shujiro Yazawa
Associate Editor: Kazumi Okamoto

Theories about "Globalization" and "Hegemonic Sciences"?

Philosophies and Ideologies of Globalization: Postmodernism, Postcolonialism and How to Go Beyond Them

Léon-Marie Nkolo Ndjodo

Introduction

Contributing to the profound changes in capitalism over the last forty years, a transformation into new radical forms mainly based on financialization and speculation, have been the French poststructuralists Foucault, Derrida, Deleuze, Lyotard, Baudrillard, Bataille and Barthes, noted for their considerations on heterogeneity, fragmentation, chaos, fluidity, flexibility, frivolity, volatility, but also circulation and itinerancy. In response to the de-territorialization of capital and the development of its structures on a world-wide scale, these authors claim that the traditional social sciences have been incapable of giving a clear concept of man and society. They mainly stress the failure of these sciences to totalize the ideas of reason, objectivity, history and truth. Following that radical deconstruction of the so-called European "rationalist," "materialist" and "positivist" heritage with its great oppositions or dichotomies (knowledge/ignorance, truth/falsity, science/non-science, matter/spirit, civilized/barbarians, man/woman, center/periphery, master/slave, domination/resistance, hegemony/counter-hegemony), the poststructuralists proclaim the "end of modernity" and the rise of a new post-philosophical, post-historical, post-esthetic, post-humanist and post-ideological world. In their disciples Fukuyama, Vattimo, Bell, but also Rorty, the rejection of sense and reason in general is closely combined with the apology for irony, intuition, metaphor, symbols, images, religious thought and legends. How this project of deconstruction of modernity plays a coherent part in the consolidation of the power of global capitalism, with the ideological purpose to present as a natural necessity the contemporary developments of this authoritarian mode of production, is what we aim to explain. In this sense the apology for "peripheries," "subaltern social activities," "hybridism," "powers of minorities" perfectly accompanies and reinforces the hegemony of neo-capitalism. Our main work hypothesis is that there is a philosophy and an ideology that justifies contemporary and free-floating contemporary capitalism, and it has a name: postmodernism. Postcolonialism, obsessed by diasporas, exile, double consciousness, "identity" presented as "hybrid," is its replication in the Third World (Africa, Caribbean islands, Asia, Latin America). To give sense to our hypothesis, we make four observations.

1.

The history of globalization is necessarily bound up with modern history's bourgeois mode of production; consequently, globalization is the late age or logical result of capitalist development: the multinational age.

Three aspects need to be taken into account to explain the emergence of contemporary or neo-capitalist modernity:

The political aspect

This first aspect implies the decline of the nation-state and the passage to the reality and concept of Empire.

In historic terms, we have to remember that by the sixteenth century Europe was characterized by the waning of feudal structures, the constitution of monarchic power, the birth of the state as the dominant social form, the formation of nation, the emergence of a unified bourgeoisie as the dominant social class establishing its political control on society during the French Revolution (Bloch 1968; Elias 1985; Hauser and Renaudet 1938; Heers 1966; Mandrou 1980).[1]

In Hobbes, Rousseau, Kant, Hegel and even during the imperialist period of the nineteenth century, we observe the theorization of the idea of the political sphere as the space of democratic articulation of private and public, the citizen and the individual, the space where all social contradictions must be rationally, metaphysically and practically resolved. That marks the key moment of political modernity with its two key concepts of sovereignty and territory. In Hegel, for example, State power represents the manifestation of Spirit. The State realizes the end of history, the destiny

---

[1] This is a long and complex process where we can see the struggle between three social figures: the ancient nobility became aristocracy, royalty and bourgeoisie.

of humankind rationally moving towards freedom, law and justice beyond the chaos of particular and egotistical interests of an economic civil society with its needs and desires (Hegel 1940a: 258–260).[2]

But with the collapse of socialist ideologies in the 1990s, the criticism of the State has become the rule. The emergence of new non-official and non-institutional actors (the "new civil society") has marked a new age characterized by the end of imperialism giving way to "Empire." This ideology of Empire, as we can see particularly in Hardt and Negri (2000), is the one which precisely designates the transition from modern social organization to a postmodern social situation. Now the latter is clearly the current phase of capitalist globalization. The "death of the State", the "end of the Nation" have imposed a concept of a new global and cosmopolitan world that privileges micro-organizations like tribes, clans, religions, villages, sexual identities, etc. This cosmopolitanism tries to rethink the Kantian notion of hospitality and has also introduced a new notion of subsidiarity against the modern concept of sovereignty (Hardt and Negri 2000: 132). Globalization is the triumph

---

[2] Hegel developed an organicist conception of the link between State and civil society. The first one is the incarnation of the universality of reason while the second one is the manifestation of desire, instinct and interest. Their reciprocal articulation imposes a logic of superiority of the political sphere that guarantees and maintains the economic sphere without destroying it. By his theory, Hegel gave an original definition of what the modern State is: the unification of the citizen and the individual.

of particularisms, the reign of fragmentation and locality (Elshtain 1998: 31; Schambra 1998: 51–53; Wolfe 1998: 19). While identities are not ever fixed, or do not have any foundations (Vattimo 1987), while identities are unstable and mobile, the subject of postmodern globalization is then a "hybrid man" who revendicates diversity, migration, statelessness, etc. He does not belong to any social, national, political or ideological organization: he is a citizen of the world.

The economic aspect

Another perspective in approaching globalization is given by studying the economic evolution of capitalism. As I. Wallerstein, F. Jameson or Ernest Mandel have said, three phases characterize the multiple historic transformations of capitalism: the market stage, the industrial stage and the consumerist stage. The first stage is marked by the freedom of economic actors, as we can see during the sixteenth and seventeenth centuries and discussed by such classic authors as A. Smith, A. Ferguson, and J.-B. Say; this stage marks the birth of a new economic and social system based on the infinite process of production, reproduction and accumulation of capital, a process of auto-expansion with this fundamental consequence: the commodification of all social activities and the transformation of public space into a unique commercial arena where particular interests are at war (Wallerstein 1990: 11–14)[3].

The second stage of capitalism is marked by the monopoly obtained by the State and the fusion of the economic and the administrative spheres, as we can see in Lenin; at this particular stage the need to concentrate capital through industrial development and financial activities pushes the capitalist system to transform into imperialism, meaning the military domination of the world (Lenin 1967: 14–21). The third stage is characterized by the hegemony of the financial structures of the economy, which give a multinational dimension to contemporary capitalism, or consumption. This multinational capitalism is the postmodern one, founded on the new virtual economy of media which makes capital more mobile, volatile, flexible and completely unregulated (Jameson 1991). Determined by the technological revolution of information and communication on the one hand, and the destruction of the "Fordist compromise"[4] on the other, this postmodern stage is the late stage of

---

[3] We know through Marx, Engels and Fernand Braudel that the freedom of economic activities claimed by classical economists in the first stage of capitalism is a complete illusion.

[4] According to the model of managerial capitalism introduced by Henry Ford the possibility exists of a concordance of interests between workers and the capitalist class. This idea is the basis of the theory of "l'embourgeoisement du salariat." The collapse of this theory during the 1970s opened the way to the neo-liberal forms of the capitalist economy.

capitalism (Boltansky and Chiapello 1999; Vakaloulis 2001: 70–100).

The cultural and esthetic aspect

Globalization has a cultural aspect. During its first period, capitalism produced a cultural figure, realism, as the true representation of reality and daily life in all its aspects (Balzac, Flaubert, Sand, Zola, Courbet). Realism gives priority to observation, experimentation, experience and objectivity; in literature, music, architecture and painting the bourgeois class tries to contest classical and aristocratic esthetic values by opening new forms or styles which aim to produce an imitation of nature. In a particular historical context where social struggles arise, the adoption of the positivist method, which tends to describe facts, is crucial for the artist. The second cultural period of capitalism is marked by the emergence of modernism with its cultural enthusiasms for machines and industrial civilization (Baudelaire, Le Corbusier, Mies van der Rohe, futurism, cubism). However, the apology for the machine is not made outside of a certain reaffirmation of the power of imagination and passion in a sense reminding the esthetics of Enlightenment (Shaftesbury, Dubos, Hutcheson, Hume, Diderot, Rousseau) ; modernism will then be defined by Baudelaire as the conjunction, or the fusion, in art of rationality, universality, eternity, objectivity, essential with passion, transitoriness, fashion, fantasy, the inessential, the singular, the bizarre (Baudelaire 1992: 237–254). The third cultural and esthetic period of capitalism is defined by the complete integration of the economic and cultural spheres with the idea that art is a pure commodity. Since Baudrillard's remarks on "consumption society" one can observe the transformation of cultural productions into commodities (Baudrillard 1970). The commodification of art is then the first characteristic of the current stage of capitalism, marked by the universal triumph of exchange value (Jameson 1991: 16). As immediate consequences of this commodification of life and art are the waning of notions such as author, personal style, creativity, beauty, sense and significance of art constructions, coherence of esthetic forms, utopia of esthetic creation, revolutionary art, separation of beauty from the market, exactly in the terms of what was severely criticized by some authors as the "ravages of the cultural industry" (Adorno 1989: 33–36). Postmodern esthetical productions are therefore deeply chaotic, anarchical, instable, fragmented, heterogeneous, but also superficial, insignificant and free-floating (Barthes 1973). In parallel, due to the disappearance of the notion of the "work of art," each object can be considered as esthetic. According to Jameson, the esthetization of the realm is the second great feature of contemporary capitalism (Jameson 1991: 15–16). Both processes of commodification of culture and esthetization of reality are the characteristic of postmodernism that designates the ensemble of cultural productions proper to global and multinational capitalism. Postmodernism is "the cultural logic of late capitalism" (Jameson 1991: 22; 31–32).

So globalization is the late stage of capitalism considered as a system. What about the philosophy and the ideology which ratify it as a historic force?

2.

There exists a philosophy and an ideology of globalization, or late capitalism: postmodernism

As a philosophy, postmodernism aims to consider the instability and the chaos of contemporary times through a severe criticism of the Enlightenment with its modern ideas of reason, science, emancipation, freedom, justice, progress, history, totality, sense, revolution, coherent art, etc. (Lyotard 1979: 7–9). The ambition of postmodernism is, contrary to the great construction of the Eurocentric approach (Descartes, Spinoza, Rousseau, Voltaire, Diderot, Kant, Hegel, Marx...), to "re-open reason" with the promotion of "alternative logics and rationalities," the reinvestment of memory and the return to archaic forms of thought such as instinct, intuition, the sacral, religion, myth, desire, sensation, etc. Postmodernism seems to open the way to a new irrationalism. The trend is then to promote "ethno-sciences" and "ethno-methods". For a better comprehension of this process, the following points are fundamental.

Nietzschean genealogy

Nietzsche's philosophy represents the basis of postmodernism while it expresses a violent reaction against the true spirit of modernity and all the ideals of the Enlightenment. Nietzsche belonged to the imperialist period of Western thought, and his approach is characterized by the destruction of reason and an apology for social inequality (Habermas 1988: 105–108; Lukàcs 1958: 267–348; Nietzsche 1993a: 933–1024). Against Hegel's dialectics and the historical materialism of Marx, Nietzsche called for hardening and barbarizing social relationships through the return, using the metaphor of Dionysus, to instinct and primitivism (Nietzsche 1994). His disgust for concept and philosophy led him to trust what he considered as non-rational productions of spirit: poetry and music. To him, as to the sophists, his masters, discourse must avoid any rational contagion by the new privilege given to illusion, irony, tragedy, perspectivism, metaphor, aphorism, etc. The critique of the depthless, the hatred of metaphysics and of any approach governed by Being signals in this philosophy the complete victory of body, appearances and surfaces (Nietzsche 1993b: 28–33). Through his recognition of the power of myths and symbols (Nietzsche 1993c: 1239–1260), Nietzsche is the hero of contemporary and postmodern relativist nihilism. Since this philosopher, the conviction in the indifferentiation between truth and non-truth, science and non-science, knowledge and falsity, the acceptance of the idea of pluralities of knowledge is a common thread in the discourse of philosophy.

Heidegger's phenomenology and hermeneutics

Heidegger was a disciple of Nietzsche's. His ambition was to rethink Western metaphysics with the objective of permitting its escape from the closure of reason, subject, consciousness imposed by the Aristotelian approach. To him the great error of the ancient thinkers was to have handled Being through a theoretical method implying the use of reflection, concept and categories: Form (Aristotle), Idea (Plato), Reason (Descartes), Category (Kant), Spirit (Hegel), Matter (Marx). His conviction led him to an immediate certitude of Being which excludes any notion of Substance. This nonsubstantial and anti-intellectual approach brings out the mystical idea of a "pre-comprehension of Being." Heidegger claims: "We do not know what "being" is. However, once we ask 'what being is,' we are already installed inside a certain comprehension or understanding of the "is" without giving it any conceptual figure [...]. An ordinary and vague comprehension of being is a fact" (Heidegger 1964: 21). Phenomenology means that Heidegger considers Being outside of sense by involving domains such as anguish, fear or all that which designates the "otherness of reason" or its "difference" without corresponding to the Hegelian dialectics of self-consciousness of Spirit (Heidegger 1964: 165–178, 257–274). That "difference" does not need to be explained and theorized, but it corresponds to what Heidegger calls "banality." That banality needs to be submitted to interpretation. Heidegger achieves his philosophy with an appeal to esthetic sensibility and art that he considers opposed to the work of science, concept, technique and analytical philosophy. A matter of esthetics and interpretation, truth is also a matter of faith, revelation and secrecy. At this stage Heidegger's phenomenology joins H. Gadamer's hermeneutic approach with his notion of a "nonmethodic truth of human sciences" (Gadamer 1996). The apology for language and discourse (being-language) in a neo-pragmatist philosopher like Rorty is the direct consequence of this hermeneutic philosophy.

Poststructuralist relativism

Poststructuralism is a tendency of contemporary philosophy represented by the posterity of Nietzsche, Heidegger and Lévi-Strauss, as we can see in Foucault, Derrida, Barthes, Bataille, Deleuze, Guattari, Kristeva, etc. The "French theory" privileges the criticism of subject sovereignty, continuity of history, rationality of reality and the capacity of philosophy and the social sciences to give sense to human reality. The "death of the subject" is one of the most famous statements of Foucault, who is both a neo-Nietzschean and a neo-pragmatic philosopher. The big concern of poststructuralist thinkers is "structure": autonomous, symbolic and emancipated from any anthropological and rational foundation for the benefit of assemblages and juxtapositions (Deleuze and Guattari 1975: 7–10; Derrida 1967). Inspired by Lévi-Strauss, these thinkers are interested in the historical genesis of ideals, the historical nature of scientific or moral concepts, but with the ambition to show that origins cannot be unique, and that each social or human production responds to a system of norms and rules which make it coherent without any intervention of clear reason or theoretical thought: "The particularity of norm, rule and system in regard to the conflict, to the function and significance that they determine and make possible, is not to be attributed to consciousness" (Foucault 1966: 372). It is important to note that these thinkers pursue a long tradition of the European ethnology coming from Lévy-Brühl with his great idea of a "primitive mentality" based under mysticism, but having its own "logic" because depending from "collective representations" of "inferior societies" (Levy-Brühl 2010: 84–118). Poststructuralists then have stressed the plurality of rationalities and rediscovered the "savage" within each culture. To them, as to Lévi-Strauss, science is not universal, rationality is contextual depending on unconscious structures of each society or culture, objectivity even in the domain of history is illusory (Lévi-Strauss 1962: 342–348)[5].

Knowledge and values are a matter of what Lévi-Strauss calls "bricolage" (ibid. 26–28): juxtapositions, super-positions, hazard, concreteness, etc. Foucault calls for the "insurrection of subjugated knowledges " (Foucault 1997: 8–13). Each system of knowledge is a pure discourse or a whole system of pure signs playing against each other (Foucault 1969). Thus, all discourses (science, philosophy, literature, myth, religion, sorcery...) have rigorously the same validity. To poststructuralists, epistemological relativism is strongly combined with the analysis of language and hermeneutics.

---

[5] We can remember Lévi-Strauss's assertion that the French Revolution is a subjective construction depending on the psychological constitu-tions or neuronal conditions of the person who is talking about that event.

Philosophies of the "End of History," doctrines of "Empire," theories of the "Clash of Civilisations" and Cultural Studies

These terms designate the galaxy formed by thinkers such as Fukuyama, thinking that liberal democracy is the achievement of human progress (Fukuyama 1992); Huntington, for who the world is an ensemble of people engaged in a global, tribal, racial, religious and cultural war, knowing that cultural elements take the place of economic and material infrastructures in the analysis of social facts (Huntington 1997); Appadurai, who considers that very far from being a factor of homogenization, globalization is, on the contrary, through the influence of global media and the work of imagination, a vector of the restored cultural heterogeneity and diversity of the world (Appadurai 2000); Hardt and Negri, for who imperialism, because of the cybernetic revolution, is dead, and the postmodernization of the economy has led to the end of boundaries, the modern State, ancient class oppositions of bourgeoisie/proletariat to bring out the new "multitude" which, alone, would be able to subvert Empire from below (Hardt and Negri 2000). These philosophical expressions stress the new role played by the circulation of a considerable number of people throughout the world. These people are supposed to escape any kind of attachment and affiliation, opening the great space of the world to all kinds of encounters.

All these doctrines have the specificity that they do not fundamentally contest the material and economic basis of contemporary capitalism. They have created an illusory opposition on the cultural level by avoiding confrontation with the historical reality of a violent economic system. By assuming the end of "class war" proclaimed by neo-liberal authors, the position of postmodernism is definitively that capitalism is an inevitable and a necessary process. The world has a structure which is immovable and unchangeable. The wise decision is not to destroy this structure, because this is impossible, but to play inside it. It is then necessary to try individually, subjectively, to turn the system to one's own advantage by finding in its interior a little space for "new forms of life," presented as "alternative" and even "revolutionary" (Foucault 2001): drug consumption, nudist movements, street arts, marginal sexualities, and so on. In this perspective the utopia of an end to capitalism is decisively unrealistic. As stated by H. Lefebvre, the structures of the capitalist system are founded on constraints defined by global technocratic power, bureaucracy and markets. To give the impression of eternal capitalism, the new technocratic hegemonic class feels the need to undermine the rational, moral, esthetic, humanist and scientific bases of modernity. Regarding these poststructuralist, neo-pragmatic and postmodernist philosophies which give preeminence to formalism through the rejection of the dialectic approach of life, reality, society and history, Lefebvre and Nkolo Foé use the same expression: "philosophy of constraints" (Lefebvre 1971: 10, 25; Nkolo Foé 2008: 65–70).

The aim of these "philosophies of necessity," opposed to the "philosophies of freedom and emancipation," has methodically led to the theorization of fixity, stability, opportunism and pragmatism.

These philosophies finally constitute ideologies, meaning systems of thinking aimed clearly at the consolidation of capitalist social order with its unequal social relations. These theories of fragmentation first avoid the description of the process of new capital which needs to be more volatile and fragmented in order to create the conditions for a more intensive accumulation process. These theories are then the ideological aspect of the global capitalist hegemonic process. As underlined by F. Jameson, postmodernism is, once again, the "cultural logic of late capitalism," the ideological ratification and justification of neo-liberalism. If we consider the theory, proposed by Nkolo Foé, of the "double level" playing inside the vertical structure of capitalist practices—liquefaction at the inferior level of market interests and ossification at the superior level of global scale (Nkolo Foé 2008: 165–168)[6]–postmodernism can be reasonably considered diversion and mystification.

---

[6] According to Nkolo Foé, postmodernism is a philosophy and an ideology produced for the middle-class of the Western world. The objective is to disarm through rhetoric of cosmopolitanism and universalism. That demagogic discourse is necessary when capitalism needs to conquer new territories. Once that goal is achieved, meaning at the level of State power and global structures, the capitalist system responds with racism and apartheid, as we can see in Samuel Huntington's theory of the clashes of civilizations.

3.

Capitalist globalization has an African aspect: Structural Adjustment policies. As capitalism proper to social formations of peripheries, these policies have been philosophically and ideologically prepared through postcolonial theory.

In this order, we have to notice the following elements:

Structural Adjustment is the face of globalization in the Southern countries

Structural adjustment was the name given in the 1980s by a series of austerity plans imposed by the IMF (International Monetary Fund) and the WB (World Bank) to Southern countries in order to force their insertion into the new global process of accumulation requested by the expansion of capitalism. In Africa this insertion in the neo-liberal economy was particularly brutal: privatizations of state enterprises; deregulation policies and flexibility of the labor market; destruction of public wealth, education and transportation systems; the waning of peasant agriculture and a rural exodus; deflation of social protection systems; emergence of pandemics such as malaria and AIDS with millions and millions of victims; the collapse of salaries and remunerations for workers in both public and private sectors; the financialization of the economy; price inflation; the opening of national industry productions to world competition through multiple economy agreements between the EU (European Union) and ACP (Africa-Caribbean-Pacific) countries, and the list goes on. The results of all these neo-liberal processes by which multinational enterprises took over the control of African national economies can be seen in the general misery of the majority of African populations, the increase in poverty, the growth of socio-economic disparities and the intensification of social and ethnic conflicts everywhere inside the continent.

This material and historic enterprise of the liberalization of African economies has been made possible by philosophers inspired by Nietzsche, French poststructuralists and Oriental "critical" thought

These Southern authors have introduced, by the complete abandonment of the concept of class struggle as a methodical tool for the comprehension of the changes taking place in Southern societies, the ideas that Western modernity is not able to totalize the whole human experience. To them modern rationalist epistemology does not completely express the practices and the situations of non-European cultures with their periphery, subaltern, indigenous or endogenous practices. Consequently, they have decided to explore the "borders of modernity," the "marginal existences" of peoples of Southern countries. In Chakrabarty, for example, the limits of the Marxist model are underlined in its incapacity to take into account some local and singular Indian experiences involving gods, spirits, demons, angels, magic, etc. These authentic human experiences are supposed to operate outside of the universal concept of capital which, therefore, seems to have ignored them. Chakrabarty gives a name to these practices which "escape any kind of generalization produced by language": "difference," "resistance" (Chakrabarty 2009: 113–114, 119–123). Said shows that Oriental(ism) as well as Occidental(ism) were pure inventions of an imperial(ist) order (Said 1980). He pursues his demonstration by noting that beyond—but more precisely below—the great history of imperialism as a process of domination of some races, nations, people under other races, nations and countries, there exist some "micro-historicities" made from "fantastic encounters" between individuals and groups. Imperialism is not only a process of destruction; it has also offered a chance for people to create new cultural fusions. The idea of a "transnational culture" could then be formulated as well as one of a "new post-imperial humanism" based on migrations and diaspora populations (Said 2000: 20–28). Appadurai formulates the idea that due to the double influence of mass media and displacements of populations throughout the world, the imaginary and the imagination are now playing a central role in contemporary processes giving them a transcultural aspect (Appadurai 2000). Bhabha agrees fundamentally with Said and Chakrabarty on the issue represented by the "ambivalence" of imperial relation and the hybridist character of cultures (Bhabha 2007: 28–46).

The hybridism of cultures, the recognition of "cultural difference(s)" in an "international world," the cosmopolitan nature of identities which are fundamentally heterogeneous: these are some key principles of postcolonial theory. For this theory, globalization is not the problem, but the solution, not an obstacle but the opportunity, the occasion for the encounters of cultures and traditions. The crucial issue is not economy, but culture. We can then see that what characterized properly that postcolonial doctrine is the acceptance, despite an apparent criticism, of the world of global economic capitalism with its needs of social marginalization and exploitation. The notable difference here is that now domination, exclusion, marginalization, exploitation are theorized, claimed and assumed by the dominants themselves.

African postcolonialists like J.-F. Bayart, Kwame A. Appiah, A. Mbembe, J.-G. Bidima or Mudimbe, inherited this tradition of new cosmopolitanism or internationalism favorable to globalization. They have theorized the idea of a "historicity" proper to the African societies, which are viewed from a Western rationalist point of view as chaotic, instable, incoherent, ruled by intuitive and instinctive forces, fundamentally hedonistic, mystical, magical and corrupted. All these features make them unable or incapable to be conceptualized by the norm of logic of identity drawn by Western culture. Bayart develops a specific intellectual attitude aiming to recover African societies in their "banality" by showing that those societies are simply "similar to the others" in this particular sense that they develop their own endogenous anthropological and political logic (Bayart 1989: 27, 317). At this stage, African societies dispose of some "internal dynamics"[7] of containment of official hegemony

---

7   Bayart develops the concept of African civil society created by strate-gies and tactics (sacral, rejection of certain agricultural productions, refusal to work,

produced by the State and Science. These local and indigenous dynamics coming "from below" are ignored by classical political science (Bayart 1983). Time has come to rehabilitate them. To Appiah, like Mbembe, Africa's "proper historicities," which escape the rationality defined by the tradition of the Enlightenment, must be respected in an international coexistence of equal cultures, the "Babel of cultures" as their master Said said. Mbembe demands that African people deny the heritage of modernity with its positivist principle of "social utilitarianism of the human sciences" (Mbembe 2000: 26–27)[8]; he attempts to persuade them to "go out of the ghetto," to "get out of the great night" (Mbembe 2010) by responding to the appeal of a global world of flux and international exchanges.[9]

We can see that there is solidarity between an apology for mysticism on the one hand and a support given to globalization on the other. It is also the sense of the Appiah's calling for a "new cosmopolitanism" (Appiah 2008).

---

irony and humoristic attitudes) by which people try to de-totalize the hegemonic control of the public sphere by political power.

[8] Mbembe is convinced of the existence of forms of knowledge distinct from scientific knowledge, but having equal validity: faith, religion, paranormal phenomena, myth.

[9] This is the meaning of Mbembe's postmodernist and postcolonialist concept of "Afropolitanism." This concept claims to replace "dogmatic" and "racist" ideologies of African liberation and unification: pan-Africanism, socialism, Marxism, nationalism, rationalism, etc.

The conviction that African progress towards modernity depends on the way that African political elites would use brutality, violence and constraint to develop a new form of capitalist system is the key position in African postcolonialist theories.

Common to all Indian and African postcolonialist thinkers is their general and massive apology for social inequalities. If one notices the de-dramatization of the consequences of colonial and imperial domination in Bayart as well as in Said, Bhaba, Appadurai, Chakrabarty, one can also certainly observe a strong tendency to justify violence. To Bayart, the main weakness of the African State rests on its incapacity to convert violence into productivity. The merit of a concept of "civil society" will then consist in undermining the State in order to permit the constitution of a dominant class whose duty as well as "historic mission" will be the reinforcement of social and economic exploitation. Bayart believes that Africa is an "unexploited continent where the power to produce violence is not achieved by the economic power of putting in work" (Bayart 1989: 45). To achieve this goal, it is necessary for the emerging postcolonial African bourgeoisie to move towards the "intensification of an internal exploitation" of subordinating populations (ibid.: 321). It is quite clear to Bayart that without economic and social subordinations of inferior categories of African societies no progress is possible.

That neo-Nietzschean vision was, on the level of philosophy and ideas, a response to the new neo-liberal demands of global capitalist accumulation addressed to the African continent. To Mbembe, that postcolonialist philosophy–now ideology–rests on this unbelievable and racist conception that African societies are ontologically ruled by corruption and charismatic leaders, and that necessity has now come to create the institutional conditions of primitive accumulation by the inscription of social exclusion in the Constitutions of African States and the codification of social domination through institutional texts. The African challenge, according to Mbembe, is the challenge of productivity. And this is impossible without trying to know how to build intensive systems of social inequality: "Africa cannot face the challenge of competition in the actual configuration of the world economy without increasing its productivity regimes, meaning definitively without putting in place intensive ways and severe means of construction of inequality and organization of social exclusion" (Mbembe 2000: 92–93).

The real problem and the true difficulty with the African bourgeoisie is that they are not coherent by privileging hedonism. That is the position of the postcolonial theory in Mbembe as well as in Bayart. To Bidima it is important to rediscover the unconscious, sexual and libidinal basis of African societies in order to liberate the "revolutionary potentialities of informal social practices" founded on crime (Bidima 1993: 240). That rediscovery of certain practices proper to African life and impossible to theorize through the dominant philosophical discourse of "identity" and "concept" pursues one objective: knowing how African people, each individually, can be a part of a world-system (Bidima 1995); not being outside of the capitalist system, but being an active element inside of that system. The category of Kairos (Bidima 1993: 240–245) in that way plays an important role because the indeterminism, the destabilization, the fugacity, the frivolity and the chaos of things it suggests opens a large space to the rationalization or the justification of crime, manipulation, trickery, domination and immorality as cardinal principles of African contemporary societies in their quest of modernity. It is clearly the apology for social violence.

All these postcolonialist thinkers are convinced that instead of fighting against the capitalist system, the most important solution for African and Southern people is to "play" with the system, to trick it, to find a place inside its stomach (not outside of it), to be "opportunistic" by turning it to their advantage. That is the reason why Nkolo Foé presents postcolonial theory as the accomplice of the violent insertion of Africa into capitalist globalization (Nkolo Foé 2008). Charles Romain Mbele holds that this doctrine is a "code of inequality" (Mbele 2010). We can finally see that the epistemological position in favor of the scientific and cultural relativism of values leads directly to political conservatism (Ngah Ndongo 2008).

4.

Going beyond postmodern and postcolonial capitalism is an urgent task. Now the criticism of contemporary capitalism is inseparable from the criticism of the limits of postmodernism and postcolonialism.

Chaos, indeterminism, violence, nihilism and domination cannot represent human destiny. That necessary enterprise of going beyond postmodern and postcolonial capitalism supposes some conditions. These are some of them:

Thinking "de-fragmentation"

This concept of "de-fragmentation" means that from the points of view of metaphysics, epistemology, esthetics and politics, nihilism is not a pertinent horizon. The error of postmodernism is to overestimate and misunderstand the power of difference, singularity and marginality.

Metaphysically since Heraclites, Hegel and Marx, we know that reality is made of conflict, contradiction and the harmony of contrary forces: light/darkness, cold/warmth, fairness/unfairness, goodness/wickedness (Heraclites). Being is a mix of being and non-being, and only the power of negativity can generate reality and things themselves. Things conserve in their interiority the opposition which denounces them as well as constitutes the justification of their existence. Hegel said that the "greatness of spirit is to lose its proper being and then, through this operation of giving death to itself, to find its true existence" (Hegel 1940b: 11). Reality is composed of pairs of contradictory elements which form a process going from immediate, virtual and uncertain forms to more and more elaborated and powerful ones (Hegel). Matter, spirit and society through economic forces are ruled by the law of dialectics (Marx, Lenin). With this perspective, negativity is not left alone or isolated or taken apart; difference is constantly reattached and linked to unity and identity. Negativity and difference are themselves an integrative part of the totality which itself is movement, progress, transition, relation. Difference belongs to totality and totality belongs to difference. Postmodernism is wrong by cutting this bridge between the two. It is the reason why mysticism, magic and irrationalism are called for.

From an epistemological point of view the dialectics of reason shows that Reason is not rigorously opposed to other faculties like sensation, desire, intuition, sensibility, reflection. Analytic is only one part, one aspect of Reason as a movement that supposes indeterminism, contingency, chaos coming from other forms of the human spirit (art, religion, economy, myth...). But chaos and contingency need to be reattached to necessity and objectivity in order to build sense and coherence through the totality of truth. The dialectics of reason assumes the limit inside the thought, nevertheless accepts at the same time, to go beyond it. Only in that way can truth be considered "not as a substance, but as a subject" (Hegel 1940b: 17). Truth and science refer to the activity of the spirit that, itself, is essentially activity. And what is named concept is not the product of sole reflection, but is the totality formed by reflection, emotion, intuition, sensation, desire, praxis, etc. Concept, or Reason, means the power of the human spirit to produce generalization and systematization, in other words to give sense and to bring up significance and clarification into anything. The perspective drawn by dialectic and historic materialism is also very clear on the fact that the relativity of each scientific, moral or esthetic truth corresponds to the limits of individual thought; but on the level of humankind, thought is infinite and absolute (Engels 1973). This is the way that dialectical materialism in Marx, Engels and Lenin solves the top question of the opposition between the relative and the absolute.

That "dialectical relativism" was rediscovered by Lefebvre, who showed in his criticism of poststructuralist and technocratic relativism that the dialectic method must rigorously reinvest the contemporary sites of indeterminism and the transitory, giving however to them a different orientation susceptible to re-opening the future (Lefebvre 1961: 40–45). The dialectic method will then mean the return to "life", "history" with their oppositions, aspirations, deceptions, struggles, conflicts, failures, dreams, etc. Esthetics, sensibility, meaning the praxis taken in the sense given by Marx, will play a central role here in this new communist approach applied to the new global society (Lefebvre 1961: 50). Thinking de-fragmentation does not merely mean being "against fragmentation" (Taylor 1994: 115–126), but being aware to the fact that that fragmentation must be considered as the ironic part of reality, the initial moment for totality, the revolutionary totality. This approach involves the rehabilitation of the totality of human senses through the rehabilitation of usage value. So the indiscriminate criticism of modern reason made by postmodern theory is an error. That error mainly consists in closing one's eyes on the real problem of modernity, which is how to go beyond capitalism by solving the hiatus between the economic modernization and the social modernization process. We can see even in Habermas the same need to open the future or utopias towards socialist forms of social organizations (Habermas 1981: 951–965). A non-capitalist modernity is a historical necessity. Compared to that project, postmodernism can be considered as part of a neo-conservative attitude.

In Africa as well as in the entire global South, the notion of "de-fragmentation" could mean going outside of the ideologies of identity and difference.

According to the Cameroonian philosopher Marcien Towa, the proliferation of these ideologies of identity and of the identities themselves is the symptom of a profound cultural crisis (Towa 1977: 598). That crisis appears only in a context of economic dependency and domination. The reason for this cultural crisis is clearly mentioned: the world system of domination and oppression by which capitalist imperialism destroys the productive forces of societies under its control (ibid.: 599–608). Parallel to that domination, this imperialism establishes alliances with the traditional forces of inequality inside these societies (feudalism, slavery, traditional religions, mystical movements, superstitions and mythologies). The consequence is the loss of creativity for the people, the loss of what Aimé Césaire called the "dialectics of needs." This concept supposes that each culture rests on the satisfaction of some intellectual and material aspirations proper to the concerned people and responding to their desire and will. Because of a colonial or imperial situation that left behind ruins, diseases, death and pillage, we participate in the collapse of indigenous cultural references, which are replaced by those of the masters (Césaire, 1956: 194–195)[10].

The personality of the colonized man is then double, fragmented, illusory and ambiguous. He considers himself a hybrid man. But hybridism is a biological fact and not a cultural one. Races, ethnic groups or clans can be biologically hybrids. But on the level of representations, ideas, ideals, aspirations, morals, knowledge, that is, the sphere of culture, the concept of hybridism, indeterminism, ambivalence, double consciousness no longer works. What is pertinent at this level is the will of all groups of society to methodically pursue a goal, an ideal, an objective, depending on what they have defined as value, depending on the options they have chosen for themselves (ibid.: 192). By doing so, the society will acquire a personality, an identity, a spirit, a specific style (ibid.: 200–201). And here is where culture lies: "the power, the capacity of each society to give to itself the richness of content" (ibid.: 191). In other words, culture is the creative power of the people, which gives them the possibility to be free. Senghor was wrong as were postcolonialist theorists.

---

[10] According to Césaire (and Fanon), the idea that imperialism has provided an opportunity for people throughout the world to meet is properly a heresy. Imperialism has been a factor in the separation of cultures.

The only way for African societies to emerge from the identity crisis is to become autonomous and conscious living centers for auto-production and auto-transformation.

This is not possible without destroying the system of domination and oppression, meaning without the destruction of capitalism itself (Towa 1977: 606). In this sense, postmodernism/post-colonialism is unhelpful, relativism is not the solution, because these "isms" do not recognize the "generic human identity" and replace it with a vague notion of "hybridism" or "internationalism" that gives support to culture disaggregation. Towa gave a severe opinion against both naturalization of identities and relativization of cultures. Both of them lead to inextricable contradictions and contribute to a unique process: cultural essentialism. Borrowing from Marx, the concept of generic identity means that human reason, in its universal power of conception, thinking, realization, is everywhere the same. This power of creation, beyond the differences of particular cultures, is the unique basis of each constituted culture. The only explanation for cultural differences, which Towa refers to as specific identity, comes from creation proper to each group of people. The younger Marx shows that the universality of man's action necessarily finds a site of specification once human praxis is confronted with different natural and social environments. In this regard, if praxis that aims to transform nature by transforming human nature itself is universal and constant, the results of that praxis will necessarily be different (Marx 1996: 113–116). But the only condition is to stop capitalist alienation (ibid.: 121). So it is important for African people to rediscover what Towa called the "transcendence" of their own culture through which they will be able to join the rest of the human community as free and proud people. This supposes the reconquest of their power to create, to manifest again, through a collective struggle, what Marx considered as the esthetic power of man, his power to change and organize his life fairly and freely. This has not been the way taken by African postmodernism.

"Transcendence" supposes a definition in advance of the means of struggle and the needs that must be satisfied.

Now some of these means can be borrowed from the dominant culture. According to Towa, all "constituted cultures" can be useful in that perspective because those elements have been put at our disposal so that we can use them and adapt them to this particular objective or need which is our own: freedom of choice (Towa 1977: 608–610). Césaire gave a magisterial name to it: "historical initiative" that supposes "historical audacity": courage, willpower, determination, obstinacy, self-confidence (Césaire 1956: 202). There is no other way for emancipation, which means recognizing as ours each cultural figure produced by any people throughout the world. It is the case with modern science and technology, which are not the property of any specific people who are presented as "rationalist," "positivist" or "materialist" (Western people), but are the common heritage of humankind developed everywhere: ancient Negro Egypt, ancient Greece, Persia, India, China, pre-Columbian

America, pre-colonial Africa (Ethiopia, Tombouctou, Gao...). African contemporary cultures can perfectly borrow these cultural elements that constitute real progress for all of humankind. Despite the great wave of mysticism that has invaded African intellectual spheres over recent years, there has been no serious proof showing incompatibility between the African spirit and modern science. Even Hebga's claim to release an "African scientific rationality" referred to as the "paranormal" (Hebga 1997) suffers from a lack of pertinence because of the multiple misunderstandings of certain fundamental categories of contemporary physical sciences (Lebeyina Ngah 2011).[11]

The urgent task for Africa is to know how to unify and integrate the different cultural elements coming from outside to create a harmonious response to challenges proposed by nature, society and history. This is freedom. The postmodernist criticism of the "Eurocentrism" of Western science has taken a false road if the objective is to pretend that the values of the Enlightenment are incompatible with non-Western societies. Criticism of positivism and pragmatism in the social sciences is quite necessary, as suggested by Habermas. But when both postmodernism and postcolonialism claim that no truth is likely to be universal or that values depend only on the "episteme" proper to each culture (Foucault) or to each discourse formation (Derrida, Hebga), this position itself is likely to encourage a regressive attitude, creating precisely the

---

[11] Considering that the Einstein's theory of relativity is a support given to relativism of scientific knowledge is a complete nonsense.

promotion of global capitalist pragmatism. This new pragmatism plays with the confusion of two levels of human practice: culture and science.

Mastering industrial civilization is finally a crucial issue for African societies.

The capitalist domination of the world is closely related to the control of matter by the social forces controlling capital. According to Towa, it is really possible that the main danger for African cultures and societies does not come from industrial civilization itself, as claimed by postmodernists and postcolonialists, but rather from capitalist imperialism. Towa states that "peace and brotherhood can be possible amongst men only on condition of a relative equality on the level of material power" (Towa 1977: 611). Neither religion nor morality, law, literature or even art can be helpful. Culture as an independent structure cannot help unless we give it the technological dimension necessary to construct a real power on the scale of the entire unified African continent. The question of nation conserves a central importance here, because, as formulated by Fanon, only a national liberation and autonomy for the people in the form of nation give the condition for African progress (Fanon 2002: 222–230). Does this perspective represent the return to technocratic and bureaucratic domination? Certainly not. On the contrary, this is the domination of the real and historic life carrying its proper needs for justice onto technocratic structuralism and the world of the machine put to the service of markets. The major issue for African people is not to become colonialists like modern Western countries, but to not be colonized anymore in anyway by anyone: "We must make ourselves non-colonisable forever" (Towa 1971: 45). This is the goal to achieve, the option to be taken: freedom and justice. From this point onwards, postmodernism and postcolonialism, both characterized by indecision and apology for imperialism and capitalism, seem to carry a logic of confusion. Only the collapse (and not the maintainance) of the capitalist and imperialist system of domination will liberate the creativity of people open to each other and now able to communicate freely. In Towa, Césaire, Fanon, Nkrumah, Cabral, this is the guarantee for a true multipolar or multicentered world.

Conclusion

Becoming hegemonic thanks to the cybernetic revolution, contemporary capitalism has needed a philosophy to justify itself. Postmodernism, to us, is that philosophy. The chaos of financial processes, the anonymous development of multinational enterprises, the contingency, the volatility and the fragmentation of neo-capital demands an abstract form. This conceptual side or moment that aims to justify the hegemony of global capitalism has been provided by postmodernism with its concepts of indeterminism, transitoriness, non-sense, incoherence, fragmentation, chance, itinerancy, migration. Applied to the social sciences, the postmodern turn produces a relativist, subjectivist, pragmatist and nihilist idea of knowledge which is presented as dependent on each individual context, culture or society. If criticism of the positivism of social science is necessary and inevitable, if it is necessary to fight the way the modern sciences have been turned into radical forms of imperialist domination, it is perhaps not pertinent to totally reject the idea of a universal rationality. Because if the Enlightenment has failed in many domains, maybe modern reason, as suggested by Habermas has its own principle of achievement inside itself. Could modernity be an unfinished, unaccomplished project? By refusing the principle of understanding social reality through a universal concept, postmodernism, like postcolonialism which replicates the philosophy in the global Southern countries by giving credit to the idea of "multiple epistemologies," is making a mistake. In parallel, the proliferation of identities is not the sign of the vigor of a culture, but is the symptom of a culture's progressive extinction under the law of commodity. The analysis needs to be more prudent and vigilant. Nowadays, coherence, totality, and sense, as postulated through the instrument of dialectics, remain useful.

References

Adorno, T. W. (1989) Théorie esthétique. Paris: Éditions Klincksieck.

Appadurai, A. (2000) Après le colonialisme. Les conséquences culturelles de la globalisation. Paris: Éditions Payot.

Appiah, A. (2008) Pour un nouveau cosmopolitisme. Paris: Éditions Odile Jacob.

Barthes, R. (1973) Le Plaisir du texte. Paris: Editions du Seuil.

Baudelaire, C. (1992) Écrits sur l'art. Paris: Le livre de Poche Librairie Générale Française.

Baudrillard, J. (1970) La Société de consommation. Paris: Gallimard.

Bayart, J.-F. (1983) La Revanche des sociétés africaines, in Politique africaine, Paris: septembre.

——(1989) L'État en Afrique. La politique du ventre. Paris: Librairie Arthème Fayard.

Bhabha, H. (2007) Les Lieux de la culture. Une théorie postcoloniale. Paris: Éditions Payot.

Bidima, J.-G. (1993) Théorie critique et modernité africaine. De l'École de Francfort à la "Docta Spes africana." Paris, ouvrage publié avec le concours du Conseil scientifique de l'Université de Paris I (Panthéon-Sorbonne) et de l'Institut de Missiologie de Aechen.

——(1995) La Philosophie négro-africaine. Paris: PUF.

Bloch, M. (1968) La Société féodale. Paris: Les Éditions Albin Michel.

Boltansky, L. and E. Chiapello (1999) Le Nouvel esprit du capitalisme. Paris: Gallimard.

Césaire, A. (1956) Culture et colonisation, in Présence Africaine N°8–9–10, pp.189–203.

Chakrabarty, D. (2009) Provincialiser l'Europe. La pensée postcoloniale et la différence historique. Paris: Éditions Payot.

Deleuze, J. and F. Guattari (1975) Capitalisme et schizophrénie I. L'anti-oedipe. Paris: Les Éditions de Minuit.

Derrida, J. (1967) L'Ecriture et la différence. Paris: Éditions Seuil.

Elias, N. (1985) La Société de cour. Paris: Éditions Flammarion.

Elshtain, J. B. (1998) La société civile n'est pas une panacée. Elle crée des citoyens, elle ne résout pas les problèmes, in E. J. Dionne (dir.), La vie associative, ça marche ! Le renouveau de la société civile aux Etats-Unis. Paris: Nouveaux Horizons/Brookings Institution.

Engels, F. (1973) Anti-Dühring. M. Dühring bouleverse la science. Paris: Éditions Sociales.

Fanon, F. (2002) Les Damnés de la terre. Paris: Éditions La Découverte/Poche.

Foucault, M. (1966) Les Mots et les choses. Une archéologie des sciences humaines. Paris: Éditions Gallimard.

———(1969) L'Archéologie du savoir. Paris: Éditions Gallimard.

———(1997) Il faut défendre la société, Cours au Collège de France. 1976. Paris: Editions Seuil/Gallimard.

———(2001) L'Herméneutique du sujet. Cours au Collège de France. 1981–1982. Paris: Éditions Seuil/Gallimard.

Fukuyama, F. (1992) La Fin de l'histoire et le dernier homme. Paris: Flammarion.

Gadamer, H. (1996) Vérité et méthode. Les grandes lignes d'une herméneutique philosophique. Paris: Éditions du Seuil.

Habermas, J. (1981) La modernité : un projet inachevé ?, in Critique N°413, pp.951–967.

———(1988) Le Discours philosophique de la modernité. Douze Conférences. Paris: Éditions Gallimard.

Hardt, M. and A. Negri (2000) Empire. Paris: Exils Éditeurs.

Hauser, H. and A. Renaudet (1938) Les Débuts de l'âge moderne. La Renaissance et la réforme. Paris: Librairie Félix Alcan.

Hebga, P. M. (1997) Rationalité d'un discours africain sur les phénomènes paranormaux. Paris: Éditions L'Harmattan.

Heers, J. (1966) L'Occident aux XVIe et XVe siècles. Aspects économiques et sociaux. Paris: PUF.

Hegel, G. W. F. (1940a) Principes de la philosophie du droit. Paris: Éditions Gallimard.

——(1940b) La Phénoménologie de l'esprit (1). Paris: Les Éditions Montaigne.

Heidegger, M. (1964) Être et temps. Paris: Éditions Gallimard.

Huntington, S. (1997) Le Choc des civilisations. Paris: Odile Jacob.

Jameson, F. (1991) Postmodernism or, the cultural logic of late capitalism. Durham: Duke University Press.

Lebeyina Ngah (2011) L'interprétation de Copenhague et la question de la réalité en physique quantique. Une lecture de Physique et philosophie, la science moderne en révolution de Werner Heinsenberg. Mémoire en vue de l'obtention du DIPES 2, ENS, UYI.

Lefebvre, H. (1961) Introduction à la modernité. Prélude. Paris: Les Éditions de Minuit.

——(1971) L'Idéologie structuraliste. Paris: Éditions Anthropos.

Lenin, V. I. (1967) L'Impérialisme, stade suprême du capitalisme. Moscow: Les Éditions du Progrès.

Lévi-Strauss, C. (1962) La Pensée sauvage. Paris: Éditions Plon.

Lévy-Brühl, L. (2010) La Mentalité primitive. Paris: Flammarion.

Lukàcs, G. (1958) La destruction de la raison. Les débuts de l'irrationalisme moderne de Schelling à Nietzsche. Paris: L'Arche Éditeur.

Lyotard, J.-F. (1979) La Condition postmoderne. Rapport sur le savoir. Paris: Les Éditions de Minuit.

Mandrou, R. (1980) La Raison du prince. L'Europe absolutiste : 1649–1775. Paris: Nouvelles Éditions Marabout.

Marx, K. (1996) Les Manuscrits de 1844. Paris: Éditions Flammarion.

Mbele, C. R. (2010) Essai sur le postcolonialisme en tant que code de l'inégalité. Yaoundé: Clé.

Mbembe, A. (2000) De la postcolonie. Essai sur l'imagination politique dans l'Afrique contemporaine. Paris: Éditions Karthala.

———(2010) Sortir de la grande nuit. Essai sur l'Afrique décolonisée. Paris: Éditions La Découverte.

Nietzsche, F. (1993a) La Généalogie de la morale, in Œuvres. Paris: Éditions Robert Laffont.

———(1993b) Le Gai Savoir, in Œuvres. Paris: Éditions Robert Laffont.

———(1993c) Le Crépuscule des idoles ou comment on philosophe au marteau, in Œuvres. Paris: Éditions Robert Laffont.

———(1994) La Naissance de la tragédie ou Hellénisme et Pessimisme. Paris: Librairie Générale Française.

Ngah Ndongo, V. (2008) Les mensonges du nouvel africanisme politique, in Identité culturelle et mondialisation, Annales de la Faculté des Arts, Lettres et Sciences Humaines de l'UY I, Actes des "Mercredis des Grandes Conférences", Numéro Spécial, pp.71–90.

Nkolo Foé, (2008) Le Postmodernisme et le nouvel esprit du capitalisme. Sur une philosophie globale d'Empire. Dakar: CODESRIA.

Said, E. W. (1980) L'Orientalisme. L'Orient créé par l'Occident. Paris: Éditions du Seuil.

——(2000) Culture et impérialisme. Paris: Librairie Arthème Fayard, Le Monde diplomatique.

Schambra, W. (1998) Il n'est de communauté que locale, la clé du renouveau de la société civile aux États-Unis, in E. J. Dionne (dir.), La vie associative, ça marche ! Le renouveau de la société civile aux États-Unis. Paris: Nouveaux Horizons/Brookings Institution.

Taylor, C. (1994) Le Malaise de la modernité. Paris: Les Éditions du CERF.

Towa, M. (1971) Essai sur la problématique philosophique dans l'Afrique actuelle. Yaoundé: Clé.

——(1977) Identité et Transcendance. Examen d'un dilemme de la pensée africaine moderne. Nanterre, Thèse de doctorat d'État (publiée aux Éditions L'Harmattan à Paris en 2010)

Vakaloulis, M. (2001) Le Capitalisme post-moderne. Éléments pour une critique sociologique, Paris: PUF.

Vattimo, G. (1987) La Fin de la modernité. Nihilisme et herméneutique dans la culture post-moderne. Paris: Éditions du Seuil.

Wallerstein, I. (1990) Le Capitalisme historique. Paris: Éditions La Découverte.

Wolfe, A. (1998) La société civile est-elle obsolète ? Rappel sur les prédictions sur le déclin de la société civile dans Whose Keeper, in E. J. Dionne (dir.), La vie associative, ça marche ! Le renouveau de la société civile aux États-Unis. Paris: Nouveaux Horizons/Brookings Institution.

"Hegemonic Science": Critique Strands, Counterstrategies, and Their Paradigmatic Premises

Michael Kuhn

Introduction

Following the postcolonial critique of the universalized European sciences, the era of globalisation and the new wave of internationalisation of sciences initiated by the global competition of nation-states about knowledge has confronted the so-called "Western" social sciences with a new wave of critique, the most radical version of which is the notion of "intellectual imperialism" and the like (for example, see Alatas 2000). In this chapter I will discuss the most typical variations of the critique the so-called Western sciences are facing today.

Four types of theoretical critiques populate the current critical discourses about the world science arena focusing on the universalisation of the "Western" concept of science and theories:

A. Critiquing theories of the Western sciences

B. Critique of the world science arena

C. Critiquing the Western way of theorizing, their epistemologies

I hold that these types of critiques represent the currently most prominent theoretical oppositions to the European model of theorising in the social sciences. I will not make any attempt to collect all the numerous examples and authors across the world, which could illustrate my discussions. The fashion to support arguments by quoting the more authors the better is part of a discourse style that seems to believe that the more theoreticians share a theory the more it must be theoretically convincing.

I discuss these types along the typical argumentative architecture of their thoughts, representing a typical type of argumentation; again, representing not in any quantitative sense, but with regard to their argumentative structure and their ways of proving thoughts.

I also need to make a remark about the object of these variations of critique, the so-called "Western" sciences and theories. I hold that attributing a geographical space to a theory or a particular way of theorizing, is a cognitive creature of the very "Western" science model it criticises. To put it in other words: The notion of a spatially constructed concept of science, the distinction of science along a "where" is the result of the very view of the science model created by the European science approach, that has been developed through the scientific revolution starting from the seventeenth century and from there universalized across the world.

I also hold that the following discussed variations of critiquing the bourgeois sciences can only be created by the way of thinking the bourgeois sciences have established with their critique of the classical philosophies and successfully spread across the world as the universal model of science.¹

Thus—this is what I will try to show—this critique, more precisely their particular way on constructing their critical thoughts, is the very creature of the science model it—often—so radically claims to oppose.

---

[1] The bourgeois model of scientific thinking means the sciences that have been established through the scientific revolution starting from the seven-teenth century replacing classical philosophies. This approach to science is based on a particular relation between the thinking subject and its objects, characterized by the subordination of thoughts under the commands of the reified social objectives incorporated in the objects of thoughts. Opposing the speculative nature of the classical philosophies which developed their theories from ideas, the bourgeois concept of scientific thinking approaches the objects of thoughts with a variation of speculative thinking, ex ante constructed models they measure against the objects of thoughts, thus cognitively travelling between their ex ante ideas and the empirical ap-pearance of their object of thoughts. They thus enthrone the nonunderstood appearance of things as an instance proving or disproving their modeled theories. This is the epistemological contradiction of a cognitive realism, the cognitive element of the bourgeois concepts of thoughts, Comte so clearly discloses in his tautological notion of "studying the real facts." See Michael Kuhn, The World Social Science System (forthcoming).

Critique Strands

A. Critiquing Western "Nonsuitable" Theories—Provicialising Social Thinking?

The postcolonial critique of the Western sciences summarized its opposition against Western sciences under the notion of "Eurocentrism," accusing the Western sciences and theories of imposing the Western interpretations of the world and interpreting their society model as the mission of mankind of the world. The critique of concepts such as "modernity," presenting the Western society model as if the Western model of society, economy, and politics was representingthe natural development of mankind's history, represented an opposition to the Western sciences, arguing against the naturalisation of the Western society model that oppressed the world, namely the world of the developing countries.

Obviously aware of a possible misinterpretation of this critique of "Eurocentrism," Said (2001 [1978]) thought he should warn against this critique of a local ethnocentrism toward a science world that replaces the monopoly of the Eurocentric worldview by a science world that consists of a multiplicity of ethnocentrisms.

This is exactly what the critique of the Western science in the era of globalisation does, obviously after any model of an alternative society had been abolished from the world's landscape with the dissolution of the Soviet Union and critical thinking had been intellectually expropriated of the option to think in alternative society systems and, thus, in systemic thinking as such.[2]

Abjuring the option of systemic thinking and critique, the postcolonial critique of the Westerns sciences dropped back into claiming against the monopole of the Western world interpretations to allow for a complimentary the parochial view replacing the monopole of the parochial view of the European sciences with the multi-plicity of parochialisms. Exactly this, creating a world of multiple parochialisms, is the idea of the current global concept in organisations like the International Sociology Association, the idea of regionalising the social sciences, put into practice by localising the social science theory production that has its theoretical point of departure in critiquing Western theories with the notion of the "here nonapplicable" Western theories.

The most typical critique of the "Western" theories in the era of globalisation coming from various global regions argues that theories created in the Western sciences are "nonsuitable" or "not applicable" to particular local context and do not allow an analysis of the social beyond the Western societies. There are numerous variations of this type of critique questioning the local applicability of theories born in the Western sciences, starting from the complaint

---

[2] See Michael Kuhn, "Facing a Scientific Multiversalism—Dynamics of International Social Science Knowledge Accumulations in the Era of Glob-alization," In Michael Kuhn and Doris Weidemann (eds.), Internationali-zation of the Social Sciences: Asia—Latin America—Middle East—Africa—Eurasia (S. 379–409). Bielefeld: transcript.

of a mismatch between the Western theories and the particularism of local phenomena and continuing to the nonapplicability of Western theories beyond the Western societies.

There is no doubt: The Western sciences succeeded in populating the world of sciences with their ideological worldviews. Theories about "modernity" and alike have established the naturalised Western society model as the model of "civilisation," and the "rest of the world" as on its way towards what time will bring about anyway—just as if these Western ideologies wanted to cartoon the historical automatism of "Historical Materialism." These Western ideologies have attracted massive critique, which has been quite easily absorbed by the Western sciences and meanwhile made part of its mainstream thinking, peacefully coexisting in a pluralistic science world—a coexistence that was always denied by the Western sciences to social theories emanating from the former Soviet Union. Unlike many critics, I argue that it is the dogma of a pluralism of thoughts, the many variations of denying the objectivity of thoughts (latest popular version Bashkar[3]) and its epistemological

---

[3] Bhaskar's variation (1997 [1975]) to confirm the dogma of the bour-geois sciences, denying the objectivity of knowledge, reveals how much thinking can obey the thinker's purpose of what he wants to prove. Concluding from the fact, that we "transform" our knowledge once we face new developments in the world, that we correct or amend our knowledge, that therefore, this knowledge is never ob-jective, only proves what this thinker thinks about knowledge, he can obviously only perceive as a unquestionable dogma or an ever relativized knowledge.

relativisms, that is the strongest weapon of the bourgeois sciences against any critique, and that it is this relativism that absorbs the critique of the knowledge this science created and creates—given that the critique shares this epistemological relativism. In most case it does.

Indeed, looking at how this critique argues, looking at the argumentative structure of thoughts critiquing Western theories by questioning their geographical reach can be considered as a classical example for critiquing theories without questioning their thoughts and, instead, rather complimenting them with other, mostly own, local thoughts. How does the critique of a theory that accuses this theory with the argument that it cannot be applied to a local context argue? Most obviously, this critique implies the assumption that the so critiqued Western theories are acceptable theories in the context of the Western societies, but elsewhere not. However, how is this possible to argue that a theory might be correct, somewhere else, in the West, but not beyond, in other parts of the world? How does this work, that a theory can be a right theory there and is a wrong theory here?

The first option, phrasing a critique of a theory as nonsuitable for a particular local context, appears as if it was a—purposeful—misconception of the object of the critiqued theory: If this critique of a nonapplicable theory wants to say that the Western theory is not suitable, because it is a theory about phenomena that do not exist in the non-Western local context and can thus not be valid in the non-Western social world, then this is not a critique of the

Western theory or its validity, but just stating that the Western theory is about another object of thought, which only exists in the Western social reality but not elsewhere. If the local context is not the same context as the critiqued theory is about, then this is not a critique of this theory and its lacking applicability, but the simply the observation that the objects of theorizing are not the same. Accusing a theory of not reflecting on the topic the critique wishes to reflect on, is not a critique of that theory. It just states, that the opposed theory does not think about the things the criticism would like it to think about.

Given the second option, that the critiqued theory however insists that it is about the very same objects of thought, then one cannot accuse this theory of not being here or there not applicable, but must discuss the theoretical faults of this theory–here and there. A theory cannot be a theory that is a theory about the same objects of thoughts and that is valid somewhere and nonvalid somewhere else, as long as it is about the same objects of thoughts.

However, though the critical notion of a "nonsuitable" theory is presented as if it is implies a critique of the "nonsuitable" theory, reflecting on the thoughts and arguments in this type of critique of a theory by accusing it of being not applicable is not the real purpose of this format of critique. If this was the case it would disprove the arguments of this theory no matter what the local context or the object of this theory is. A critique that wants to know if a theory is false or not would have to trace the theory's arguments no matter where the social phenomena exist and where not. The notion of a locally nonsuitable theory, however, does not say that a theory is wrong or right, no matter where. It does not even want to discuss the thoughts of the theory. It rather seeks to reject theories without discussing their thoughts. It thus establishes claims, instead, to compliment thoughts its does not want to question or even discuss, with other thoughts, without saying what is wrong or right about the thoughts, which this notion though discusses through the gesture of an opposition.

Indigenisation: Opposing the Western science monopole with the parochialism of thinking

Sato's thoughts (2010) about how to oppose the nonsuitable Western knowledge and to compliment it with "authentic" knowledge are very instructive to understand the nature of indigenized knowledge: Both methodologically as content wise the indigenisation of knowledge rejects, not critiques, Western thoughts and Western thinking and constructs the suitable knowledge as a variation of Western theories and theorizing. This is not to say, that there are no theories that originated from the knowledge traditions beyond the Western sciences they excluded from their concept of scientific knowledge by discriminating this knowledge as indigenous knowledge. It is the indigenization of theorizing as a scientific strategy against the Western science that opposes the Western theories by reproducing both their theoretical constructs as their way of theorizing. (See also D. Weidemann in chapter 6 in this volume.)

Methodologically it constructs its knowledge as a comparison between the indigenized knowledge and the rejected Western knowledge, taking the rejected Western knowledge as the discrete implicit tertium comparationis. Content wise it introduces, here the East Asian, categories, here "aidagara" and "guanxi," rejecting the Western category, here "social capital," as the more appropriate East Asian interpretation of these very categories. Aidagara or guanxi in Sato's critique of the notion of social capital are promoted to better understand what both the Western and the East Asian categories share; and what they share are the theoretical abstractions articulated in the notion of social capital originating from the Western society model this comparison seemingly considers as the nature of thoughts about the social.

Thus, indigenized knowledge consists of a gesture of critique that not only never questions the Western theories nor the Western way of theorizing, but ennobles Western thoughts as the categorial reference basis for the indigenised knowledge as variations of the Western thoughts.

How far away this gesture of opposition to Western theories is from critiquing these theories can be seen if one has a glimpse at an example of a theory that accuses a Western theory of being "nonsuitable" in a local context, in our example a discussion about a sociological topic, the "Western" category of "social capital," which is accused not being applicable to East Asian contexts and its East Asian complimentary categories aidagara for Japan and guanxi for China.

Taking Sato's critique and discussion of the above categories as an arbitrary example from the numerous variations of this format of critique populating the world of theorizing mainly in developing countries, in this case in East Asia, and what he says about the difference between the Asian and the Western categories of "social capital"[4] and "aidagara," illustrates how much this critique insinuates itself as being a critique of Western categories and how far away such critique is from really critiquing these Western thoughts, which stereotype East Asians with the well known scientific cliché as "collectivists." (The most prominent example are Hofstede 1984 or Ruth Benedict.) Indeed, the Asian categories, may they be the Japanese version aidagara or the Chinese version guanxi, within Sato's discussions about the question "why is social capital, and not "aidagara," "en" or "guanxi," the universal sociological concept that describes social relations" (Sato 2010: 193), even reproduce in their comparison with the Western categories the racist stereotypes Western theories have created about East Asia: Beyond any critique of the false dichotomy of individualism versus collectivism Sato's critique of the nonapplicable notion of social capital in an East Asian contexts just reverses the stereotype value judgments by accusing the Western theories not of any false thoughts in this di-

---

[4] It is another sociological Marxist's, Bourdieu's privilege to have cre-ated a concept, social capital, that no Asian scholar wants to critique. Is it not so difficult to see the theoretical mistake, not to mention the political purpose, establishing those, the have-nots, who have nothing but "durable networks" with a sudden "capital," capitalists would never need, since they own capital?

chotomy, but of an a Western individualism that, as he feels he needs to say, is ignorant about the collective, methodologically phrased, what he calls the "contextuals":

> Unlike individuals, "contextuals" which represent actors in methodological contextualism, do not give priority to autonomy and independence but are dependent on other "contextuals" (ibid.: 14).
>
> Constructing "contextuals" without being individuals is as false as the whole idea of thinking about societal subjects without societies and then to denounce societies as collectives without individuals or as individuals that do not respect the "contextuals." While the first version of an false sociological opposition of two false abstractions aims at casting aspersions on Asians as "collectivists," the critique coming from the "contextualists" aims at casting aspersions on Westerners as "individualists."
>
> In our example Sato even realizes that his interpretation of the Asian categories substantially do not differ from the critiqued Western terms.
>
> Why is social capital, rather than aidagara and en, popular among sociologists worldwide, even though the terms are similar? (ibid.: 193)

So what is the problem about social capital if it is so similar to the Asian categories? Since his critique is not a critique of the Western categories, they are according to him even "similar," his critique that pretends being a critique of the Western categories, is a critique about the global intellectual leadership, their global popularity. Discussing the explanatory value of theories is not a concern of the critique that accuses Western theories as elsewhere being nonsuitable, applicable, and alike. This critique only plays with the gesture of a critique of theories and rather discusses the question, Which theory, which provincialism, has the say in the world of theories?[5]

---

[5] As if Sato wants to prove my argument that critically reflecting on theo-ries and raising the question about who dominates the global discourses are opposing issues, Sato argues that theories become more dominate the shallower they are: "I would argue that thin concepts spread faster among sociologists than thick concepts, which are loaded with local meanings. This is because when individuals are exposed to a concept and try to un-derstand it, a thin concept has lighter cognitive burdens on its receivers than a thick concept" (Sato 2010: 197). If one leaves aside that this is not a compliment for the world social sciences, his argument clarifies this: To compete with Western theories about who has the say in the global science arena, he calls their international popularity, and without any hesitation he suggests the creation of a local theory that is shallower as any Western theory could ever be: "The second strategy is a particular-ism-to-universalism-to-particularism strategy. Using this strategy, the Japanese sociologist would invent a broad concept that covers both Japa-nese and the Western types of social relations, as well as the Chi-nese type. The Japanese sociologists could then derive local concepts such as aidagara and guanxi from the more general concept. Generally, this is an authentic scientific strategy and is, therefore, preferable" (ibid.:199). The "preferable" strategy for creating new global "popular" theories is: "Inventing" a theory that is "broad," "thin" and "authentic." The conceptual conservatism uncritically fostering the national histories in this opposition against Western thoughts is obvious. This, not critiquing but competing with Western theories

In fact, as this example shows, this critique, of a nonsuitable theory not only does not critique the Western stereotyped value judgments about "Asians," it builds on their false abstractions, reproduces their argumentative structure as their racist categories, reverses their value judgments, and thus supports the universal reign of the Western theories. This critique has not only learned its lesson from the bourgeois science, it is a very part of its way of thinking as of its way of disputing.

Departed from the critique of a nonsuitable theory and once arrived at the critique of the global leadership of Western theories, various strands of arguing are from here being developed and elaborated. They range from creating alternative, mostly "Southern" theories, which are in most cases also no critique of Western theories, but alternative views based on the same Western approach of thinking, towards quarrelling about how the Western leadership could be eroded, as Sato does in his case for the global ambitions of the Japanese academia.

What all these variation of critiquing Western theories as being nonsuitable theories have in-common is that they do not question or erode the persuasive basis of Western theories that is, by critically tracing the cognitive architecture of their thoughts. They do in some cases argue against their main ideological messages and thus

---

via conserving uncritical national historical concepts is the concern of critiquing Western theories in the era of globalisation in which competition about the global popularity of thoughts is ascendant; in such a competition, sound thinking is—very frankly—considered as being quite disturbing.

question the Western theory monopoly (the most current prominent example is Connell 2007), but they rarely attack their theories by critically tracing the argumentative structure of thoughts through which the Western theories are constructed and through which they gain their intellectual credibility.[6]

Thus, by leaving the cognitive basis of the Western theories, the argumentative structure of their thoughts, not only untouched but in many cases even reproducing and arguing with them and creating an alternative ethnocentrism, as in the above case about East Asian sociology, it is not only not surprising that such kind of critique does not only not erode the persuasive basis of the Western theory bodies. It rather also transforms the universalisation of the

---

[6] Maybe the most striking examples of critiquing the ideological effects of Western theories without critiquing the theories are the notions of "mo-dernity" for sociology and the notion of "globalisation" for economics. While the critique of the ideological effects of the notion of "modernity," claiming that the Western model of society represents the history of mankind, is most common, and the "notion" of "globalisation," a term spatialising a nameless something, might also raise some concerns about its ideological implications, the theories summarized by the these notions have rarely been critically contested. It is this circumscribed opposition, restricted on critiquing these theories' ideological impact, that leaves the arguments from which these theories are constructed untouched, and thus allow them to be acknowledged worldwide as an explanation of what is happening in the world. The rest, the extent to which such theories are acknowledged, is a matter of nonscientific means of imposing such theories as the global theoretical standards.

Western parochial knowledge toward a global knowledge arena consisting of a multiplicity of competing and coexisting parochialisms, competing about which theory has the leadership in the global science arena.

Indeed, accusing Western theories via a new figuring of the notion of "Eurocentrism" in the era of globalisation is an interpretation of an older question that asks: How do the Western theories shape the "captive minds" of academics? (Alatas 1974), except that now the question has become: Which parochial sciences dominate the scientific discourses in the globalising science world? No doubt, it is the European sciences, which have imposed their views about the world on the world. However, making the opposition to the European sciences a matter of the global scientific leadership and shifting the theoretical leadership from the European monopoly toward a multiplicity of parochial world interpretations, does not only leave the Western theories uncritiqued; just as if they want to ignore Said's warnings, this critique of elsewhere locally nonapplicable theories rather aims at replacing the Western theoretical leadership with the multiplicity of spatially restricted ways of theorizing, the final globalisation of very bourgeois concept of science introduced to the world with the most active support of those who might believe to critique the Western model of science or their theories. It is another irony of the world sciences that its major current approach critiquing Western theories in the era of a globalising science arena helps to strengthen and globalise the position of the Western way of theorizing.[7]

---

[7] It is a very particular double irony in the history of the world sciences that it is the correct opposition of academics from developing countries against a false opposing theory, their critique of the "Historical Materialism", an ideology the Soviet Union had established against the Western ideology production and spread across the world as an opposing world view, mainly into the colonised world supporting their fights for independence, that this critique of the Soviet Union ideologies has helped to established space, the epistemological creature of the bourgeois sciences, as a worldwide acknowledged epistemological dimension, more than the universalisation of the bourgeois concept of science itself ever could. Chakrabarty's error in his opposition against "Historical Materialism"—a historical epistemolog-ical twofold accident, the wrong self-critique of a wrong theory, the ideology of the Soviet Union, an interpretation of Marx as a type of scientific reli-gion—is that he critiques Marx via critiquing a caricaturelike Marx inter-pretation, that could not more contradict Marx's theories. It was Engels, who was often critiqued by Marx, when Engels used the term "Marxism," thus transforming Marx theories about capitalism into an approach to science, who perpetrated the caricaturelike notion of the "Historical Mate-rialism." First, uncritically adopted by social movements against colonial-ism and used for the independence of colonial countries, then, once the former colonies became independent, critiqued by the same academics in the new states as an intervention into their local national identity-building process, this science ideology of the Soviet Union was seen by theorists from the periphery as a theory that did not know any "where," that is, did not allow the creation their own local worldviews. In fact, the Soviet

B. The World Science Arena—A Battlefield of National Science Communities?

A second strand of critique spread across the world and mainly articulated by social scientists in the so-called developing countries critically discusses not the Western theories, but the world science arena. It opposes mostly with very radical terms the world science system, ranging from the more modest notions about inequalitities toward the more radical version of accusing the Western sciences of a "scientific imperialism" (Alatas 2003) and alike. (See chapter Okamoto in this book.) This critique accuses the Western sciences of "dominating" (...) hegemonizing (....) an "unequal" or "asymmet-

---

ide-ology subsumed the whole world under its odd dogma of an historical au-tomatism, in which authorities in the Soviet Union did not themselves believe. The impact of introducing the "where" as an epistemological di-mension of thoughts since then has flourished as an opposition against the Western sciences, under the notion of indigenous sciences, Southern sci-ences, and the like. In any case, it was and is this opposition against the Western theories that paved the way for universalising the "where," space, mostly politically defined, as a worldwide epistemological dimension of science, thus extending the bourgeois concept of science in away the bour-geois sciences never could, due to its own very political, i.e., nationalized "where." Since then, the world of sciences consists of the global theoretical roundabout of no-where valid theories. On international science discourses, the circle of a spatialised expertise about the local "wheres" of knowledge results in the global nondiscourse culture among the many local expertises.

ric" (Keim 2008) science system, mainly arguing that the "peripheric" sciences are ruled by "scientific centres"—and do not notice that all these complaints about the conditions under which social scientists around the world accumulate knowledge operate with the major constructs of this science system that implies these conditions as its—inevitable—outcomes.

Though one could argue that the critique of the world science arena in which social sciences around the world produce knowledge does of course not oppose the thoughts reigning the world knowledge productions, since this is not their topic, one could assume that such critique, that excludes the theoretical substance of thoughts from their agenda, cannot be of such an importance. However, more than any critique of thoughts and theories, it is this critique of the world science system that represents the most prominent opposition to what is called the "hegemonic sciences," a critique originating from the developing countries, meanwhile shared as a kind of global synonym for a critique of the global science world.

In the following section I will not discuss all the different variations and aspects of this critique strand of the world science arena, but just raise some questions about the key scientific subject populating all those critical reflections about the global science arena, that is the "national science communities," the unquestioned construct also uncritically used by the above radical critique of the global science arena. Discussing this, the subject all these variations of critique argue with the notion of a world science system consisting of "national science communities," discloses the tragic errors of this critique as its affirmative standpoint.

Indeed, this idea of a science community as the subject populating the world science arena, shared by the most radical critique of the global science arena, is one of these typical constructs of the bourgeois sciences, namely sociology, everywhere seeing "communities," constructed from wherever sociologists find people who have nothing in-common but competing or opposing interests. In this case, the subject populating the world science arena, the "national science communities," are constructed— again mainly by sociologists, however used by all disciplines in their discourses about the world sciences—from the very competitive and opposing interests academics have within the Western concept of science via the organisation of science as a competition about knowledge.

National social science communities, the nowhere questioned subjects of the world science system, are imagined as the internationally competing subjects, organisational entities of academics constructed from simply sharing the same nationality. This notion of national science communities seriously seems to believe that academics working internationally are on an international mission representing a national entity in their battles against other national science communities about how much they, the national science communities, participate in what this critique calls the "growth of knowledge." Do they seriously want to say that scientists attending conferences, publishing books, reflecting on theories from other scientists abroad or collaborating in research projects, according to the imaginary world of these critical theories, are all trying to contribute to a competition among national science communities to beat each other in producing more knowledge than the other national science community? They do. Are they seriously thinking an internationally acting academic is a kind of intellectual soldier gathered and organised in national science entity fighting a battle between national science organisations from different countries?

One could already learn from a glimpse of the historic emergence of the disciplinary specialisation of social sciences that the Western model of nation-based societies organises its knowledge production as a scientifically specialised disciplinary service and by no means as a national entity or a national organisation. This is why such a thing as a national science community, gathering the social sciences under a national entity, nowhere exists, neither via a national institutional body nor via a nationally unified theoretical approach (see for example, Wallerstein et al. 1996).

There is no such thing as the French, Japanese, or Indonesian social sciences. There are social sciences in these countries, working under the same conditions, rules, and infrastructures of national science policies, but the sciences are not a nationally constructed entity. Sciences anywhere in the world are constructed along their scientific specialisations and the according disciplinary organisations, and the history of science is the history of a battle among disciplines about their disciplinary, nonnational "territories" (Becher and Trowler 2001).[8]

---

[8] See Wallerstein et al. (1996); more recently, see Becher and Trowler (2011).

These disciplinary organisations share scientifically much more with disciplinary organisations in other countries than they share with any other science discipline within the same countries. No academic in any country shares as a theorist anything national with all other academics that would allow them to scientifically gather as a national science entity as the category of national science communities, according to all the critical discourses populating the world sciences, insinuates. Academics in all countries and across the disciplines are subordinated to their specific national science policies, funding policies, and laws framing their academic activities. However, this joint political infrastructure does not constitute the academic subject of a national entity.

People in the post-World War II world project of a world consisting of nation-states are constructed as national subjects, citizens, and as scientists that the bourgeois model of sciences constructs in the world of science along a specialisation of knowledge, a specialisation that reflects the knowledge needs of the bourgeois society, its economy, and its politics, not along their nationalities and their accordingly constructed science disciplines. More than that, the era of globalisation has created science as a global resource the globally competing nation-states and global "players" are trying to get under their local command.

In this globalised sciences world, the construct of national science communities only occurs in the practical political and institutional access that nation-states establish on academics, treating all academics alike by disregarding their scientific peculiarities and disregarding their nationalities *as if they were* nothing else but a national resource for the international economic battles nation-states initiate and supervise.

Moreover, those who propose the notion of the "national science communities" have apparently not yet noticed that in the era of globalisation, the globalisation of capitalism under the global supervision of those imperial nation-states, who have a global reach, the whole world is considered as a resource for economic growth, if possible invoiced in the currencies of the imperial powers, including the world's people and also including the world's professional thinkers. One's nationality is the least thing a globalist imperialist would care about. A glimpse on the nationalities of academics in the leading Western universities would reveal how irrelevant nationalities today in the practice of national science policies are. Only critical academics, who believe and seeming share the nation-state view of the era of colonialism, are concerned about national science communities and consider, caught by their blind and vain view of their rankings about global prestige, the nationality of academics as a relevant category under which they gather academics in their imaginary subject of the global science arena.

From this—very outdated—political perspective, and only from this perspective, the critique of the world science arena, which uncritically accommodates its views and operates with this view of the national political elites on the world science arena, these critical reflections about the world sciences—very consequently—occasionally finds allies in the political elites or even in the—very updated—political and economic imperialism of the real world powers. Accordingly, the same critique rarely detects the political elites in the—developing—countries of their own nationality as those who do dictate the "unequal," "asymmetric," or "imperial" conditions under which their "national science communities" are expected to compete and occasionally sympathize with and speculate on how shifts in the global imperial power balances between the political and economic imperialists could have an impact on the global ranking of their "dependent" science communities.[9]

C. Critiquing the Western Way of Theorizing

Unlike those two above critique strands caught in the Western science concept and in the political national missions of academics in a globalised (science) world, there is also a critique that questions the bourgeois concept of science. This critique focuses on two aspects of the bourgeois sciences:

---

[9] As an example F. Alatas, who frankly speculates and expresses his disappointments about the imperial power of Japan and its effects on the global science power distribution: "Here it would be interesting to speculate about how academic dependency may be affected by the shifts in the balance of economic power. It is not uncommon in Asia to hear optimistic views to the effect that if Asian economies overtake the West, Asian culture will become more dominant globally: . . . But, it is doubtful that any Asian nation or Asia as a whole would become dominant in the social sciences on a global scale. The case of Japan is instructive in this case. Japan is a world economy power but it is not a social science power by any means" (Alatas 2003: 605).

Concerned with the observation of a world guided by armies of scientists and the ideological effects the Western theories have on the world, namely, the world of the developing countries, the rationale of–what this critique calls–the Western concept of rationalism becomes a subject of critique. The other version of critique critically discusses another very correct observation that is that despite of all the armies of scientists, social sciences theories play a very ideological but no practical role in practical considerations of citizens; instead they are mainly the subject of the exclusive discourses among the professional knowledge experts, the academics. Those who subscribe to this critique rightly observe that the world employs masses of people who are professional thinkers, but the knowledge they create does not anywhere guide anyone's practical life, except the academic disputes among the professional thinkers about their thoughts.

Critique of theories and of the way of theorizing is an elementary ingredient of the Westerns concept of science. As long as one respects the rules of the Western science, that is his or her methodological apparatus, which defines what can be acknowledged as scientific knowledge and what not, one can write any nonsense and present this as sound scientific knowledge.[10]

---

[10] To illustrate this with one example, here from economic theories: The title of the book of the latest Nobel Prize winner, Sims, is "Macroeconomics and Reality." Within the bourgeois model of thoughts, stating that thoughts are the product of the fantasy of the thinker he then compares with the real world, are reward with a Nobel Prize. In fact, his book title already frankly reveals that

Discussing the favourite assumptions of a demand/supply equation he states: "In principle we realize that it does not make sense to regard 'demand for meat' and 'demand for shoes' as the products of distinct behaviour, any more than it would make sense to regard 'price of meat' and 'price of shoes' equations as products of distinct categories of behaviour if we normalized so as to reverse the place of prices and quantities in the system. Nonetheless, we do sometimes estimate a small part of a complete demand system with part of a complete supply system—supply and demand for meat say. In doing this, it is common and reasonable to make shrewd aggregations and exclusion restrictions so that our small partial-equilibrium system omits most of the many prices we know enter the demand relation in principle and possibly include a shrewdly selected set of exogenous variable we expect to be especially important in explaining variation in meat demand (e.g., and

---

the "Macroeconomics," his thoughts about the macro-economy must be no thoughts about the real macro-economy, otherwise these thoughts could not be compared with the "Reality." The other pole of his comparative construct, the "Reality," presented as the most possible radical abstraction possible, the reality, can also not be any phenomena in the real economy, since this economy cannot be theoretically grasped with the notion of the "Reality." While thinking about the economy the highly rewarded thoughts of this thinker obviously travel between hypothetical assumptions he calls "Macroeconomics" and a "Reality" he creates for his cognitive journey between his theoretical models and a reality he has modeled for this journey. Thoughts like this are therefore not at risk of being ruled out of contention for the Nobel Prize.

Easter dummy in regions where many people buy hams for Easter dinner)" (Sims 1980: 2). Where the modeled thoughts do not coincide with the modeled reality, the reality is adjusted to the model via shrewd aggregations. This is the most common free floating way of speculative thinking in the bourgeois sciences, rightly rewarded with a Nobel Prize. However, if one critiques these definitions, defining what science is and what not, adherents of European science are very good at denouncing those who dare disregard or oppose their holy enlightened definitions of science. It is the missionary view on the world that European science have,[11] con-

---

[11] To illustrate this cognitive attitude of Western social scientists I quote from a book titled Nations Matter by Craig Calhoun. According to the book cover, "Nations Matter argues that pursuing a purely postnational politics is premature at best and possibly dangerous." The first sentence of the "President of the Social Science Research Council" in this book is this one: "Nationalism is not a moral mistake" (all Calhoun 2007). My point quoting this is not to argue about nationalism. A world of nation-states are the project of the US post-World War II imperialism and that a president of the social science research council celebrates nationalism as the analyt-ical perspective for social scientists confirms that he is the best president. I only quote this to point out the religiouslike jargon of a leading Western social scientist, an attitude in which his views are presented to the world as if they the sacred commands from a world social science messiah. Similarly Wallerstein: Though Wallerstein is not a person one would suspect of harboring US imperial thoughts, in his latest publication, arguing heavily against "European universalism" (Wallerstein 2006), he discusses at length under the headline "Whose Right to In-

vinced about their model of science as the science of mankind, that prevents them from responding to critique with critique, but rather with denouncing their critics. Societies and scientists around the world have thus received their racist labels.[12]

Their insulting weight is politically carefully distinguished and dosed dependent on how much they are politically predetermined as an enemy for the US imperialism's ambition to decide about the "good and the evil." While Africans are (today) politically irrelevant to the global Western crusaders, they nonetheless are insulted as being "incurably obscure," while the Islamic world, which dares to refuse adjusting their societies to the Western model, and who

---

tervene? Universal Values against Barbarism", bothering the world with the scruples of left US intellectuals with the question, what circumstances would cleanly legitimize military interventions and discusses the missionary activities of Las Casas, most obviously to build a congenial memorial for Immanuel Wallerstein.

[12] As an example, Nisbett, who has gained a reputation as being sym-pathetic with with East Asian thinking, denounces his students coming from East Asia in the more sophisticated style of a Western science patri-arch: "The truth is, however, that this linear rhetoric form is not at all common in the East. For my Asian students, I find that the linear rhetoric form is the last crucial thing they learn on their road to becoming fully functioning social scientists" (Nisbett 2005: 196). See also the chapter in this book by Okamoto.

create their own Islamic science approach, receives as a response the threat of a "clash of civilisations" (Huntington 1996).[13]

C1. Critique from African Thinkers—Trapped by the Cognitive Warship of Facts?

The critique coming from African scholars as from other parts of the world about the Western way of theorizing always assembles around an opposition of the notion of the rationalism of Western sciences, which is a response to the Western critique of an "incurable religious Africa," which means an irrational Africa. I will neither trace nor discuss in this section all the elaborated philosophical arguments implied in the most elaborated critique African scholars have about the Western concept of science. Since the notion of an "incurable religious Africa" is anyway only an insult about their incurable nature and which rejects any critical discussions with African scholars about their critique of the Western science, these insults are also not my issue.

In this section I just want to draw the attention to one implication, one assumption in the critique African scholars phrase when opposing the "Western rationalism." African scholars consider this Western rationalism "as no longer valued without contestation"

---

[13] The more diplomatic version, phrased by the scientific spokesmen of an imperial power, that would like to question the US science imperialism, is articulated in the so-called Metris Report, written on behalf of the Eu-ropean Commission by an Expert Group with leading European scholars (European Commission 2009). So what is this critique that attracts such insulting responses?

(Mbembe 2000: 27) and advocate "the recognition of the existence of forms of knowledge distinct from scientific knowledge...the multiplicity of worlds and forms of life, the existence of narrative knowledge distinct from scientific knowledge, the plurality of forms of invention of difference and the universal, the redefinition of relations between objectivity and representation" (ibid.).

Logically very similar to the aforementioned critique of Western theories as "nonapplicable" to the non-Western world, it is remarkable to notice that the critique coming from African scholars also contests Western rationalism by advocating the recognition of other forms of knowledge "distinct from scientific knowledge." Their opposition to the Western concept of science is not opposing the Western form of scientific knowledge, but its exclusive definition of what counts as scientific knowledge.

This is remarkable since advocating other forms of knowledge as a critique of the Western concept of science, the Western concept of theorizing as an exclusive rationalism, apparently considers the Western rationalism as a rational way of thinking.[14]

The modern Western social sciences—thoughts traveling between their imaginary theoretical ex ante models, assumptive the-

---

[14] See also J. B. Quedraogo and Carlos Cardoso, Reading in Methodol-ogy, African Perspectives (CODESRIA, 2011). This volume focuses on crit-ical epistemological and methodological discussion of the Western science approach. It should however be stressed that as much as such epistemo-logical debates help theory go beyond the level of social science engineering, they cannot replace any critique of the Western theories.

ories, hypotheses, and the like, and their descriptive perception of the facts, a never understood and methodologically manipulated phenomenology, established as the instance for proving what they call the "evidence" of thoughts—this is supposed to be rationale? Theories, compressed in concepts like "modernity," the market imagined and proved with accordingly constructed facts as an equalizer of demand and supply, an economic theory taking scarcity as the founding element of an economy that dumps and produces everyday values this theory does not even know how to count, not to mention to explain, political theories thinking the nation-state as ever solving problems only a nation-state can ever create, and so on and on—all these most inconsistent and preoccupied thoughts, an epistemology that preferably proves the impossibility of objective science the Western sciences believe they are practicing, all this is supposed to be rational theories and a rational approach to theorizing?

Is this African critique, that hesitates to oppose this way of theorizing other than complimenting it with other types of knowledge, may be also a victim of the reflexive realism, the descriptive view of the bourgeois science, they here apply to their reflections about the Western science approach, trapped by the methodological apparatus of the Western sciences? Does this critique possibly mix up the rationale appearance of the bourgeois concept of science, presented via its sophisticated methodological apparatus with the irrationalism of the cognitive architecture of Western theories? Do they mix up in their critique the rational appearance with a theoretically irrational thinking not drawn from the Western theories but from the ideological impact Western thoughts have on thoughts in Africa, and believe this to be the result of a Western rationalism. Do they possibly mean that the effects Western theories have on African thoughts is the result of a scientific rationalism, because they, the Western theories, present themselves as being methodologically rational? Is this critique also a victim of looking at the very facts about the Western science, trapped by their warship of facts, here by the fact of a methodologically presented rationalism, that allows the presentation of the most bizarre preoccupied thoughts as rational, once they can prove these to be constructed according to the rules of their methodological apparatus. Is there anything this concept of science cannot prove, preferably in their epistemological departments proving the impossibility of rational knowledge?

C2. Critique from the Islamic Social Science Approach – Opposing the Expropriation with a Twofold Expropriation from Knowledge

The most striking irrationalism of the Western societies, of the global capitalism and their political systems, democracy, certainly is that this society has established and institutionalised sciences to a greater extent than ever before in history, established institutions, universities, with armies of professionally thinkers—and denies the knowledge they produce has any say in the decision makings of this society. Not only in the sense that the political decisions can only be made by another professional elite, the politicians, and are strictly a matter of the political spheres, decisions in which the knowledge of sciences is not allowed to take part, unless as the provider of nonbinding advice; this society also distinguishes its citizens as professional knowledge holders and knowledge consumers (See Kuhn 2007: 11ff). The latter get pieces of knowledge to prove their appropriateness for the higher level of jobs, ruling the rest. More than that, the creation of knowledge has even gained the ideological status of governing a "knowledge-based society" while at the same time in a very fundamental sense decisions about any aspects of people's lives are not taken in relation to knowledge but to the rules, lawful considerations about life priorities, transformed into indisputable moral principles, and finally established with the political power of the political elites and the ideological power of the professional thinkers. Decisions guided by knowledge but violating laws are thought not a matter of debates, but of sanctions.

This political definition of the role knowledge does and does not play in a society that creates knowledge for other purposes, disempowering people's decisions from knowledge and subordinating their decisions under the power of laws, internalised as the moral principles of life, is the political reason for the dogma of a relativism of scientific knowledge, which many epistemologically engaged philosophers have so passionately proven to be a necessity of the nature of scientific thinking. Indeed, if knowledge must be ever subjective it cannot serve as an instance of any decision making.

It is precisely this mind set separating knowledge from the practical concerns and considerations of decision making in the bourgeois concept of science,[15] "Knowledge" falls short of expressing all the aspects of *'ilm*. Knowledge in the Western world means information about something, divine or corporeal, while *'ilm* is an all-embracing term covering theory, action and education. (Ahktar, n.d.)

Their critique hits the above-mentioned point when they critique the Western concept of knowledge. The notion that the concept of ilm embraces "theory, action and education" opposes the Western concept of science by insisting on knowledge as a means for the concerns of societal practices.

However fueling the lacking practical dimension of knowledge with the moral ideas of the religion of Islam does make knowledge a practically relevant instance in thinking, but it introduces cognitive instances that define thoughts beforehand with the moral ideas of this religion and directs thinking toward given results, postulated by their religious beliefs. Thus the Islamic concept of knowledge, which considers knowledge as an instance of the societal practices, binds this thinking to the moral framework of their religiously preoccupied assumptions.[16]

---

[15] The notion "This is only theory" illustrates the role theorizing plays in the mind architecture of the bourgeois citizen. Theory is denounced as being practically irrelevant, theory is wishful thinking. implied in the dogma of its knowledge relativism, that the Islamic critique addresses in its opposition to the Western approach to science.

[16] Introducing the moral principles guiding thinking toward religiously defines societal practices also conflicts with the ideas of knowledge, as the controver-

In addition to this, in the Islamic concept of knowledge, rightly critiquing the split mind in the Western concept of knowledge delegating knowing into a sphere separated from practically thinking about the world of action, the concept of *'ilm* implies a religiously motivated variation of the Western politically motivated elite distinction in knowledge holders and knowledge consumers. It distinguishes *'ilm* into a hierarchy of knowledge levels the highest one of which can only be reached by a religiously defined elite.[17]

---

sial discourses among the Islam sciences show. Their ongoing debate about whether scepticism can be considered as a creative element in the creation of thoughts or eroding the basis of believing illustrates the epistemological contradictions of introducing the moral ideas of a religion into scientific thinking. "It is generally believed that in Islam, as far as belief is concerned, there is no place for doubting and questioning the existence of God, the prophethood of Hadrat Mu-hammad (S) and the Divine injunctions, that Islam requires unequivocal submission to its dictates. This general belief is a misconception in the light of Islam's emphasis on 'aql. In the matter of the fundamentals of faith (usu-l al-Din), the believer is obliged to accept tawhid, nubuwwah and ma'd (in the Shi'i faith, 'adl, i.e. Divine Justice, and imamah are also fundamentals of faith) on rational grounds or on the basis of one's exis-tential experience. This ensures that there is room for doubt and skepti-cism in Islam before reaching certainty in Iman" (Ahktar).

[17] "The sufis have described iman as consisting of three stages: 'ilmal-yaqin (certain knowledge), 'ayn al-yaqin (knowledge by sight) and haqq al-yaqin (knowledge by the unity of subject and object). The last stage is attainable by an elect few" (ibid).

Once the Islamic concept of knowledge distinguishes between the type of thinking of an enlightened cognitive elite, exclusively gaining the stage of "knowledge by the unity of subject and object" and thinking that never reaches this unity guided by the ideas of religious beliefs, this thinking cannot know, it compliments the interventions of a lawful thinking the Western societies provide for the ordinary knowledge holders as the way of building their obedient minds with a twofold morally guided and a lawfully thinking mind, supervised by an chosen political and religiously enthroned elite.

Rightly arguing against the Western concept of knowledge that expropriates thinking from its societal practices and reserving the highest level of knowing for a chosen elite, and complimenting the subordination of thinking under a lawful thinking in the Western concept of knowledge with the subordination of thinking under the moral ideas of the Islamic religion, is a critique of the Western sciences, but a critique that adds another binding moral instance to an already morally misguided concept of knowledge.

Conclusions

The history of thoughts seems to progress via an opposition constructed in alternative ways of doing the same.

The strongest, if not the weapon of the Western sciences against their critics is their concept of critique. More precisely critiquing theories is the mode this approach to science has established together with the universalisation of its concept of science.

The relativism of hypothetical thinking implies a concept of critique that discusses theories via investigating the methodological apparatus with which the theories are constructed, not the thoughts of the theories themselves. Any theory is acknowledged that supports its whatever preoccupied thoughts, its hypotheses, with their proof through the facts, facts the theory constructs with the methodological apparatus through the perspective of its hypothetic thoughts; thus there are no facts the methodological apparatus could not provide for the hypothetical thoughts, since the facts are nothing but the constructed illustrations created and interpreted through the assumptive thoughts. This circular relation between the thinker and his object of thinking implies the epistemological necessity that all thoughts that can be proved by the facts this thinking constructs for its proof, proving them as "evident" thoughts.

Relativizing thoughts, in the first place relativizing thoughts that articulate critique, is an epistemological necessity in this bourgeois concept of thinking. In this model of thinking, critique can only articulate alternative thoughts, alternative assumptive theories also proved by the facts it constructs for its proof.

It is only this format of critiquing theories that can intervene into theorizing in this concept of thoughts by complimenting other, in the same way proved thoughts, created and proved with the same circular procedure. It is this format of critique that stimulates critique as an ever-reactivated impulse for the creation of an ever-relativized knowledge and that at the same time immunizes knowledge against a critique that would trace any thoughts.

In this circular world of competing proved and relativized theories, the discourses among the holders of this knowledge can only prove the validity of their relative thoughts against others by monopolizing the production and publication of relativized theories. Monopolizing relativized thoughts is the only way to relativize their relativity. Monopolizing, that is, aiming at a leadership of thoughts by dominating the world of thoughts, is therefore the way this concept of science serves the cognitive impetus in scientific thinking seeking knowledge, its concept of cognition denies.

It is a tragic mistake to oppose the Western monopoly on theorizing, since monopolizing thoughts and arguing about the monopolisation of thoughts is the essential part of the Western sciences. Questioning this monopoly and building alternative local knowledge regimes opposes the Western sciences, but it opposes them by imitating, thus reinforcing the Western science approach, responding to the Western leadership in theorizing by struggle over scientific leadership.

Questioning the thoughts of the Western theories, and thus eroding the universal reign of Western thoughts, is not what the above discussed variations of critique do. Critiquing, not complimenting, thoughts is not an option the Western model of thinking knows. However, the fact that Western sciences only know this format of a relativized critique does not mean that it is not possible.

It is epistemologically "forbidden." That is why it is necessary and the only way to critique.

References

Ahktar, S. W. (n.d.) The Islam concept of Science, part 1, Al-Tawhid, A Journal of Islamic Thought and Culture 12, no. 3.

Alatas, S. F. (2003) Academic Dependency and the Global Division of Labour in the Social Sciences, Current Sociology 51: 599–613.

Alatas, S. H. (1974) The Captive Mind and Creative Development, in International Social Science Journal 36 (4): 9–25

——(2000) Intellectual Imperialism: Definition, Traits and Problems, in Southeast Asian Journal of Social Science 28 (1): 23–45.

Becher, T. and P. R. Trowler (2001) Academic Tribes and Territories. 2d ed. Ballmore, UK: Open University Press.

Bhaskar, R. A. (2008[1975]) A Realist Theory of Science. Oxon, UK: Routledge.

Calhoun, C. (2007) Nations Matter: Culture, History, and the Cosmopolitan Dream. London: Routledge.

Chakrabarty, D. (2000) Provincializing Europe: Postcolonial Thought and Historical Difference. Princeton: Princeton University Press.

Connell, R. (2007) Southern Theory: The Global Dynamics of Knowledge in the Social Science. Cambridge: Polity Press.

European Commission (2009) Emerging Trends in Socio-economic Sciences and Humanities in Europe, The Metris Report 2009, Retrieved from http://ec.europa.eu/research/social-sciences/pdf/metris-report_en.pdf (Last access on 5 July 2012)

Hofstede, G. (1984) Cultures's Consequences, London: Sage.

Huntington, S. P. (1996) The Clash of Civilizations and the Remaking of World Order. New York: Simon & Schuster.

Keim, W. (2008) Vermessene Disziplin, Zum konterhegemonialen Potential afrikanischer und lateinamerikanischer Soziologien. Bielfeld: transcript.

Kuhn, M. (2007) Inside Global Learning Societies—The "War of Ideas" of the Good World in the Global Battle of Cultures, in M. Kuhn (ed.), New Society Models for a New Millennium—The Learning Society in Europe and Beyond. New York: Peter Lang.

Kuhn, M. and S. O. Remoe (eds.) (2005). Building the European Research Area: Socio-economic Research in Practice. New York: Peter Lang.

Kuhn, M. and D. Weidemann (eds.) (2009) Internationalization of the Social Sciences and Humanities. Bielefeld: transcript.

Kuhn, M. and J. Kabbanji (eds.) (Forthcoming, 2013) Arab Social Thoughts in International Knowledge Encounters.

Mbembe, A. (2000) De la postcolonie. Essai sur l'imagination politique dans l'Afrique contemporaine, Paris: Karthala coll. "Les Afriques."

Nisbett, R. E. (2005) The Geography of Thought. London: Brealey.

Said, E. W. (2001 [1978]) Orientalism: Western Conceptions of the Orient. New Delhi: Penguin.

Sato, Y. (2010) Are Asian Sociologies Possible? Universalism versus Particularism, in M. Burawoy, M. Chang, and M. F. Hsieh (eds.), Facing an Unequal World: Challenges for a Global Sociology Vol. 2, Asia. pp.192–200, Taiwan.

Sims, C. A. (1980) Macroeconomics and Reality, Econometrica 48, no. 1: 1–48.

UNESCO, International Social Science Council (2010) World Social Science Report 2010: Knowledge Divides., Paris: UNESCO.

Wallerstein, I. (2001) Unthinking Social Science: The Limits of Nineteenth-century Paradigm. 2d ed. with a Preface. Philadelphia: Temple University Press.

———(2006) European Universalism: The Rhetoric of Power. New York: New Press.

Wallerstein, I., C. Juma, K. Fox, J. Kocka, D. Lecourt, V. Y. Mudimbe, K. Mushahoji, I. Prigogine, P. Taylor, and M.-R. Trouillot (1996) Open the Social Sciences: Report of the Gulbenkian Commission on Restructuring of the Social Sciences. Stanford: Stanford University Press.

What is Hegemonic Science? Power in Scientific Activities in Social Sciences in International Contexts

Kazumi Okamoto

Introduction

International scholarly activities in the social sciences are no longer special and unusual, and interactions between social scientists across geographical borders can frequently be seen through coauthoring, international conferences, joint research projects, scholar exchange programmes, and other international activities. Although these activities have brought collaborations to social science scholars, and have enabled them to build wider academic networks beyond the national context, they at the same time seem to have revealed an imbalance of research fund distribution, unevenness of material resources and facilities, and unlikeliness of non-English-native speakers to be able to publish their work in well-recognized, worldwide academic journals. This imbalance has been labeled as "hegemony," the domination of certain countries such as the United States, the United Kingdom, and some other Western European countries in the social sciences. As part of a recent discussion on internationalization of the social sciences, numerous articles can be found that discuss the North-South divide (Connell 2007), centre-periphery (Altbach 2002) relationship, academic dependency (Alatas 2003), and hegemonic power in the social sciences. These imply that there are two parts of social science communities: the North (or West), which is the centre of hegemonic power, and the other is South, the dependent periphery. The Western, which generally means North American and Western European, social science communities are deemed as the dominant power which globally sets research problems, relevant theories, and standard of academic practices in the social sciences, while academic communities in other countries are described as victims of domination by the Western social sciences. That is, they have fewer resources for research funds, facilities, publications, and other academic activities that are considered as relevant and necessary than the dominant academe.

In the above descriptions of the world social sciences, it seems that the key terms such as hegemony, power, and domination used to describe the position of Western social sciences over the rest are taken for granted and the meaning of these almost synonymously used categories are rarely carefully scrutinized. Rather, these terms are discussed as if they were "common sense" phenomena in the world of social sciences. Moreover, other common terms such as inequality are often considered as analogous to situations in which non-Western social science communities are dominated and ruled by certain Western counterparts. For instance, "inequality" seems to be mixed up with notions of hegemony and/or domination when discussing international academic activities in the social sciences such as cross-national research projects, publications, and theorizing. While the notion of hegemony includes the idea of antagonism between the divided science communities, the term inequality rather implies the idea of gradual differences. While inequality means that sciences do not operate under the same conditions and addresses the circumstances under which international science work, domination refers to the relation of hierarchies among the scientific subjects and subordination among scientists.

This paper, therefore, tries to clarify the different implications of the above-mentioned terms in order to better understand them and to enable us to discuss the current situation in the social sciences with regard to so-called scientific hegemony, which is widely perceived as a great obstacle, especially for social scientists coming from neither North America nor Western European countries in discussions about international scientific activities. I would also like to discuss issues that seem interrelated with the notion of hegemony, power, and dominance of the Western social sciences, such as the structures of social science knowledge generation, forms of valid knowledge in the social sciences, and reasons motivating social scientists to discuss international social sciences using the above categories. By stocktaking these aspects, it would be clearer for us what the topic is, and why and how we should tackle one of the important issues on the social sciences in the era of globalization.

The Definition of Hegemony and Perception of Hegemony among Social Scientists

Before we start discussing what scientific hegemony is and what is not, it might be helpful to have a brief look at the definition of hegemony and other related terms. Looking up some online English dictionaries is an instructive beginning. The meanings of the major terms are defined in the following way:

> Hegemony: leadership or dominance, especially by one state or social group over others (Oxford online); a situation in which one state or country controls others (Longman online).
>
> Dominance: power and influence over others (Oxford online); the fact of being more powerful, more important, or more noticeable than other people or things (Longman online).
>
> Power: the capacity or ability to direct or influence the behaviour of others or the course of events (Oxford online); the ability to influence people or give them strong feelings (Longman online).
>
> Inequality: difference in size, degree, circumstances, etc.; lack of equality (Oxford online); an unfair situation, in which some groups in society have more money, opportunities, power, etc than others (Longman online).

Though there are overlaps in the definitions of these words, it seems wise to neither mix up the particular relations between subjects in these categories nor—most importantly—to apply these categories, which originate from the world of global politics and global economies, to the world of science.

The general perception is that the North/West is the dominant power in the hegemonic social science world, in which inequality, dependency, and unfair opportunities for funding, publications, and scientific knowledge provision can be found. Despite the different spheres from which these categories are taken and applied to the world of international sciences and despite of the very different meaning, describing the international sciences with the above categories seems a common sense understanding in many discourses about the international science world.

However, do these categories really represent the current status in the social sciences? And is it really possible to apply these categories from the world of global politics to the world of international sciences? What is the motivation of scientists to discuss topics related to hegemony, domination, and inequality in the world of international social sciences?

Hegemonic Power of a Language?

Globalization of the social sciences seems to bring more challenges than benefits to social scientists. For instance, as its subtitle "Knowledge divides" indicates, the World Social Science Report (International Social Science Council 2010) focuses on rather negative effects from current international scholarly activities in the social sciences. Indeed, details of what they mean by "knowledge divides" are expressed as the chapter titles and their contents (e.g., chapter 3: "unequal capacities,"; chapter 4: "uneven internationalization,"; chapter 5.1: "Hegemonies and counter-hegemonies"). Generally, the majority of the contributions implies and/or exemplifies how social science knowledge is divided. Let us take some examples from the report. The most popular and probably the only approach to gauge internationalization/globalization of social sciences is the bibliometric approach, which references the International Social Sciences Index (ISSI) to observe which regions'/countries' social scientists are cited more frequently than others, which nationality collaborates with which other nationalities, what language is the most popular for such publications, and so forth. Chapter 4 of the World Social Science Report (2010) broadly takes this approach, and concludes how "uneven" knowledge generation and dissemination in the social sciences is. Despite that Frenken et al. note that the above-mentioned resources are "known to be biased" (ibid.: 145) as the majority of the journals that are counted are English language journals, they nevertheless exploit the resources and conclude from such admittedly biased resources that "research collaboration in the social sciences is dominated by North America and Western Europe" (ibid.: 148). Therefore, according to Frenken et al., the divide between "core and periphery" in the social science has persisted during past decades. For Gingras and Mosbah-Natanson, "the globalization and internationalization of research have essentially favoured Europe and North America, the regions that were already dominant" (ibid.: 153). Ammon goes into details about the role of English language in international scientific activities. He claims that English is "an asymmetric global language whose benefits are unequally distributed" (ibid.: 155). Thus, for him, the usage of English language in scientific communication including publications and conference presentations could only benefit English native speakers, and there is a limited flow of information, and funding, and publication opportunities for non-English speakers due to the strong structural linkage between Anglophone social science communities, which could be part of the reason for their domination. Although he suggests some solutions for improving the current situation, Ammon thinks that the English language could hamper non-English native social science scholars from participating in international activities.

As has been mentioned, gauging the level of international scientific activities via certain citation indices indicates an English-only language bias. Since these citation indices greatly rely on English journals, naturally only articles written in English would be visible beyond each science community. It is therefore not surprising that the authors cited above contributing to the World Social Science Report arrive at the same conclusion that the world social sciences is divided between North America-(Western) Europe and the rest, as they exploit the same resources. According to Archambault et al. (2006), such citation indices vastly overrepresent English-language publications while underrepresenting articles written in languages other than English. Hicks (2005) points out that there are other traditions and conventions for academic publications, especially in Social Science and Humanity (SSH), such as publishing books and other nonacademic media articles rather than journal articles. Despite these negative views about relying only on citations indices to gauge international scholarly activities in SSH, this approach has been used and attained a certain level of respectability among SSH scholars. Why do we use this approach, even knowing that it would not lead us to a reasonable picture of international scholarly practices?

As is widely known, citations are one of the most influential elements in university ranking such as Time Higher Education University Ranking and Academic Ranking of World Universities by Shanghai Jiaotong University, and, in a similar way, the citation indices seem to be used to decide world winners of scholars in international scholarly activities. In this sense, measuring so-called "internationality" via such obviously biased resources results in the same biases as noted above. As the World Social Science Report declares, the world of social science is divided into two parts-winners and losers-with nothing being mentioned about hegemony, power, and dominance, or that the latter is ruled by the former. Seemingly, notions of hegemony, power, and dominance could merely be a way to disguise the losers' irritation and frustration toward winners.

Some scholars such as Ammon find the use of English as the lingua franca of international academic social science studies problematic. Certainly, it is not so easy for any non-native English scholars to publish and/or to participate in international conferences in English. For instance, the very difficulty of the English language in a context of international scholarly activities has also been discussed among Japanese social and human science scholars (Japan Society for the Promotion of Science, 2011) in order for them to more participate in scientific discourse beyond the national level. Japanese SSH scholars have discussed concerns such as infrastructure for translation service for academic publication, budgetary matters, and whether publishing scholarly work in English bring authors any incentive at all would also exist in non-English-speaking countries. Nevertheless, efforts to improve the situation relating to English publications in non-English-speaking countries are not necessarily made because English is "hegemonic" language as Ammon strongly claims. No one is forced to publish in English, but English is the language which has been broadly used when scholars from different global regions gather and try to carry out any scholarly activities together. In such cases, there is a need for using one common language to communicate. Otherwise, it would be impossible to carry out such international activities.

Whatever language is chosen as the international scientific lingua franca, what Ammon describes as problems in using English would not disappear unless everyone was able to understand and to command many languages in the world. Of course, it is undeniable that English native speakers do have advantages in carrying out any scientific activities under this circumstance in terms of linguistic ability compared with non-English speakers. However, being able to speak, read, and write perfectly in English does not mean that only English native speakers can generate relevant scientific knowledge worldwide. There are surely excellent works done by non-English speakers in languages other than English. The more important point is that such works written in languages (e.g., Japanese) that are not widely understood by non-native speakers remain only in their national context, which hinder scholars of these works from having scientific dialogues with their foreign counterparts. Thus, since we are not really "forced" to use English as the academic language, English itself cannot be "hegemonic." Behind the complaints of Ammon and other scholars who question the use of English in social sciences, must be another unstated message: We, non-English native speakers, have many fewer advantages, or many more difficulties, in using English for academic purposes than English native speakers when we compete worldwide. Indeed, this has little to do with the English language itself being hegemonic, but rather it blames English because of the difficulty that non-English native speakers have in taking full advantage as native speakers do to show their presence in the world social sciences.

What we could see from the above selected discussions in the World Social Science Report is that the authors have the common grounds for what they call hegemonic, uneven, and divided world social sciences. That is, there is the dominant group of social science scholars, who tend to be located in North America or Western Europe, and they have much better conditions to play important and influential roles in the world social science. It seems that those who criticise this situation want to complain that they cannot be themselves dominant due to their working environment, conditions, and being non-English native speakers. We have seen in the previous section that dominance literally means the status by which one party influences others. Apart from the relation with power, being more important and/or more noticeable is also understood as the status of dominance. Being important and noticeable has a connection with the fact that other parties find a person or group (or some groups) of people important, since one cannot be important by oneself. Being important and therefore noticeable is the consequence of the fact that other people acknowledge certain person/people as important. Without this recognition by others, no one can be either important or noticeable, and therefore dominant. Thus having influence over others could also be the consequence of becoming important and noticeable.

What, then, is the real objective of the critique phrased with the notion of a hegemonic language? A different distribution of acknowledgments? Making the winners the losers and vice versa would indeed shift their roles. But would it abolish hegemonic relations?

Being "Dominant": A Means against Dominations?

Alatas's article on academic dependency (2003) has the same direction as the above-mentioned World Social Science Report. He refers to academic imperialism, which was originated from suzerain-colony relations in the nineteenth century and until the Second World War. This academic colonialism influenced colonized countries' social scientific thoughts, as the Edward Said's well-known work "Orientalism" (1978) describes and analyses. According to Alatas, the economic dependency has led to neocolonialism in the world of social sciences, and as the result, academic dependency has emerged. He defines the West as the following countries: the United States, Great Britain, and France, which "we may call the contemporary social science powers" (2003: 602). This is so because these countries:

> (1) generate large outputs of social science research in the form of scientific papers in peer-reviewed journals, books, and working and research papers; (2) have a global reach of the ideas and information contained in these works; (3) have the ability to influence the social sciences of countries due to the consumption of the works originating in the powers; and (4) command a great deal of recognition, respect and prestige both at home and abroad. (ibid.: 602)

Alatas's definition of the West and his reasoning why these Western countries can be taken as "the contemporary social science powers" (ibid.) appears to be very widely shared in discussing the issue of the skewed social science world as seen in the above-mentioned Social Science Report. Indeed, this structure of Western dominance related to producing a lot, disseminating in well-known, easily accessible worldwide journals results in making their work influential; thus they are more likely to be recognized, respected, and prestigious worldwide, reflecting on the taken-for-granted reality of current world of social science in respect to globalizing/internationalizing academic work. Therefore, it is not hard to concur with the Alatas's claim that the Western "monopolistic control of and influence over the social sciences in much of the Third World are ... (determined) rather by the dependence of Third World scholars and intellectuals on western social science in a variety of ways" (ibid.: 602). In short, he seems to express that Third World countries are academically dependent, as the aforementioned Western countries are too dominant to dismantle the structure of their dominance.

When we discuss the dominance of certain groups of people in the social sciences, often a certain tone crops up that can be understood as viewing the dominant groups as the ones that impose their influence too much on nondominanton groups. However, they cannot become dominant only by themselves. As discussed, recognition by others plays an important role for them to reach this dominant status. This is quite tricky because nondominant people also contribute to raise certain dominant people's status higher by referring to their work in their papers and presentations. Why do the nondominant people do it? The answer is simple: They also want to be recognized by referring to some of those well-known scholars' work to show others that he/she knows what these well-known scholars are doing. This means that, whether consciously or unconsciously, nondominant groups of scholars join this recognition game in the social sciences which the dominant group play.

What Alatas claims as "academic dependency" of the Third World scholars in social sciences on the Western social sciences, in the above sense, seems rather another way of expressing that those who have not yet been dominant in the world social sciences also somehow want to be dominant and influential in the future. While people are intensively discussing about such academic dependency as if it was the reality that has been created and imposed by "Western" countries, the core of the discussion is more geared toward the point why we, nondominant group(s) of social science scholars cannot also have chances to be winners of the world competition of the social sciences. The reward for the winners is certainly "a great deal of recognition, respect and prestige both at home and abroad" (Alatas, 2003: 602), which nondominant people could not obtain in the current situation. Similarly, Beigel (2011) refers to the World Social Science Report and notes the following: "Academic prestige was progressively concentrated and a set of international hierarchies was established–separating research completed in more prestigious academic centers from marginal knowledge produced and published outside." From this notion, Beigel also seems to concentrate on the prestige of social science scholars. Thus, we could now slightly see some possible reasons why advocates who are against Western social science power, hegemony, and dominance are so keen to discuss these issues in relation to the international social science scholarly activities. From some literatures, we could see the relationship between being dominant/influential/powerful and recognition/prestige of individual scholars. After all, it seems that a number of social science scholars are keen to become dominant, therefore influential and noticeable, because such status would bring them reward, namely, prestige in the world. That is probably why winning the social science competition is very important.

Globalization/internationalization of the social sciences has surely brought competition to social science scholars worldwide. However, getting recognized and becoming prestigious are not only characteristics of the global competition but the same could be seen in the "dominant" West, namely, in science communities in the United States and Great Britain. Becher and Trowler (2001) attempt to exhibit ways in which academic disciplines operate, ways to define and/or decide borderlines between disciplines, how subdisciplines emerge and are operated, how academics are rewarded and acquire prestige in their disciplines as well as what roles ethnicity and gender play in relation to their promotions and work styles, on the other. Their empirical studies and the literature exploited in their work are not limited to the social sciences, however; their main focus is to understand academic culture(s) in which work of academic people and the establishment of their career as academicians are operated. While Alatas (2003) gives us the impression that the Western dominant countries have monopolized opportunities for publications, research funds, and academic prestige, Becher and Trowler's work indicates that there is severe competition between academics working within these dominant countries. Since their empirical work took place in rather prestigious research universities in the United States and United Kingdom, we could draw a conclusion that location in the dominant West does not necessarily mean that members of such dominant academic communities are always academically dominant and powerful. For instance, as many non-Western scholars argue, publication is, as Becher and Trowler admit, important and a formal "criterion for recognition" (ibid.: 78); however, "it is not only what you write but who you are and where you come from that counts" (ibid.). They refer to some other similar studies relating to academic prestige and recognition, and come to a conclusion that one must study at a "right" —in this context prestigious— university, at least, for his/her doctoral study, and moreover, that they should be supervised by one of the "leading figures" (ibid.: 79) in the field he/she studies for his/her own future prestige. Although their work is not particularly focused on issues of internationalization/globalization of academe, it is interesting to glimpse at ways so-called Western academe in the U.S and the U.K operate. The work of Becher and Trowler somehow indicates that members of the dominant West also engage in a series of struggles and competitions among them to be recognized in any field of science.

It could be mentioned that internationalization/globalization have introduced this worldwide "winner-loser" relationship. Of course, before scientific activities acquired international dimensions such as several styles of collaboration with foreign partners, this competition was seen within the level of a national science community. One publishes more than others in a discipline in a country, and some might be better known in the field than others.

Similarly, some people from certain universities in a country tend to receive more funding, facilities, and equipment for research activities than colleagues from other universities. Besides, there are so-called prestigious research universities in a country, which receive more admiration and fame because of their status as elite universities. In this sense, what people advocate as "inequality" in relation to the international social science activities seems to exist before the social sciences took an international dimension.

As Becher and Trowler (2001) suggest, the majority of academicians are motivated toward individual prestige in their career. How prominent and famous they are in a disciplinary field is crucial, because such a status would bring a person more opportunities to get promoted within a university or to a better or more prestigious one. Once they are recognized in a country, they would have better chance to get acknowledged by foreign research institutions. This could make him/her more visible in the international scene rather than only in the national context. Again, as I quote the work of Becher and Trowler (2001), not everyone in the dominant West could have such opportunities for academic recognition. That is, one needs to start one's academic life as a student in a very prestigious university, and preferably, one needs to be supervised by a science celeb. This is simply because such connections in a particular environment would provide him/her a much better and often more privileged condition to promote him/herself than the others that do not have such connections. If one does not have such a condition, he/she should create a condition by networking, publishing a lot, and by other means which make him or her very visible in the science celeb circle. If and how the international sciences contribute to the progress of knowledge is seemingly not an issue such discourses seem to raise. Is the international and noninternational science world after all about the prestige of scientists?

Who Is Often Quoted Must Be RIGHT: Democracy in the Social Sciences?

Hegemony connotes the meaning of dominance, although interpretations of both words might vary from one person to another. When some people talk about hegemony and/or domination, sometimes they seem to be confused with the notion of majority. One would say that a hegemonic/dominant group of scholars get scientific approval from the majority because of the quality of their work. This seems a relevant statement; however, validity and quality of scientific work could not be measured by a number of the votes, and this assumption is only based on the number of citations in the aforementioned resources like the Social Sciences Citation Indexes and Arts and Humanities Citation Index. Relying on the number of citations, therefore, can hardly be an appropriate and reliable way to evaluate scientific contents. However, though certainly nobody believes in such a way of measuring the quality of sciences in international context counting citations—the majority counts. Historically mistakes and incorrectness in the natural sciences occurred by similar ways to this democratic approach relying on the majority's approval. For instance, the geocentric theory of the universe was believed to be a scientifically valid theory by the majority, but Copernicus's heliocentric system finally proved to be the one scientifically true. In this sense, it is risky to introduce the democratic approach (or the "majority rule" in science) when consistency of one's scientific work is judged. Yet, as long as the number of citations is the only mechanism to judge excellence of work in the social sciences, people would blindly believe in such a mechanism, and would be keener to have their work appear in journals that are adopted as credible in the citation indices. It might be, therefore, this strong belief in and the taken-for-granted reliability of the citation indices in the social sciences that makes scholars worldwide believe that it must be excellent work if one's work is cited and is appeared in the said citation indices. This is how the democratic approach in the social sciences has received its popularity as well as reliability from social scientists in different global regions, although this belief and its mechanism seem not to be logically sound. Thus, talking about a majority as being something influential to others in the social sciences seems rather redundant. However, again, we could find a certain connection between the mechanism (the citation indices), recognition, and the notion of majority in relation to the hegemonic social science structure behind the notion of majority.

To sum up the above discussion, one of the core issues on the hegemonic science structure seems to be recognition. Especially in the era of globalization in the social sciences it is crucial to get recognized in the so-called Western science circle, needless to say, via

Western norms and conventions of scientific work. The more non-Western scholars participate in this competition, the more strongly this competitive Western science system is supported. The irony of this system is that once a non-Western scholar who has complained about this system gets recognized in Western science circles, he or she can easily shift from the side of the losers to the winners. At that point, this competitive system is no longer a concern for him/her.

What Is Missed by All Knowledge Counting: True Hegemonic Knowledge

When one would like to observe how Western scholars understand thoughts (or mechanism of thought) from parts of the world other than the West, a book by Nisbett (2005) is interesting. As the starting point, Nisbett informs us about a small episode of interaction between his Chinese student and himself. For him, it was natural to think that people in the world, more or less, perceived things in the same ways as he normally did. However, one of his Chinese students pointed out that Chinese people have different ways of seeing the world. This discussion brought him to write The Geography of Thought: How Asian and Westerner Think Differently—and Why (2005). As a social psychologist, his main focus is to clarify differences that seem to occur due to cultural differences between Asian and Westerners, and to analyse them. Based on a number of social psychological studies, he examines how Asian and Westerners are different and what the reasons are for that. The most interesting part in this work in relation to the structure of scientific work is where he discusses how these Western-Asian differences affect ways of scientific work. He exemplifies a part of these effects by indicating the number of Nobel Prizes awarded in 1990s to scholars from the United States, Japan, Germany, and France. Especially, he mentions that while only one Japanese scientist was awarded the prize, forty-four U.S scientists were awarded, Germany got five, and France three, despite that the funding for science in Japan was much more than Germany and France. This, therefore, suggests that it does not seem to be a matter of how much money a country could spend on science. Nisbett reveals that "some Japanese scientists attribute the deficit in part to the absence of debate and intellectual confrontation" (ibid.: 195). He continues: "Peer review and criticism are rare in Japan, where such things are considered rude and where there is not widespread acceptance of their role in clarifying and advancing thought about scientific matters" (ibid.). Although he does not clearly say that Japanese scientists are not as good as their Western counterparts from the United States, Germany, and France in terms of the number of Nobel Prize laureates, we could see that he implies that Japanese scientists are lacking some of the conditions that are required for generating and developing scientific thinking. Similarly, the rhetoric seems also a problem for Asian scholars.

Most Westerners I speak to about this format[1] take it for granted that it is universal: How else could one communicate findings and recommendations briskly and convincingly or even think clearly about what one is doing? The truth is, however, that this linear rhetoric form is not at all common in the East. For my Asian students, I find that the linear rhetoric form is the last crucial thing they learn on their road to becoming fully functioning social scientists. (ibid.: 196)

This notion indicates that it is, indeed, for him universal that anyone that attempts to construct scientific arguments should be able to follow the Western linear rhetoric form. Therefore, it is unbelievable that Asian students who would like to be "fully functioning social scientists" find this rhetoric form least crucial. Later in this book, he also expresses how hard it is to educate such Asian students in American universities according to American or Western standard of higher education (ibid.: 211). Thus, some of Nisbett's observations on Asian students seem relevant for understanding how a Western social scientist finds problematic the behaviours and thoughts of Asian scholars/students when it comes to scientific activities. More importantly, he strongly believes that the Western ways of science are universal despite a number of findings he and his colleagues could exhibit about the differences between

---

[1] It takes the form of: background; problem; hypothesis or proposed proposition; means of testing; evidence; arguments as to what the evidence means; refutation of possible coun-terarguments; and conclusion and recommendations. (Nisbett 2005: 196)

Asian and Westerners in the ways how they see things and think. The fact is that he finds different ways of thinking does not prevent him from measuring any way of thinking against what he most naturally considers as the thinking of a "fully functioning scientist."

This view, that thoughts that do not fit into his definition of what scientific thinking is, must be not fully functioning thinking, is not only Nisbett's own personal view but a view broadly shared by Western scientists when they do research about Asian students studying at Western Higher Education institutes. Scholars and educators often discuss why Asian students tend to face challenges studying in Western universities, and how these challenges can be lessened, and indeed, many seek for reasons in different national cultural characteristics between West and East (e.g. Brown 2008, Durkin 2008). However, the noteworthy point about Nisbett is that he, unlike the above theorists about students, refers to scholars who are no longer academic trainees. Especially in the case of Japanese scholars his remarks about peer review and criticism seem a criticism on the absence of "normative" scientific convention in the Japanese social sciences. For Nisbett, therefore, it is beyond his imagination how Japanese and Asian social science scholars could properly develop any scientific thoughts without the "universal" format, which is the linear rhetoric form. Thus, we could see his strong message that ways to generate and deploy scientific knowledge in the social sciences should be the ways which Western scholars consider "universal." This belief in the universality of conventions and norms in the Western science could imply the hegemonic science structure, since such a belief could reinforce and justify the Western social science system as the world standard. Consequently, what the articles contributed to the World Social Science Report (2010) as well as Alatas's discussion on academic dependency (2003) actually reveal is that the Western (or Anglo-American) social science system does force scholars who have different academic norms and conventions to employ the Western ways of knowledge generation and dissemination. Probably this is the belief that constructs mechanism such as the use of citation indices, overrepresentation of English language in journal articles that are currently counted as internationally influential articles, and making prioritised research topics and preferred methodology, among other things. Therefore, the most fundamental element of discussion about so-called hegemonic social sciences is not about the winner-loser relationship but the taken-for-granted structure of knowledge generation and dissemination in the world social sciences.

The Complaint about Hegemonic Sciences

If we take the definition of the West that Alatas deploys, what he considers as powers in the contemporary social sciences puts emphasis on rather quantitative aspects such as "large output" (2003: 605) and "global reach" (ibid.), which lead to "a great deal of recognition, respect and prestige both at home and abroad" (ibid.). If one agrees with his definition of the West as the dominant social science power, the quality of scientific work as a criterion for being important and influential seems of less concern. Then, if the quality of scientific work is not as important in discussing who hegemonizes the social sciences, and how and why, what is the role of quality of scientific work in this context? As discussed earlier, the quality of work in the social sciences often tends to be judged by the number of citations in certain academic journals, however, such judgments are less likely to be based on academic dialogues among social scientists from all over the world to scrutinize their logical consistency and validity. In such a situation, the more one publishes in well-known academic journals, the better one presumably is as a social scientist. Moreover, by doing so there would be more opportunities that others might cite his/her articles, then, he/she would attain a higher status in terms of appearing in citation indices. This would increase or improve one's personal academic status, which might lead them to further career promotion. In this context, it matters less what is published; instead, how much is published—in other words how visible a scientist is from the Western social science circle—is more important. As the result, people who have such personal ambitious go into this very system which they hate and criticize as Western hegemony. They might think what they practice is counterhegemonic against Western social sciences. However, what they do not realise is that it is actually the opposite of what they think. They strongly support the system, which they consider an obstacle for them to participate in international scholarly activities in the world social sciences, by participating in it. How ironical it is! As long as they practice these counterhegemonic activities within the system, little is changed.

As mentioned at the beginning of this paper, a great number of scholars understand that there is a clear division of West versus non-West, North versus South, and centre versus periphery when they discuss the situation in the world social sciences. These divisions might mislead people into taking fundamentally unsuitable directions as they discuss the basic matter(s). Certainly, unequal situations of research funding, reference resources, facilities, and other things that closely relate to research activities do exist and are dependent on a nation-state's economic and political situation. It is not to be denied that there are lots of competitions in the world we live. Under these circumstances, it is almost impossible not to judge who is more successful or who has more than others, because once a competition starts there will always be a winner and a loser. Either one critiques competition as such, but if one does not do it, it is odd to advocate competitions without winner and losers. There would be no equal competitions in which everyone could be the winner. However, I point out that so far the discussion on this matter seems to have placed too much emphasis on the nature of science competition and the significance of getting access into the science celeb circle. These aspects are orientated to the self-satisfaction of scientists. This self-satisfaction, as discussed already, relies less on the scientific quality of one's work but more on his/her fame, prestige, and popularity in the world. If one is more interested in the quality of others' work, it really does not matter if you come from the West, the South or the periphery. One's scientific thoughts are not necessarily dependent on others' ideas which are more popular and influential. At the same time, if the dominant thoughts from the West/North/centre are logically consistent, they should be scientifically appreciated.

In the context of constructing globalized social sciences, the belief in the universality of Western science conventions and norms, which were reflected in the Nisbett's work (2005), could hinder scholars who do not come from the Western science background in scientific collaborations. Japanese social and human scientists also point out such a Western-centred view as one of the difficulties in international collaborations, and they contest the idea that Japanese scholars cannot show their disagreement in scientific collaborations with their foreign counterparts (Okamoto, 2010). If the West is perceived as being hegemonic in scientific work, such a belief of the Western style of scientific work as being universal should be pointed out. Although such taken-for-granted conventions and norms in Anglo-American ways of scientific work in relation to the structure of social science work has rarely been discussed[2], it is important to realize how these influence and often create difficulties in international scientific activities, because scientific hegemony is, after all, not about the competition among

---

[2]   One of the rare works on the issue was carried out by Kuhn and Weidemann (2005). Their work depicts that even among European scholars experienced challenges in implementing joint research projects under EU Framework Programmes.

social scientists from different countries but the structure into which we have been swallowed. In order to better understand what hegemonic science is and whether or not such science exists, what we are aiming at by generating social science knowledge as well as the question of what we call as social science knowledge is to be answered. A discussion about hegemonic science or any other version of science does not make sense unless we know the answer to these questions and realize why we work in the field called science; without these answers, we only reinforce the existing structure of the world social sciences.

Most of the discussions we could find on the topic of hegemony, dominance, power, and inequality in the social sciences seem to assume that so-called the Western social science forced them to use their methodology, concepts, theories, and style of working. However, if one does not want to follow such Western trends, he/she could still carry out his/her academic work without following them. In fact, this is how it is used to be in many countries' social sciences, and probably it still is in some countries and for some scholars. Thus, contra Alatas (2003), there is no reason to be totally dependent on mainstream concepts and ideas from the West. Scholars are really dependent on the Western ideas and concepts when they are also dependent on the Western social science system as discussed above. Therefore, the West/North/centre itself is an imaginary enemy scholars have created as hegemony, dominance, and power in the social sciences. If we have to tackle issues that hinder social science scholars from regions that are not included in the West, our first target should be the taken-for-granted universality of the Western social science knowledge generation and dissemination system and of norms and conventions in the Western social sciences.

References

Alatas, S. F. (2003) Academic Dependency and the Global Division of Labour in the Social Sciences, in Current Sociology 51(6): 599–613.

Altbach, P. G. (2002) Centers and Peripheries in the Academic Profession: The Special Challenges of Developing Countries, in P. G. Altbach (ed.), The Decline of the Guru: The Academic Profession in Developing and Middle-Income Countries. Chestnut Hill, MA: Center for International Higher Education. pp.1–22.

Ammon, U. (2010) The Hegemony of English, in UNESCO, The World Social Science Report. Paris: UNESCO. pp.154–155.

Archambault, E., E. Vignola-Gagne, G. Cote, V. Lariviere, and Y. Gingras (2006) Benchmarking Scientific Output in the Social Sciences and Humanities: The Limits of Existing Databases, in Scientometrics 68(3): 329–342. Budapest: AcademiaiKiado.

Becher, T. and P. R. Trowler (2001) Academic Tribes and Territories. 2d ed. Buckingham, UK: Open University Press.

Beigel, F. (2011) Academic Dependency: Response to Sztompka, in Global Dialogue, ISA Newsletter 2(2). ISA. Retrieved from http://www.isa-sociology.org/global-dialogue/2011/11/academic-dependency/ (Last access on 12 January 2012).

Brown, L. (2008) The Incidence of Study-Related Stress in International Students in the Initial Stage of the International Sojourn, in Journal of Studies in International Education 12(1): 5–28.

Connell, R. (2007) Southern Theory: Social Science and the Global Dynamics of Knowledge. Cambridge, UK: Polity Press.

Durkin, K. (2008) The Middle Way: East Asian Master's Students' Perceptions of Critical Argumentation in U.K. Universities, in Journal of Studies in International Education 12(38): 38–55.

Frenken, K., J. Hoekman and S. Hardeman (2010) The Globalization of Research Collaboration, in UNESCO, The World Social Science Report. Paris: UNESCO. pp.144–148.

Gingras, Y. and S. Mosbah-Natanson (2010) Where Are Social Sciences Produced?, in UNESCO, The World Social Science Report. Paris: UNESCO. pp.149–153.

Hicks, D. (2005) The Four Literature of Social Sciences, in H. F. Moed, W. Glänzel and U. Schmoch (eds.) Handbook of Quantitative Science and Technology Research: The Use of Publication and Patent Statistics in Studies of S&T Systems, New York: Kluwer Academic.

International Social Science Council (2010) World Social Science Report. Retrieved from http://www.unesco.org/shs/wssr (Last access on 15 March 2012).

Japan Society for the Promotion of Science (2011) Jinbun Shakaikagaku no Kokusaikanitsuite (On the internationalization of human and social sciences). Retrieved from http://www.jsps.go.jp/j-kenkyukai/data/02h oukokusho/houkokusho.pdf (Last access on 7 July 2012).

Kuhn, M. and D. Weidemann (2005) Reinterpreting Transnationality—European Transnational Socio-economic Research in Practice, in M. Kuhn and S. O. Romoe (eds.) Building the European Research Area: Socio-Economic Research in Practice. New York: Peter Lang.

Nisbett, R. E. (2005) The Geography of Thought: How Asians and Westerners Think Differently—And Why. London: Brealey.

Okamoto, K. (2010) Challenges for Japanese Social and Human Scientists in International Collaborations, unpublished Masters Degree Thesis submitted to the University of London.

Said, E. W. (1978) Orientalism. London: Routledge and Keagan Paul.

Counter Strategies?

The Emergence of Hegemonic Social Sciences and Strategies of Non (counter) Hegemonic Social Sciences

Kwang-Yeong Shin

Introduction

Theories of the social sciences developed in the West have dominated theoretical discourses and empirical research in the non-Western world since the nineteenth century. Though modern social sciences emerged first from Middle East, represented by Ibn Khaldun, the social sciences developed in the West since the nineteenth century became the dominant mode of social sciences nowadays. As higher education and academic credentials were introduced in the colonized countries by colonial governments or religious missionaries, Western social sciences were transplanted to those countries. Thus, the university system in the non-European regions emulated the Western university system in terms of degree, academic schedule and curriculum. Universities in those countries suffered from the shortage of appropriate staffs who could teach university students. Thus, foreign born professors or local scholars educated in the West took positions at the universities.

The institution of higher education and the social sciences experienced interruption and discontinuity when colonial countries were liberated from imperialist rule after the World War II. Thus, the higher education in the newly liberated countries did not properly function as educational institutes until teaching staffs and administrative system were fully established to accommodate students' demands. At the time, the major role of universities was teaching rather than research. Mostly, the contents of teaching in the social sciences were social theories developed in the West. Indigenous social thoughts and social theories were not introduced at university curriculum yet.

Theoretical discourses in academic journals and books in the West overrode local and indigenous social discourses that persisted for several centuries in non-Western regions. "Local social sciences" at a rudimentary stage were completely removed from the modern education system as they were regarded as pre-scientific or non-scientific. The social sciences in the West have dominated the social sciences in the non-Western regions even after countries were liberated from the imperial rule.

Hegemony of the Western social sciences was already established as the West dominated non-European countries as their colonies. Newly established universities taught medicine, natural sciences, humanities, and the social sciences. Those universities had authority over modernity and power over knowledge by monopolizing symbolic spaces, and the new and highest education system. Domination on colonies by imperialist countries was not done simply by coercive power but hegemonic power which shaped the ways in which the people in colonies perceived the world they lived. The power of the Western social sciences shaped how to define issues and how to deal with the issues. To use Foucault's term

(1970), the Western social sciences affected a new episteme in the social sciences in postcolonial countries, operating as unrecognized, unnoticed and untold underlying assumption about legitimate knowledge.

Even in the postcolonial period, social theories have been produced mostly in the West and consumption or application of those social theories through translation or transplantation has been continued in non-Western regions. For example, relevance and validity of those social theories in different social, cultural, historical context have not been fully interrogated by scholars in the non-West. Cultural and social contexts of those social theories were not recognized as legitimate factors to adjudicate social theories. Thus social theories developed in the West have been considered as abstract universal theories beyond spatial and temporal boundaries.

In this paper, I explore the nature of hegemonic social sciences, revealing institutional bases of hegemonic social theories after the World War II. Analyzing modernization theory and neo-classical economics, I address how the state, institutions, and market jointly operate in shaping hegemony of social theories. After that, I will discuss double indigenization, symmetrical comparison, denationalization so as to seek for the possibility of alternative social sciences which intends the non-hegemonic social sciences. Double indigenization refers to theoretical reflection through re-contextualizing Western social theories in the West and contextualizing local social theories in the non-West. Then I propose asymmetrical comparison to overcome limits of comparative approaches that contribute to undermine the hegemonic social sciences since the late twentieth century. I also suggest the necessity of rethinking the unit of the social sciences. Implicitly the nation state has been assumed to be equal to society. Mostly the social sciences in the West equate the nation state to society. Globalization has been restructuring boundaries of "the social" beyond the national state, transforming conventional conceptions of society and sociological discourses themselves as well.

What Do Hegemonic Social Sciences Mean Today?

While dominance of the Western social sciences has been an undeniable truth since the colonial period in non-Western countries, there have been different understandings of the meaning of dominance of the Western social sciences. While some social scientists in the non-Western countries regard it as natural since the social sciences in the West have been advanced much earlier than those in the non-Western countries, others perceive it as continuation of knowledge production controlled by the West in the name of universal science. Social theories and empirical research by scholars and institutes in the West dominated the global academic fields. Institutional bases of knowledge production such as publication of books and journals were also established much earlier in the West than in the non-West, as the knowledge market, selling books and journals and possessing copy rights, became lucrative. The West preoccupies the position of knowledge producer and supplier, whereas the non-West tends to import those produced knowledge, including social theories and research output not through academic activities. Unbalanced knowledge markets affect not only the flows of knowledge from the West to the non-West but also relations of knowledge power between the West and the non-West, operating through ideas and institutions.

Hegemonic social sciences of the West have established as scholars in the non-West accepted concepts and theories of the social sciences of the West. Modernization theorists, for instance, suggest a general framework for social development in non-Western countries, identifying key factors promoting social development such as technology, education and literacy, rational personality, achievement motives etc. (Inkeles 1974; McClelland 1961). Industrialization and technical changes contribute to emergence of free enterprises and autonomous civic organizations. Backwardness of the third world was considered as an outcome of underdevelopment of technology and sciences. The final stage of social development is democratization in which rational and autonomous citizens engage in political process (Lipset 1960). In addition, developed countries in the West can be a model of the future of less-developed countries when they are modernized enough in the long-term perspective. Thus, endogenous social changes are necessary for overcoming backwardness of non-Western countries, following the trajectory of social progress of the Western countries.

Ascendance of modernization theory in the 1960s and the early 1970s influenced discourse on development in the social sciences including economics, political science and sociology in the Third World. In particular, the Third World countries pursuing economic development accepted core arguments of modernization theories in their government policies. Politicians and scholars who were influenced by modernization theory attempted to transplant economic and social policies of the advanced societies into their countries, emphasizing the endogenous factors.

One of critical weaknesses of modernization theory is that it fails to recognize historical processes of social changes in a longer perspective. Assuming that social development of the West was an outcome of endogenous factors within each Western country, modernization theory completely ignores the fact that the imperialist experience of core Western countries was a significant factor for development of the West over two centuries (Frank 1970; Cardoso and Falleto 1979). As the cold war system was intensified, however, core assumptions of modernization theory became adopted by the Kennedy government and modernization theories went beyond academic circles (Latham 2000). Thus, modernization theory was charged with highly politicized social theory in the 1970s and 1980s. Ironically, however, as political democracy and market economy become a dominant social system in an era of globalization, "a loose or weak version of it is experiencing a revival in the academy as well" (Berman 2009).

We can discern another type of hegemonic social sciences reinforced by institutions including the market, different from modernization theory directly engaged by the state. Because of increasing theoretical struggles among the social sciences theories, some social theories in the West do not dominate the whole intellectual fields. However, it sets the limit of critiques or the boundaries of discontents by emphasizing the nature of the social sciences as a scientific endeavor, defined by narrow disciplinary doctrine. For instance, neoclassical economics and economists preoccupy major institutions such as university and economic institutes and reproduce neoclassical economists, excluding different economic theories and research (Blaug 1997). Thus issues that cannot be proved or disproved due to limits of analytical technique or empirical data are regarded beyond academic discourses. Or heterodox economics with different perspectives and different analytical methodology are completely excluded from the academic discourse. For a while, for instance, critical theories on globalization have been ignored by mainstream economists simply because some arguments are hard to be proved or styles of writing are not confirming to the standard economists' format. The practice of boundary maintenance has been accompanied by professional education at graduate level. Even after the financial crisis in the USA in 2008, the model of education of students in mainstream economics remained intact simply because those who initiate reform are subjects to be reformed or because those who are educated in heterodox economics experienced hard time to find jobs after graduations (Alberti 2012). Though economists trained in the USA recognize the failure of academic economics, the principle that "analytical rigor is everything and relevance is nothing" was internalized among economists (Colander et al. 2009). In short, as Rosenberg (1992) argues, economists did not succeed in providing economic theories of real economy. Nevertheless, they do not know how to escape from the dilemma yet, simply because they are parts of institutions composed of professors, students and curriculum which are not replaceable in a short period.

From the above discussion, we can identify three modes of the hegemonic social sciences. The first one is hegemony based on paradigms developed in the West. Some paradigms prevail over the global academic fields including both the West and the non-West. As Kuhn (1962) argues, a paradigm determines legitimate problematic, research methods and mode of presentation of research results. While dominant paradigms in the social sciences are much less than in natural sciences, there are many weak versions of paradigms in the social sciences. In the social sciences, there are contending social theories. However, there are dominant social theories accepted by scholars in the Third World. Translation and transplantation of social theories in the West has contributed to the dominance of Western social theories in the non-Western countries.

The second is an institutional hegemony by which some concepts and theories dominate graduate schools, academic journals, research funding organizations and economic organizations. Those who do not follow those rules are excluded in the game. Research articles that do not accept dominant perspectives are not accepted by major journals. Thus, the dominance of particular concepts and theories is associated with power explicitly associated with institutions. In addition, it is also strongly linked with languages used in analyzing issues. Thus, though there are several official languages used in international academic meetings, English is the most commonly used language and dominates academic discourses. Language barrier plays a significant role in marginalizing local concepts and theories written in other language than English in the global social sciences.

The third is the contested hegemony that refers to the situation in which concepts and theories are regarded as less valid and questionable but alternative concepts and theories are not available yet. When there is not a theory with better explanatory power than the existing one, in spite of serious problems, the existing theories cannot be rejected. To use Lakatos' term (1978), the existing concepts and theories persist until a "progressive research program" emerges. The less valid research program will be replaced by an alternative research program only when the alternative research program will be available. For example, scholars in the Third World accept agenda and research topics defined by the existing theories in the West, even though they are critical of those theories.

Search for Non-hegemonic Social Sciences

New tides

Recently, comparative historical approaches and cultural psychology provide good example to incorporate spatial and temporal context in the social sciences. Above all, acknowledging cross-national differences, comparative research has emerged as less hegemonic social sciences in the West. One of the most significant contributions to the social sciences is made in the field of comparative historical analysis over the past decades (Steinmo, Thelen and Longstrech 1992; Mahoney and Rueschemeyer et al. 2003; Crouch 2006). Comparative political economy and comparative historical sociology begins to emphasize the limit of universal social theories by contextualizing them with regard to institutions or socio-political dynamics. The growth of comparative historical perspectives in the social sciences undermines relevance of social theories mostly developed in a single country rather than reinforces them. Comparative approaches seek social theories based on particular culture and society, recognizing variation of social systems due to differences in history, culture and institutions. In other words, comparative historical approaches contribute to perceive the reality in one country within a spatial-temporal context, usually captured by "temporal process and path dependence" (Mahoney and Rueschemeyer 2003: 6). Furthermore, it also allows us to conceive concepts and theories in the West from a comparative perspective.

The rise of comparative research in the late twentieth century shows two distinct things. One is that while cultural dimension was emphasized in the human sciences in the nineteenth century, institutional dimension is more accentuated in the social sciences in the twentieth century. For example, GiambattistaVico (1668–1774) and Johan Gottfried Herder (1744–1891) advocated a new understanding of human sciences, suggesting peculiar culture in each society. Unlike natural sciences, they argue, cultural forms such as literature, customs, a *volksgeist* shape different historical paths in each society. Comparative historical researchers in the social sciences in the twentieth century, such as Barrington Moore (1966), Theda Skocpol (1979), Gøsta Esping-Andersen (1990), Charles Tilly (2004), did not pay much attentions to culture.[1]

Instead they focus on the state, policies, economic changes, social and political movements etc. Looking at historical trajectories of political transformation or systemic variation, they compare socio-political changes across among countries at the macro level.

Another is that while comparative research in the social sciences undermines relevance of the internal (theoretical) hegemony of the social sciences in the West, it also does not significantly change the external (institutional) hegemony of the social sciences in the West. Most of comparative research has been produced by American so-

---

[1] The meaning of culture here is very different from that in cultural studies in which culture covers from ideology to popular culture or sub-cultures. For varieties of usage of culture, see During (2005).

cial scientists, though they do not claim overarching general/universal theories.[2]

Accumulation of data and information about other societies requires advanced information technology, sufficient financial resources and long term engagement of researchers. Without much research funds and trained researchers, it is impossible to do comparative research in a large scale. Thus only top research universities in the West provide financial supports for comparative research for several years. Thus the rise of comparative research in the social sciences is not directly related with the development of the social sciences in the Third World. It is a new trend only for scholars and research institutes with more efficient technical and institutional bases in the West.

Cultural psychology is an alternative approach to universal and unified psychology, by uniting culture, society and psychology. It challenges the mainstream psychology that assumes psychology of human being as universal. Instead, it emphasizes that psychological processes are culturally bounded and culture shapes emotion, cognition, value and attitude (Fiske et al. 1998; Nisbett 2003; Shweder 1991). It also assumes that there are qualitatively different cultures across countries or regions. Although geographic boundary is not necessarily equivalent to cultural boundary, multiplicity of cultures persists and generates different cognitive and emotional psychology. In other words, cultural psychology tries to understand

---

[2] One exception might be Kiser and Hechter who argue that a general theory is necessary to test the research conducted (1998).

"ethnic and cultural sources of diversity in emotional and somatic functioning, self-organization, moral evaluation, social cognition and human development" (Shweder 2000: 210). Instead of searching for psychological concepts and theories universally applicable, cultural sociology seeks for locally valid multiple psychologies. Contrary to mainstream neoclassical economics, cultural psychology considers social actions and economic decision making as an outcome affected by culturally inherited cognitive factors (Valsiner and Rosa ed. 2007: 23–39).

However, emphasis on culture generates some difficulty in defining culture. Does China have one culture? Can East Asia be considered to have same culture? Some suggests cultural group as a unit of analysis in cultural psychology. For example, Hwang (2005) argues that religious groups such as Confucian, Muslim or Buddhist groups are suggested to be object of research because of distinctiveness of life styles, beliefs, cognitions, emotions and behavior. It might be reasonable to agree that cognitions and emotions are solely dependent on religion. But it might be also reasonable to assert that there are variations in cognitions and emotions within the same religious society. Furthermore, many societies are multi-religious societies which deny any simple classification of a country by religion. We can conclude that as Elster (2007: 160–161) correctly argues, some emotions are universal and other emotions are not universal. How we classify countries by religion remains as an unsettled issue.

Double Indigenization

Focusing on spatiality and temporality of the social sciences, we discuss two issues associated with hegemonic social sciences of the West and the possibility of non (counter) hegemonic social science in non-Western regions. The first one is double indigenization: The first order indigenization refers to consider the Western social sciences as indigenous social sciences rooted in the West. For example, Karl Marx's theory and Max Weber's theory are derived from social changes in the Western Europe or Germany. They tried to capture the nature and direction of social changes in the Western Europe in the nineteenth century. The validity of their theories can be judged not only by the internal logics in each theory but also by its relevance with social changes in the Western Europe in the nineteenth century (see 1 in Figure 1). Indigenization of sociology and development of local social sciences emphasize specificity of each society by contextualization of the social sciences in the West and re-contextualization of local knowledge. Contextualizing the Western concepts and theories within the Western societies allows us to comprehend the relationship between theories and societies at the spatial-temporal dimension, identifying unique contextual factors tacitly incorporated in the theories. It implies that the Western concepts and theories can be considered as indigenous concepts associated with the Western societies.

The second order indigenization is to compare the relationship between social theories and social reality in the West (1 in Figure 1) with that in the local societies in the Non-Western World (4 in

Figure 1). We need to understand both society A and society B so as to compare the relationship between theory and society. Without contextualizing social theories in the West, they can be directly applied to other societies (3). While some regards (4) as the indigenization of the social sciences, it is incomplete in that it does not pay sufficient attention to the applicability of theory A to society B. Neoclassical economists among others display strong disposition to apply abstract theories developed in the West to the Third world, mimicking physics in natural sciences. Sometimes, mathematical models displaying a relationship among economic factors are considered to be universal economic models to be applied to any economic system. Without critical reflections, concepts and theories developed in society A are introduced to society B (2). The second order indigenization requires reasonable understanding of both A and B, which might be demanding for sociologists in the society B as well as the society A. Through the process of double indigenization we can reach at theory B, applicable to society B.

Limited generalization refers to an attempt to generalize within a restricted condition. Though overarching generalization of the social sciences is impossible, we should avoid unrestricted and limitless plural social sciences. Thus the compromise between universalism and localism is a limited generalization which searches for the social sciences valid under the certain conditions. Which conditions are required to talk about limited generalization? The elaboration of the conditions is the major concern of those who search for the non-hegemonic the social sciences.

Regardless of radical or conservative social theories, all social theories are indigenous social theories. However, we can move from a single society to more broad societies by double indigenization. Without double indigenization, an imposition of radical theories or conservative theories developed in the West to the non-Western society could distort the reality of the non-Western society. In short, it fails to promote better understanding of local societies as well as Western societies. The core of double indigenization is that Western social theories themselves should be considered as indigenous social theories based on Western countries.

Symmetrical Comparison

As we observe, resurgence of comparative historical research in the social sciences significantly contributes to weaken hegemonic social sciences in the West. Today comparative research, which was considered as a marginal field in sociology, political sciences and psychology until 1980s, becomes a core research field among major universities. As globalization proceeds, comparative perspectives are gaining more attentions from academics as well as business. As global communication through the Internet and other communication technology has been advanced, knowledge and information about other societies has been drastically increased. The growth of comparative perspectives has changed the tide of academic research in the social sciences in the West.

However, comparative research in the social sciences in the West tends to marginalize small countries in the non-Western countries, mainly focusing on big countries in the West or big countries in the non-Western countries. Small and less developed countries in the Third World are easily ignored by social scientists in their comparative research. There has been asymmetrical relationship between big countries and small countries and between advanced countries and less developed countries in comparative research in the West. The Third World countries are not so visible in comparative research in sociology and political sciences. Thus the society and the people in the less developed small countries are forgotten in major theoretical discourses in the social sciences.

In order to advance the social sciences reflecting social change and culture, social scientists should expand their scope of comparative research by incorporating small and less developed countries in their research. Biases skewed toward advanced countries or big countries undermine validity and reliability of research outcomes. In order to test theoretical arguments developed from the research on big countries, comparative research on small countries might be a good research strategy to promote more comprehensive or universally applicable social theories. It can serve as method for hypothesis test and parallel demonstration of theory for theory development (Skocpol and Somers 1980).

How do we do comparative research in the social science? There are many good text books on comparative research methods (Ragin 1987; Landman 2000; Bradly and Collier 2004). I would not address new methods or technical issues. Rather here I discuss meta-theoretical issues that might be addressed in the tradition of current comparative research and suggest symmetrical comparison as an alternative to it. The current comparative research has distinct features that restrict a full-fledged comparative perspective in a global era. Regarding meta-theoretical issues in comparative research, I will focus on two related issues; one is ontological and another is institutional.

An ontological issue is related with the local asymmetry underlying in the comparative social science research. Researchers are trying to capture causal mechanism which operates across societies. However, some comparative researches have a limited spatial scope in their analysis but they do not make a statement clearly by assuming their research results as universal or by ignoring other societies excluded in their comparative research. For instance, comparative researches on varieties of capitalism (VOC) (Hall and Sockice 2001) and welfare regimes (Esping-Anderson 1990) mostly focus on European cases or societies in the West. Since they do not include other societies in Africa, Asia, and Latin America, they are completely Eurocentric. However, their theories are treated as universal theories on capitalism and welfare regime. Thus they contribute to recognize heterogeneity of social formation in contemporary capitalist countries but they still reflect the unequal distribution of global power (Quijano 2000; Wallerstein 2006). Even though the theory can be a starting point of discussion, it will be possible to discuss more varieties of capitalism by symmetrical comparison by which other institutional characteristics can be captured by comparison of the West and the non-West in a balanced way.

Another issue is an institutional asymmetry in comparative research. Comparative research has been done mostly by social scientists in universities and institutes in the USA and some European countries. Thus the ascendency of comparative research is not a global phenomenon but an academic phenomenon in the advanced industrial countries. Consequently it contributes to the dominance of a weak version of academic hegemony of the West over the rest. A weak version of academic hegemony refers to the hegemony of academic research in one society or one regime over the rest, based on the natural monopoly of academic discourse by one society or by one region. For instance, the USA takes the dominant position in the global academic ecology, restricting diverse local voices and local perspectives of the Third World countries. The voices and perspectives of the powerless are not visible not because of the lack of validity or reliability of their voices but because of the powerless status of scholars of the Third World in the global academic ecology. While academic imperialism ended up with the end of colonial system, the weak version of academic hegemony of the West persists in various new forms after the Cold War and in the era of globalization.

Changing Boundaries of the Social

One of the most striking developments of the contemporary world is the compression of space and time in a remarkable pace. Globalization has completely transformed the economic environment and life of the people in the world, destroying traditional national territory and national identity. Mobility of commodity, capital, labor power, information and culture has been precipitated since the late twentieth century.

Globalization gives rise to serious doubt to the validity of traditional sociological theories which assume the national state as a natural unit of analysis. The meaning of "the social" in sociological discourse was regarded as equivalent to the social within the nation state. Globalization begins to blur the meaning of geographical territory of the nation state. Through the Internet and telecommunication, the boundary of imaginary community has been expanded beyond territorial unit. The formation of multicultural society through migration has transformed cultural identity shared by racial or ethnic groups living in a given territory.

Globalization generates fluidity of symbolic demarcation accompanied by geographic territory and classificatory boundary. Thus traditional concepts and theories based on the nation state produce difficulty in explaining newly emerging social and political phenomena. For example, while there has been the continuous rise of class inequality, the working class struggle has been weaken in the non-West as well as in the West. The flow of migrant workers and the formation of the transnational capitalist class have revealed the limit of the traditional working class struggle, shattering the social base of class conflict (Robinson 2004; Sklair 2001).

Globalization changes the traditional conception of the social that has been rooted in the nation state. The social as a foundation of the traditional sociology has been changed through ever increasing fluidity of symbolic and cultural boundaries and ever expanding imaginary communities via Internet and mobile networks. To use Bauman's term (2000), liquid modernity, emerging global system has brought the unprecedented fluid state of life world of human being. Shifting boundary of the social has also brought the new possibility of articulating new concepts and theories rooted in the local, lower unit than the nation.

Concluding Remarks

Knowledge production in the social sciences has been organized by complex political, institutional and material power of a society. While the boundary of the nation state has weakened with ever accelerating globalization, the social sciences in the world have persistently shown the dominance of the Western social sciences over the rest. Over the Cold War period, the social sciences in the USA dominated the global social sciences, influencing research agenda setting, research questions and theoretical perspectives in other countries. Both the state and the market power increasingly have affected social scientific research in the USA during the Cold War period and even in the post-Cold War. Thus the hegemony of the Western social sciences, particularly that of the USA, still has not diminished in the era of globalization. The social sciences of the advanced or big countries dominates the social sciences of the less developed or small countries. In particular, the social sciences in the Third World have been strongly affected by the social sciences of the West.

The rise of East Asia opens a new way to reconsider the issue of the hegemony of the social sciences in the West over the rest. In the 1970s, dependency theories in Latin America provided an opportunity to critically examine the hegemony of modernization theory. Indigenous social scientists in Latin America began to challenge social theories developed in the West critically, recognizing economic reality in Latin American countries. In the 1990s, social scientists in East Asia began to reconsider the validity of social theories based on European or American experiences. As classical social sciences in the nineteenth century in Europe reflected European social changes, they begin to think that new social theories based on East Asian social changes might develop. Though they are not so big in number, they might challenge the hegemony of the West in the social sciences.

This paper suggests double indigenization of the social sciences and symmetrical comparison as a new way to construct non-hegemonic or counter hegemonic social sciences against the hegemonic social sciences of the West. The double indigenization is to consider concepts and theories of the West as indigenous concepts and theories rooted in the social changes and history of the West and to evaluate them in the context of the non-West. Symmetrical comparison is to carry out comparative research in consideration of possible logical asymmetry, spatial limitation of comparative research, and institutional asymmetry, the dominance of the West in disciplinary organizations such as social scientists and institutes of the social sciences.

The rise of the social science in the earlynineteenth century in Europe has prevailed for almost two centuries. The hegemony of social sciences of the West over the rest has also persisted for that period. Globalization begins to transform the hegemony by undermining validity of social theories developed in Europe and America and by rising East Asia in generating anomaly of concepts and theories of the social sciences in Europe. In addition, critical thinking of the relationship between knowledge and power provides an opportunity of scholars in the Third World to reexamine the social sciences in the Third World in a reflexive way. Globalization has reorganized the global economy, damaging validity of traditional social theories in economics and the political sciences. The process of reorganizing knowledge and power provides a room for the possibility of alternative concepts and theories reflecting voices and perspectives of the powerless in general and the small and less developed countries in particular.

The non (counter) hegemonic social sciences remains as an open and possible issue in the twenty-first century. Unlike optimistic visions of globalization, neoliberal globalization has shattered basic rights of the mass in the Third World as well as in Europe and America. Those who do not have a chance to express their voices and perspectives are the real social base of non (counter) hegemonic social sciences. Recognizing the fact that knowledge in the social sciences in the West has reflected power unbalance at the global level is the first step for constructing the non (counter) hegemonic social sciences in the non-West. Yet, it also requires recognition of institutional weakness of social science research in the non-West.

References

Alberti, M. (2012) Mainstream Economists on the Defensive, *Remapping Debates*. Retrieved from http://www.remappingdebate.org/node/1159 (Last access on 15 December 2012)

Bauman, Z. (2000) *Liquid Modernity*. Oxford: Polity Press.

Berman, S. (2009) What to Read on Modernization Theory, *Foreign Affairs*. March 12, 2009.

Blaug, M. (1997) Not Only and Economist: Recent Essays by Mark Blaug, New York: Edward Elgar.

Bradley, H. and C. David (eds.) (2004) *Rethinking Social Inquiry: Diverse Tools, Shared Standards*. New York: Rowman and Littlefield.

Cardoso, F. H. and F. Enzo (1979) *Dependency and Development in Latin America*. Berkeley: University of California Press..

Colander, D., H. Föller, A. Haas, M. Goldber, K. Juselius, A. Kirman, T. Lux, and B. Sloth (2009) *The Financial Crisis and the Systemic Failure of Academic Economics*, Discussion Paper No. 09–03, Dept. of Economics, University of Copenhagen.

Crouch, C. (2006) *Capitalist Diversity and Change: Recombinant Governance and Institutional Entrepreneurs*. Oxford: Oxford University Press.

During, S. (2005) *Cultural Studies: A Critical Introduction.* London: Routledge.

Elster, J. (2007) *Explaining Social Behavior: More Nuts and Bolts for the Social Sciences.* Cambridge: Cambridge University Press.

Esping-Andersen, G. (1990) *The Three Worlds of Welfare Capitalism.* New Jersey: Princeton University Press.

Fiske, A., S. Kitayama and H. R. Markus and R. E. Nisbett (1998) The Cultural Matrix of Social Psychology, in D. Gilbert & S. Fiske & G. Lindzey (eds.), *The Handbook of Social Psychology* (4th ed.). San Francisco: McGraw-Hill, pp.915–81.

Foucault, M. (1970) *The Order of Things: An Archeology of the Human Sciences.* New York: Pantheon Books.

Frank, A. G. (1970) *Latin America*: Underdevelopment and Revolution New York: Monthly Review Press

Hall, P. A. and D. W. Soskice (2001) Varieties of Capitalism: The Institutional Foundations of *Comparative Advantage,* Oxford: Oxford University Press.

Hwang, K. (2005) A Philosophical Reflection on the Epistemology and Methodology of Indigenous Psychologies, in *Asian Journal of Social Psychology* 8(1): 5–17.

Inkeles, A. (1974) *Becoming Modern: Individual Change in Six Developing Countries.* Mass. Cambridge: Harvard University Press.

Kiser, E. and M. Hechter(1998) The Debate on Historical Sociology: Rational Choice Theory And Its Critics, in *American Journal of Sociology* 104(3): 785–816.

Kuhn, T. (1962) *The Structure of Scientific Revolutions.* Chicago: Chicago University Press.

Lakatos, I. (1978) *The methodology of scientific research programmes*, Cambridge: Cambridge University Press.

Landman, T. (2000) Issues and Methods in Comparative Politics: An Introduction. New York: Routledge.

Latham, M. (2000) Modernization as Ideology: American Social Science and "National Building" in the Kenney Era, Chapel Hill: University of North Carolina Press.

Lipset, S. M. (1960) Political Man: *The Social Bases of Politics*. Baltimore: The Johns Hopkins University Press.

Mahoney, James and D. Rueschemeyer (eds.) (2003) *Comparative Historical Analysis of the Social Sciences*. Cambridge: Cambridge University Press.

McClelland, D. (1961) *The Achieving Society*. New York: Free Press.

Moore Jr., B. (1966) *Social Origins of Dictatorship and Democracy*. New York: Beacon Press.

Nisbett, R. E. (2003) *The Geography of Thought*. New York: Free Press.

Quijano, A. (2000) *Coloniality of Power, Eurocentrism and Latin America*. Nepantla, No. 3, Durham, North Carolina: Duke University Press.

Ragin, C. (1987) Comparative Methods: Moving Beyond Qualitative and Quantitative Strategies. Berkely: California University Press.

Robinson, W. I. (2004) A Theory of Global Capitalism: Production, Class and State in a Transnational World. Baltimore: The John Hopkins University Press.

Rosenberg, A. (1992) Economics-Mathematical Politics or Science of Diminishing Returns? Chicago: Chicago University Press

Shweder, R. (1991) *Thinking Through Cultures*. Mass. Cambridge: Harvard University Press.

———(2000) The Psychology of Practice and the Practice of the Three Psychologies, *Asian Journal of Social Psychology* 3: 207–222.

Sklair, L. (2001) *The Transnational Capitalist Class*. London: Blackwell.

Skocpol, T. (1979) State and Social Revolution: A Comparative Study of France, Russia and China. Cambridge: Cambridge University Press.

Skocpol, T. and M. Somers (1980) The Uses of Comparative History in Macro-social Inquiry, in *Comparative Studies in Society and History* 22: 174–197.

Steinmo, S., K. Thelen and F. Longstreth (1992) *Structuring Politics: Historical Institutionalism in Comparative Analysis*. Cambridge: Cambridge University Press.

Tilly, C. (2004) *Contention and Democracy in Europe, 1650–2000*. Cambridge: Cambridge Univresity Press.

Valsiner, J. and A. Rosa (2007) The Myth, and Beyond: Ontology of Psyche and Epistemology of Psychology, in J. Valsiner and A. Rosa (eds.), *The Cambridge Handbook of Sociocultural Psychology*. Cambridge: Cambridge University Press.

Wallerstein, I. (2006) *European Universalism: The Rhetoric of Power*. New York: The New Press.

The Transcendental Dimension in the Construction of the Universal Social Sciences

Shujiro Yazawa

Introduction

The major characteristic of Western thought, centered around the notion that rational, rationalistic reasoning is real understanding, is based on the Enlightenment and progressive ideas which hold that mankind will eventually reach a single correct perception and be able to build a just society. Starting from the nineteenth century, but especially in the twentieth century, various critiques of this view have emerged. With time, these critiques seem to have advanced in number and improved in quality. However, modern rationalistic reason has not been dethroned, and its detractors have yet to offer a positive alternative, as we can learn from the expression "deconstruction."

Let me now call this problem of modern rationalistic reason and its criticism the problem of the "reflection of modern rationalistic reason." How has contemporary sociology dealt with this problem of "reflection of modern rationalistic reason"? This paper shows the achievements and the problems of its attempt, and offers a direction to advance reflexive sociology.

Let me first distinguish the two principal types of reflection that set the framework for my argument. One is "transcendental reflection"; the other is "hermeneutic reflection." According to Yasusuke Murakami, reflection in general can be divided into partial reflection and holistic reflection. Holistic reflection reflects on all objects for its reinterpretation while partial reflection limits itself to parts of objects. Holistic reflection is further divided into two sets of reflections. The first is "transcendental reflection" that centers on the post-reflective self, which is separated from the lifeworld as it transcends the lifeworld. The second is "hermeneutic reflection" which looks at the pre-reflective self that is embedded (again) in the lifeworld as its component.[1] On this distinction, sociology would mainly deal with hermeneutic reflection as a matter of fact.

The Rise of Reflexive Sociology

It was Alvin W. Gouldner who first proposed reflexive sociology in the field of sociology. With Harold Garfinkel, he showed, that the background assumption of everyday life, which is "seen-but-unnoticed,"[2] is a departing point from, and a returning

---

[1] Yasusuke Murakami, An Anticlassical Political-Economic Analysis: A Vision for the Next Century (translated with an Introduction by Kozo Yamamura), Stanford University Press, Stanford, 1996, pp. 398–408.

[2] Alvin W. Gouldner, "Sociology and the Everyday Life," in Lewis Coser ed., The Idea of Social Structure: Papers in Honor of Robert K. Merton, Harcourt Brace Jovanovich, New York, 1975, p. 422. Dis-cussions on Gouldner's reflexive sociology are based on this article. pp. 417–432. Harold Garfinkel, Studies in Ethnomethodology, Eng-lewood Cliffs, N.J., Prentice-Hall, 1967.

point to, the lifeworld and an interpretive framework for matters, and that this background assumption of everyday life and its common rules stabilize, standardize and normalize everyday life. Gouldner defines as historical what is not expected from this everyday life: what is remote, what is not everyday life. According to Gouldner, this historical existence and the everyday life constitute social theory. Thus, the special task of reflexive sociology is to focus on the everyday world as a foundation for theory. Certainly, a theorist's interpretation of history and everyday life is formed not solely from the background assumption that is not observed. The theorist's tradition of intellectual field and subculture would play an important role. Theory would be shaped through and by way of its interaction with these. A theorist naturally needs to implement professional operational codes and reveal the level of life which has been submerged under certain conditions.

When its task is defined this way, reflexive sociology can be considered as dealing with a special case of sociological task which is not so different from sociology in general. That is to say, reflexive sociology shares with sociology the task of releasing the reality that has been subordinated. Nevertheless, Gouldner considers that the task of reflexive sociology slightly differs from that of sociology as it is normally understood. The task of sociology in general is said to be one of discovering reality by finding and identifying social laws and regularities. But Gouldner thinks that the task of reflexive sociology can be better addressed as recovering what is already discovered instead of finding what is new. Another important point relating to this is that sociology involves special research that deals with humans who also look at human behavior. The target of sociology cannot simply be an object; The target is defined by humans who themselves participate, reflect, theorize and possess substantial knowledge about life. In sociology, unlike natural science, there is no fundamental difference between the subject and the object of cognition. Sociology and its target of research constitute two cognitive communities which interact and compete with each other. Gouldner thinks that one may not be able to see the task of reflexive sociology fully unless one understands this point well.

A reflection of the subject of cognition, when it rejects the perspective that treats objects as things, and accepts the reflector's kinship and common subjectivity with objects, reveals itself not only to professionals but amateurs, and becomes capable of accepting their judgments. Only when the reflection of the subject of cognition achieves this does its reflection become an "interpretation" and not merely an explanation. Accordingly, Gouldner thinks that reflexive sociology must be "hermeneutic" and thus historical reflexive sociology.

Therefore, the task of reflexive sociology is to study everyday life where its object recovers rather than discovers its features, and to help the object become less like an object, and more like a subject, more capable of understanding and controlling everyday life. Through research, sociology has no choice but to intervene in, and change, the world.

The Development of Reflexive Sociology

After Gouldner, reflexive sociology develops into Pierre Bourdieu's interpretation via reflexive sociology centered on the problem of reflection on the system level and the problem of structure and agency as discussed by Anthony Giddens and Urlich Beck.[3]

After showing that Bourdieu's reflexive sociology aims at examining reflexivity of cognition, Loïc Wacquant argues that Bourdieu's reflection differs from others' in three points. First, the main object of reflectivity is not individual but the "social and intellectual unconscious embedded in analytic tools and operations"[4] of analysis. Secondly, it is a "collective enterprise"[5] rather than an attempt assigned to an individual scholar. Thirdly, it "seeks not to assault but to buttress the epistemological security of sociology"[6].

But Wacquant rather overemphasizes the uniqueness of Bourdieu's reflexive sociology. Gouldner's reflexive sociology incorpo-

---

[3] About the history of reflexive sociology, see Barry Smart, Facing Modernity: Ambivalence, Reflexivity and Morality, Sage Publica-tions, London, 1999. Of particular interest is Chapter 3: Reflexivity, Modernity and Sociology, pp.67–87. Ulrich Beck, Anthony Giddens and Scott Lash, Reflexive Modernization: Politics, Tradition and Aesthetics in the Modern Social Order, Cambridge, Polity, 1994.

[4] Pierre Bourdieu and Loïc J.D. Wacquant, An Invitation to Reflexive Sociology, University of Chicago Press, Chicago, 1992, p.36.

[5] Pierre Bourdieu and Loïc J.D. Wacquant, ibid., p.36.

[6] Pierre Bourdieu and Loïc J.D. Wacquant, ibid., p.36.

rates the first point mainly through the "background assumption"; that Gouldner stresses the theorist's community as a medium between subject and object suggests that he also fully understood the non-individual aspect of reflection. Bourdieu's reflexive sociology must be taken as a thorough completion of Gouldner's reflexive sociology.

Bourdieu's reflexive sociology rejects all the biases that distort sociological perception. Such biases include class, nationality, ethnicity, sex, academic position and intellectualism. This can itself be called transcendental reflection since it denotes the operation where one selectively excludes the dangers that might distort cognition and build up post-reflective self. But Bourdieu's reflection is never cut off from the pre-reflective self. He has no dualism between the pre-reflective and the post-reflective self. This is because the pre-reflective self is considered the "socialized body," "the repository of the generative and creative capacity to understanding" or "the bearer of a form of 'the kinetic knowledge' endowed with structuring of potency"[7]. Thus, transcendental reflection returns immediately to hermeneutic reflection again. His reflexive sociology is "the work of objectivation of the objectivating subject"[8]. Bourdieu could show himself as a developer of "Pascalian meditation"[9].

---

[7] Pierre Bourdieu and Loïc J.D. Wacquant, ibid., p.20.

[8] Pierre Bourdieu and Loïc J.D. Wacquant, ibid., p.40.

[9] Pierre Bourdieu, Pascalian Meditations, translated by Richard Nice, Polity Press, Cambridge, UK, 2000, 256p.

When we compare his reflexive sociology with that of Gouldner's, which is characterized by dualism between consciousness and thing, Bourdieu's reflexive sociology must be evaluated as reflexive sociology at a higher stage.

The reflexive sociology built by Bourdieu analyzes the social as its object, finds thence the original, indigenous universalities and creates universality as the consummation of those operations which collect, compare and examine the indigenous universalities that have been found. This is the direction that Western sociology now pursues. When it does so, globalism and internationalism must embrace cosmopolitanism. It is essential to relativize the idea of nation-state. Certainly, cosmopolitanism is only a passing point.

Transcendental Reflection

As I said above, reflection can be divided into "hermeneutic reflection" and "transcendental reflection." Most sociology study is engaged in "hermeneutic," "historical" reflection as a "reflexive sociology." In what follows, I will advance my analysis of "transcendental reflection." It is expected that doing so further clarifies the nature and the problems of "hermeneutic reflection."

Yasusuke Murakami, who divided holistic reflection into "hermeneutic reflection" and "transcendental reflection," regards "transcendental reflection" as that which stresses the post-reflective self, cuts the "self" off from the lifeworld and establishes it as a cognitive subject transcending the lifeworld. He clarified the features of this reflection through the following logic.[10]

This reflection can never reach a holistic reflection no matter how often it repeats reflection. Thus, it must go through an endless "process of transcendentalization" and "upward progression." Therefore, "transcendental reflection" discovers historic religion (Robert Bellah[11]).

This is because historic religion exempted one from transcendentalization by "introducing absolute God or principles" and also by offering "practical guidance about transcendental or quasi-transcendental thought for human beings." Among historic religions, Christianity was especially useful for Western "transcendental reflection." This is because it offered absolute principles and was capable of directing one's attention to the lifeworld. Descartes' so-called dualism opened up a channel for the shift of interest from religion to the lifeworld. As a result, natural science developed rapidly. This is how "transcendental reflection" came to be represented by "natural scientific, lawful reflection."

Mr. Murakami's argument, shown just above, is an extremely perceptive argument deserving high consideration. But there is one big problem with this argument. Such an argument as his is trapped in a vulgar discussion of Descartes' philosophy and fails to capture the strand of thought that attempts to overcome modern philosophy, including the thought of Descartes, Spinoza, Kierke-

---

[10] Yasusuke Murakami, op. cit., pp.399–411.

[11] Robert W. Bellah, Beyond Belief, Harper and Row, New York, 1970.

gaard, Nietzsche, Marx, Freud, Lévi-Strauss and Wittgenstein. This results in the failure to grasp the differing meanings of transcendental reflection. In what follows, I will look into this point, based on Kojin Karatani's argument.[12]

First, Karatani says, modern philosophy treats subject as classification or concept, not as singularity. It transforms singularity into particularity and manages to connect particularities by placing an assumption of intersubjectivity. Singularity suggests and assumes the asymmetry or difference between self and the other as such. This is expressed through the proper noun. A proper noun does not express individuality: It expresses singularity. What should be noted further is that a proper noun exists inside and outside language at the same time. A proper noun cannot be translated in either a foreign or a native language. The externality of proper nouns in language suggests that language cannot be reduced to the closed langue and the sociality of language. A proper noun assumes a social existence rather than a common existence.[13] We should not forget this.

---

[12] My understanding of Kojin Karatani's theory is based on the follow-ing works of his: Tankyu I (in Japanese), Kodansha Gakujutsu Bunko, 1992. Tankyu II (in Japanese), Kodansha Gakujutsu Bunko, 1994. History and Repetition, edited by Seiji M. Lippit, Columbia University Press, New York, 2004.Transcritique: On Kant and Marx, translated by Sabu Kohso, MIT press, paperback edition, Cambridge, Mass. 2005.

[13] Kojin Karatani, Tankyu II (in Japanese), Kodansha Gakujutsu Bunko, 1994, Part 1, chapter 1 to chapter 5.

Moreover, according to Karatani, a proper noun denotes "none-other-than-this-ness." "None-other-than-this-ness" means not simply that "it is not other," it means "it-actually-is-even-though-it-could-be-otherwise." If so, in order to talk about a proper noun, we must think about the modalities of "possibility, actuality, contingency and necessity." A proper noun tries to maintain itself by fixating the none-other-than-this-ness and excluding the otherness=many possibilities. That assumes otherness and the contingency of relations.[14]

Thus, the problem of proper nouns comes down to the problem of communication, which cannot establish itself without "the leap of life and death."

Now, Karatani faces the task of overcoming modern philosophy in order to deal with singularity and proper nouns in a sufficient manner. The objective of that task is to overcome the dualism between mind and body. This dualism is generally attributed to Descartes. However, according to Karatani, Descartes tries to overcome this dualism. Descartes' spirit aims at rejecting this dualism. Karatani quotes the famous passage from Descartes' Discourse on Method :

---

[14] Kojin Karatani, ibid., chapter 5.

> I resolved to feign that all the things that had ever entered in my mind were no more true than the illusions of my dreams. But, immediately afterward, I took note that, while I wanted thus to think that everything was false. It necessarily had to be that I, who was thinking this, was something. And noticing that this truth—I think, therefore I am—was so firm and so assured that all the most extravagant suppositions of the skeptics were not capable of shaking it, I judged that I could accept it, without scruple, as the first principle of the philosophy that I was seeking.[15]

What does cogito ergo sum mean? According to Karatani, "in Descartes, 'I doubt' is a personal determination of will." And this 'I' is a singular existence, which refers to Descartes himself (1). In a sense, (1) is an empirical self, and simultaneously the doubting subject (2), who doubts the empirical subject (1); through this process the transcendental ego (3) is discovered"[16].

Descartes asks who I am apart from all the systems. And Descartes answers this question by saying that I exist because I think and doubt. Thus, Descartes' thinking is consciousness or self-consciousness and at the same time is outside consciousness or self-consciousness.

The location of the spirit is in the discursive space and not in the geographical space. And the spirit is shown in a formal way, deductively. But it is utterly "private" and does not have any base. What

---

[15] Kojin Karatani, Transcritique: On Kant and Marx, translated by Sabu Kohso, MIT press, paperback edition, Cambridge, Mass. 2005, p.87.

[16] Kojin Karatani, ibid., p.87.

ultimately grounds it, then, is world, nature or what can only be called God.

In summation, Karatani argues that we must stand outside the system to which self belongs and searches for the infinite idea=God. This is what Descartes did. And the person who continues this line of thought is Spinoza. Of course, this God is not God as representation (identification of language), illusion or consciousness. It is God as an idea or definition. The idea we talk about here cannot be represented empirically. But it is something whose existence we cannot deny; nor can we deny the place in which one looks at transcendence itself as representation. If we follow the arguments through the relationship between concepts, we can depict them as in the following figure.

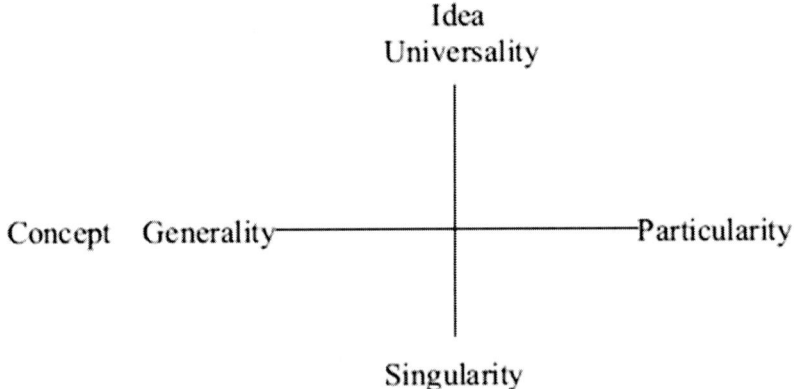

Idea and Concept, Singularity and Particularity (Kojin Karatani, *Tankyu II* (in Japanese), Kodansha, 1994, p.150)

We can understand God as an idea which differs from a concept by dealing with infinity. In infinite space, the system is closed and everything belongs to it. No dualism will be necessary, and we can put an end to endless transcendence.

Karatani tries to dig into the problem of overcoming modern thought, and focuses primarily on Spinoza. Karatani maintains that Spinoza's subject is not a cognitive subject. This fact is made clear when a cognitive subject is doubted and criticized. It can be called a transcendental subject, subject as singularity. The impossibility of transcending the world, the attitude of singularity (only this I, only this world) is different from self-consciousness or reflexivity. It is precisely this fact that creates society's thinking and universality, transcending the community's thinking and generality (common subjectivity) which stays in a single world.

The nature of the givenness of everything must be clarified by the work of the transcendental subject. This is called critical, archeological thinking. It is important that the asymmetrical relation between the self and the other is made clear by critical, archeological thinking. Karatani calls the asymmetrical relation between the self and the other as "society" and defines "community" as the symmetrical relation of having the same rules. Social science has a critical, archeological approach dealing with society as its object. Thus, social science aims at clarifying as its object the givenness of communication, transportation and exchange which appears as an asymmetrical relation between the self and the other[17].

---

[17] Kojin Karatani, Sekaishi no Kozou (in Japanese), Iwanami Shoten, 2010.

Tentative Conclusion

This paper clarifies how universality is pursued in modern sociology by tracing the establishment and development of reflexive sociology. It also elucidates the argument that stresses, in the attempts to overcome modern philosophy, the importance of the transcendental subject that does not assume common subjectivity, a notion absent in modern sociology, and the meaning of that argument. The two aspects that are reflexive sociology and the argument that stresses the importance of a transcendental subject look similar in terms of emphasizing the lifeworld, but they come to differ significantly. But does not the development of globalization and of planetarization show us the need for modern sociology to realize the importance of the transcendental subject?

This kind of sociology already exists. Alberto Melucci's reflexive sociology is one example. According to Melucci, "Finally, the planetary extension of the world system has by now acquired a total scope: countries and cultures only exist as inner dimensions of a global system. This new 'internalization' introduces a fourth dilemma, that between inclusion and exclusion. Inclusion irons out differences and transforms peripheral cultures into insignificant and quaint appendages to the few centres where languages are elaborated and diffused through the great market of the media.

Any resistance to this standardization almost inevitably leads to exclusion, spelling silence and cultural death"[18].

But Melucci also thinks that "individuals gain wider control over the formation and orientation of their action"[19]. Namely, he understands that the self-reflective capacity of individuals to produce communication and solidarity can grow at the same time. His sociology takes the body and language as "the foundations of an ethic responding to the need to cope with the problems of a planet."[20]

Therefore, his sociology is an attempt to learn to move between body and language. Through this sociology, we can understand that we are social existences and that we can live with others.

At the end of this investigation, I would like to point out one more thing related with the history of sociology. As I stated earlier, the social thought of Descartes, Spinoza, Kierkegaard, Nietzsche Marx, Freud and Wittgenstein are very important to sociology. Therefore, we have to include these social thoughts in the history of sociology and to examine the relationship between these thoughts and sociology. For example, F. Tönnies investigated the revision of the medieval world view and the philosophy of Hobbes and Spinoza.[21]

---

[18] Alberto Melucci, The Playing Self: Person and Meaning in the Planetary Society, Cambridge University Press, Cambridge, 1996, p.127.

[19] Alberto Melucci, ibid., p.3.

[20] Alberto Melucci, ibid., p.131.

[21] Ferdinand Tönnies, On Social Ideas and Ideologies, edited, translated, and annotated by E.G. Jacoby, Harper and Row, New York, 1974, Part I, pp.3–58.

Of course, we have to deploy critical, archeological research or historical sociology that deals with the asymmetrical relation between the self and the other as its object.

References

Beck, U., A. Giddens and S. Lash (1994) Reflexive Modernization: Politics, Tradition and Aesthetics in the Modern Social Order. Cambridge: Polity.

Bellah, R. W. (1970) Beyond Belief. New York: Harper and Row.

Bourdieu, P. (2000) Pascalian Meditations. Richard Nice (Trans.) Cambridge, UK: Polity Press.

Bourdieu, P. and L. J. D. Wacquant (1992) An Invitation to Reflexive Sociology. Chicago: University of Chicago Press.

Garfinkel, H. (1967) Studies in Ethnomethodology. N.J: Englewood Cliffs, Prentice-Hall.

Gouldner, A. W. (1975) Sociology and the Everyday Life, in Lewis Coser(ed.), The Idea of Social Structure: Papers in Honor of Robert K. Merton. New York: Harcourt Brace Jovanovich. pp. 417–432.

Karatani, K. (1992) Tankyu I (in Japanese). Kodansha Gakujutsu Bunko.

―――(1994) Tankyu II (in Japanese). Kodansha Gakujutsu Bunko.

―――(2004) History and Repetition. Lippit, Seiji M. (ed.) New York: Columbia University Press.

―――(2005) Transcritique: On Kant and Marx. S. Kohso (trans.) MIT press, paperback edition, Cambridge: Mass.

―――(2010) Sekaishi no Kozou (in Japanese). Iwanami Shoten.

Melucci, A. (1996) The Playing Self: Person and Meaning in the Planetary Society. Cambridge: Cambridge University Press.

Murakami, Y. (1996) An Anticlassical Political-Economic Analysis: A Vision for the Next Century (translated with an Introduction by K. Yamamura). Stanford: Stanford University Press.

Smart, B. (1999) Facing Modernity: Ambivalence, Reflexivity and Morality. London: Sage Publications.

Tönnies, F. (1974) On Social Ideas and Ideologies. E. G. Jacoby (ed., trans. and annotated) New York: Harper and Row.

Three Decades of Chinese Indigenous Psychology: A Contribution to Overcoming the Hegemonic Structures of International Science?

Doris Weidemann

"The crucial question is, what contributions does or can Asian psychology make to the study of human behavior in general and hence to the development of psychological science as a whole?"

David Ho, "Relational Orientation in Asian Social Psychology"

Introduction

Indigenous Science Approaches

Indigenous social science movements have aimed to overcome the Western bias of international science by adopting a cultural approach that allows adjusting research to local conditions.[1]

---

[1] 'Indigenous science' is not an undisputed term. While it is understood as highly denigrating by some (who would prefer the term "endogenous science" instead, e.g. Ndjodo and Patel in this volume), it is however an established notion in the field of psychology where it is used in the sense of "local" or "originating from this particular place." It is equally em-ployed with respect to Asian, African, or North American psychology (e.g., with respect to Canadian psychology (Adair 2006), or indigenized US-American psychology, Danziger

At the same time, they strive to widen the theoretical and empirical base of social science in order to formulate "derived" instead "imposed etics." Indigenous social science approaches therefore support efforts of "authentic internationalization" (Oommen 1991), that is, to create a nonhegemonic science system that would allow better representation of 'non-Western' life worlds and science traditions. It is an open question, however, if indigenous science approaches have actually succeeded in challenging the academic mainstream. Taking the case of Chinese indigenous psychology (IP) as an example this chapter investigates whether this prominent indigenous social science movement has in fact contributed to the internationalization of science in the expected way. Has it remedied the Western bias that is typical of mainstream psychology, and has it helped to counteract traditional hegemonic science structures?

Chinese Indigenous Psychology

In China as in other Asian countries academic psychology was an import from the West. The first psychological laboratory in China was established in 1917 by Chen Daqi with the support of Cai Yuanpei, educational reformer and former student of Wilhelm Wundt at Leipzig (Higgins and Zheng 2002; Jing and Fu 2001). During subsequent years Chinese psychology closely followed the Western

---

2009), and is also used in self-referential ways by Indian, Korean, Philippine, and Taiwanese psy-chologists. I shall therefore stick to the established term and speak of 'indigenous' and 'indigenized' psychology/psychologies.

model until development was interrupted by war and civil war (1937–49). After the founding of the People's Republic of China in 1949 the Soviet model became predominant and Chinese psychology reoriented itself toward Russian authors and theories. Development was once again interrupted during the Cultural Revolution (1966–76) that attacked psychology as a "bourgeois" undertaking and led to a complete halt of psychological research (ibid.). After 1976 psychology reemerged—albeit on a weak institutional basis. Since then, the number of researchers, psychological institutes, journals, and scope of research have extended spectacularly and academic psychology is fully integrated into the international science community today. While the majority of Chinese psychological research rests on Western concepts and theories, it has also become obvious to large parts of the Chinese academic psychological community that imported theories, concepts, and methods are not always fully applicable in local Chinese contexts. Consequently, calls for a better adaptation of psychology to the Chinese cultural background have become widespread.

Attempts to create a culturally sensitive indigenous Chinese psychology date back to the early 1980s (with earlier predecessors). Major proponents include Taiwanese scholars Yang Kuo-shu and Hwang Kwang-kuo (for an overview cf. Hwang 2005; Kim, Yang and Hwang 2006), Hong Kong based Michael Bond and David Ho (e.g., Bond 1996, 2010; Ho 1993, 1998), and Wang Fengyan (Wang and Zheng 2008) in mainland China, among many others.[2]

Indigenous psychology is understood "as the scientific study of human behaviour (or the mind) that is native, that is not transported from other regions, and that is designed for its people" (Kim and Berry 1993: 2). In a similar vein, the overall program of establishing an "Asian psychology" aims at "a theoretical system or school of thought in psychology rooted in, or derived from, Asian cultures" (Ho 1993: 241). Prominent topics that have been considered as essential for the construction of a Chinese indigenous psychology include "face" (*mianzi, lian*), "reciprocity" (*baofu*), "favour" (*renqing*), "filial piety" (*xiao*), "interpersonal affinity" (*yuan*), "relationships" (*guanxi*), and "self" (*ziwo*) (Gild 2010; Hwang 2005, 2012).

Considering the small scale of the indigenous psychology movement as compared to mainstream psychology in and beyond Asia, its impact has been more noticeable than might have been expected. Research contributions, especially by Taiwanese and Hong Kong authors, have found explicit recognition in international (American) media and conferences. In particular, the adjoining field of cross-cultural psychology has taken up findings of

---

[2] The program to create a "Chinese" (indigenous) psychology is pursued by researchers in China, Taiwan, and Hong Kong alike. By subsuming con-tributions from researchers from all the above places under the label of "Chinese psychology" I follow the established notion and do not mean to imply a political statement.

Chinese indigenous psychology: terms, such as face or guanxi are now firmly established in cross-cultural psychology. Closer investigation, however, shows that the hegemonic mechanisms of international science have remained largely unchallenged. I will argue that the success of Chinese indigenous psychology has benefited from the Western interest in "exotic" customs and is by and large following the rules and demands of the Euro-American science system. Topics are in accordance with Western definitions of academic psychology and—where they address local variations—are influenced by Western perceptions of Asia. Prestige and international recognition of Chinese indigenous psychology are likewise based on Western criteria.

Power Mechanisms in International Social Science

While the early years of academic psychology in Asian countries were accompanied by dependence on Western textbooks and academic training, this stage clearly belongs to the past. Academic psychology is now firmly established in Chinese higher education and research: Chinese universities train their own young academics, psychologists are organized in local professional organizations, have created local scientific journals, and have participated in the founding of international Asian associations and publication series. Drawing on his observations of the development of psychology in various countries worldwide, Adair (2006) argues that the global spread of psychology as a science discipline follows several distinct phases: the "importation" of psychology is followed by "implantation" and "indigenization" before reaching the stage of an "autochthonous" science (Adair 2006: 471–472). He identifies the following "Stages and Activities in the Spread of Psychology around the World":

1. Importation
   a. Discipline is introduced to a country
   b. becomes part of the university curriculum, and
   c. scholars are sent abroad to be trained

2. Implantation
   a. Returning scholars begin functioning as psychologists
   b. conduct research emulating Western training model,
   c. research topics selected from journals,
   d. use textbook application of methods to guide research, and
   e. teach discipline as it was taught in graduate school

3. Indigenization
   a. Scholars criticize Western models and methods as inappropriate,
   b. adapt tests and methods to language and culture,
   c. research topics in the national interest, and
   d. identify culturally unique behaviors/thoughts for study.

4. Autochthonization

a. Establish graduate training programs to self-perpetuate discipline.

b. Locally authored/edited textbooks published and used.

c. National association promotes journals, discipline, and

d. standards for research ethics and professional practice.

e. National funding reliably available for research, and

f. critical mass of mature, established scholars focus on research problems that are culturally appropriate and nationally important

(Adair 2006: 472)

Taking Adair's model as a diagnostic reference frame, it would appear that in most Asian countries psychology has reached the stages of indigenization, and, in some cases, autochthonization. It could therefore be assumed that Asian science communities have become independent and equal partners in international dialogue. Yet Adair's argumentation implicitly also demonstrates that the ethnocentrism of Western academia is undefeated: the Euro-American model, unsubjected to critique, is taken as the only plausible way of carrying out psychological research. It thus also defines the one and only end point of a desirable development towards "proper" academic psychology. In addition, by formulating the rule that the development of an autochthonous science discipline requires the "importation" of Euro-American science, this model insinuates that local sciences were either nonexistent or irrelevant. Apparently, even the fact that psychology in Asian countries has reached "maturity" does not necessarily mean that it counterbalances Western ethnocentrism. On the contrary, the fact that "maturity" is defined with respect to "Western" standards only, suggests that hegemonic structures are still in operation. Even if Chinese academic psychology can be classified as "autochthonous" by Adair's standards, this does apparently not imply that it operates beyond international hegemonic structures. It therefore seems worthwhile to revisit some of the classical findings regarding the power mechanism in international social science and to investigate whether they are traceable in the field of Chinese indigenous psychology, as well.

In his popular model Syed Farid Alatas (2003) distinguishes between "social science powers" (the United States, UK, France), "semi-peripheral social science powers" (Australia, Japan, Germany, the Netherlands), and peripheral, "intellectually dependent" (usually Third World) social science communities. An exchange mechanism between these different players involves (a) the flow of concepts and theories from the social science powers to the intellectually dependent countries, (b) a flow of students and researchers from peripheral and semiperipheral countries to the social science powers where they are trained and receive their academic degrees, (c) an unequal distribution of funds to the disadvantage of the peripheral science communities, (d) the spread of English as the global language of science, (e) unequal representation in publications to the disadvantage of researchers from the peripheral science communities, (f) general high respect and prestige of the institutions and research output of the social science powers (for an extended discussion and examples see Kuhn and Weidemann 2010). These mechanisms can be described as "hegemonic" or "imperialist" insofar as they result from or established themselves in the wake of US economic, political, and military dominance in the postwar era. They are also "hegemonic" in the sense that they regulate participation in international science, that is, control which topics are given an international agenda and whose voices are silenced. As Moghaddam and Lee (2009) observe, the American influence has been particularly strong in the field of psychology. They conclude that "the United States has dominated psychology in a way that has not been replicated in sociology, anthropology, and other social sciences" (p.170).

As space does not allow a full-scale analysis of all of the above aspects, I will concentrate my discussion on a few select facets and ask if in the field of Chinese indigenous psychology (a) dependence on Western education has been overcome, (b) whether the addressed research areas and topics are independent from Western influence, and (c) if the underlying science model can be considered "indigenous," or mirrors Western definitions of social science.

Power Mechanisms Affecting Chinese Indigenous Psychology

The Role of Western Education

While Chinese psychology is "autochthonous" with respect to educational infrastructure and academic reproduction, overseas academic training, especially doctorates and research visits at American universities, hold much prestige. They also provide the opportunity to acquire the necessary English language skills that provide access to international debates and readership. In China, not many social scientists of the middle and elder generations have been trained in English and thus face huge difficulties when it comes to writing English language articles. Chinese language contributions, on the other hand, are rarely translated into English and thus remain inaccessible to an audience that does not read Chinese. This has led to the curious effect that a very small number of Chinese researchers (those educated in North America) have come to represent "Chinese social science," and even fewer to represent "Chinese indigenous psychology." There are not nearly enough translations of relevant contributions, and clearly no attempts of the international science community to acquire the necessary linguistic and cultural skills to study Chinese psychology to counterbalance this effect.

In the field of indigenous psychology this effect is visible in the selection of authors who contribute to English language publications. A glance at select, notable volumes reveals that almost all

Chinese and Taiwanese authors are graduates of American universities (e.g., Special Issue on the indigenous psychologies, International Journal of Psychology [2006], and Kim, Yang and Hwang 2006). Prominence of authors does not solely reflect their scientific excellence but is obviously also based on affiliations with American universities and academic networks. The American academic experience provides internationally acknowledged academic titles, the ability to publish in English, and (ideally) support by renowned American co-authors who aid career development. Evidently, the status of "peripheral" authors is still granted by authority of the "academic center"; this rule applies to indigenous psychology as much as to social research in general.

Western Influence on Research Topics

Chinese indigenous psychology has introduced a host of new, "Chinese" concepts into psychological debates. Yet the organization into subdisciplines that is fairly standardized internationally also regulates research activities in indigenous psychology. The international reader will thus encounter traditional research topics, such as motivation, development, personality, child socialization, and others as familiar reference points. Subdisciplinary structures as well as their associated research fields and central concepts are apparently considered either as universal or at least as undisputable elements of academic psychology as such. Indigenous research is fitted into this general structure, and "Chinese" concepts mainly serve to describe local variants of internationally established topics.

While this strategy is effective in achieving a synthesis of international scientific standards and adaptation to local conditions that makes it compatible with international psychological discourses, it also comes at a cost. Not only does it confirm the theoretical authority of the Western research framework but also makes the "West" the central reference point for all attempts to describe local "otherness." By concentrating on comparisons between "East" and "West," or—as it is frequently done—between China (or Japan) and the United States, psychological research replicates a questionable West-East dichotomy that perpetuates orientalist thinking patterns and ignores the existing heterogeneity within both "Western" and "Eastern" societies. Cross-cultural and indigenous psychology replicate Western stereotypes of the "collectivist," "interdependent," "relational," and "holistic" Chinese (or: Asian) that is contrasted with the "individualist," "independent," and "analytical" Westerner (Hofstede 1980, 2001; Marcus and Kitayama 1991; Nisbett 2005; Hwang 2012). In an attempt to describe the distinctiveness of Chinese cultural groups local authors resort to

these established categories and often promote heterostereotypes as autostereotypes. As a result, the picture of "the Chinese" or "the Asian" is often unduly homogenous and highly stereotypical, even in Chinese indigenous psychological research. The mechanisms that underlie these conceptual choices are subtle. Researchers from Western as well as Asian countries actively strive to overcome traditional representations that more often than not are unfavorable to Asian societies and to integrate the newly arising science communities into international dialogue. Integration, however, still seems to imply either to accept mainstream topics and theories, or to place "cultural" issues in the few niches that are granted and defined by mainstream science that wants to "open up" its research to cultural diversity (cf. also Kuhn and Weidemann 2010). Interest in "exotic" customs prestructures the field of indigenous psychology, and it can be assumed that research that fits Western stereotypical expectations finds more attention and acceptance with international editorial boards and conference committees and thus stands greater chances to be published or to be supported by grants. On the other hand, international attention is not the only factor that shapes the choice of research topics and concepts. Other factors include political preferences of researchers' home countries and tradition lines that have been created by the first generation of indigenous psychologists. In combination, these factors may explain why some cultural traditions (Confucianism) are given more weight in Chinese indigenous psychology than others (e.g. Daoism, whose influential rule is, e.g., discussed by Peng 2006). It would be worthwhile to investigate the mechanisms regulating research activities in the field of Chinese indigenous psychology more closely. A comparative content analysis of internationally published English language articles and local Chinese publications could, for example, shed more light on the adaptive strategies that authors take in order to find international acceptance.

Indigenous Concepts of "Science"?

Since the start of the indigenous psychology movement focus points and lines of arguments have shifted to some degree, especially with respect to the prospects of creating an "alternative science." In accordance with the anticolonial impulse of the early IP movement, Western psychology was rejected and definitions stressed the cultural distinctiveness of research environments and the need to take local values and concepts into account. Yet, current authors tend to distance themselves from approaches that point beyond the framework of Western science. Instead, definitions clearly accentuate the adherence to the "universal" science tradition:

> Indigenous psychology is part of a scientific tradition that advocates multiple perspectives, but not multiple psychologies. [···] Indigenous psychology is a part of scientific tradition in search of psychological knowledge rooted in cultural context. This knowledge can become the basis of the discovery of psychological universals and can contribute to the advancement of psychology and science. (Kim, Yang and Hwang 2006: 9)

The indigenous psychology project is carefully defended against critical arguments that were raised during the last decades (e.g. Poortinga 1996; 1999). Much space is devoted by the same authors to explain what indigenous psychology should not be confounded with: "We need to distinguish indigenous knowledge, philosophies and religions from indigenous psychology. [...] Although they provide a wealth of information and the basis of development of formal theories, they need to be empirically tested and validated" (Kim, Yang and Hwang 2006: 9). They repeatedly assure readers that indigenous psychology is and should be firmly based on a Western philosophy of science and methodology that guarantees its status as "science" (also Allwood and Berry 2006).

The distinction that is sometimes made between an "indigenous" psychology in the narrow sense of the word and an "indigenized" psychology is helpful for describing the different standpoints. "Indigenous psychology" thus would refer to "psychological theories that were already formalized and had already integrated psychologically relevant concepts into a systematically elaborated theory before modern psychology was taken into account" (Chakkarath 2004: 34). Hindu psychology serves as one example of "indigenous" psychology that features a conceptual framework, a repertoire of methods and of set of therapeutic techniques (ibid.; another example would be Buddhist indigenous psychology, Chakkarath 2007). Allwood and Berry feel that this search for alternative knowledge systems jeopardizes scientific seriousness and warn: "the label 'indigenous psychology' risks creating confusion with older cultural traditions often stemming from religion and philosophy in a country, such as ideas put forth in Hindu philosophy or religion regarding human beings" (2006: 244). In fact, Yang (2006: 299) argues, very few psychologies would earn the label "indigenous psychology" if science philosophical foundations were to be included in the definition: "In contemporary world psychology, only psychologies in the Euro-American countries and the former Soviet Union are genuinely indigenous" (Yang 2006: 299). Even though indigenous Chinese psychology is rooted in cultural context, its adherence to the Euro-American science model classifies it as an "indigenized" rather than an "indigenous" psychology. Psychology in Taiwan, Hong Kong, and China is Westernized Chinese psychology that has been turned into an indigenized Chinese psychology (ibid.: 300).

Conclusion

Chinese Indigenous Psychology Remains within the Confines of Western Definitions

Hegemonic structures that have amply been described for mainstream social science seem to be firmly in place for indigenous psychology as well. The fact that indigenous social science has provided a small number of non-Western researchers national and international career opportunities should not be mistaken for true internationalization. The limits of the acceptable are still defined by "Western" academia and are also held up by those who return to their home countries after receiving a Western education. These limits allow for and reward the integration of a certain amount of exotic diversity, yet to the terms of Western academia. Thus, Danziger concludes:

> Although part of the program of modern indigenous psychology may involve a greater openness to local pre-modern traditions, both scholarly and folk, the movement of indigenization itself is unambiguously a phenomenon of modern psychology. A critique of current Western psychological doctrines and practices forms the starting point of proposed reforms, the advocates of the reforms have been trained and professionally certified by Western academic institutions, and most public discourse about indigenous psychology is conducted via regular professional channels. (Danziger 2009: 215)

Apparently, in order to be accepted internationally, indigenous psychological research needs to conform to several evaluative criteria that are defined by Western academia. Failure to comply with any one of the following questions leads to being disqualified from international reception: Is the employed science model "scientific" by international (Euro-American) standards? Are research topics and methods "valid" (accepted as a topic or method of academic psychology) by international (Euro-American) standards? Are contributions published in English? Is the author scientifically "competent" or even "excellent" by international (Euro-American) standards? Contributions that are filtered out include a vast number of Chinese language publications, research that is based on alternative (indigenous) research frameworks and research methods, and research that addresses topics considered as "illegitimate" by Western standards (consider e.g. research on the "transmigration of souls"). As a result, indigenous psychology is either made compatible with Western expectations (and thus turns into "indigenized psychology") or remains marginal. In short: while indigenized psychology finds international acceptance, indigenous psychologies do not.

Non-Western Indigenous Psychologies Hold Potential for Advancing International Psychology

While the integration of indigenized psychologies has enriched psychological research, it is my belief that the exploration of truly indigenous approaches could yield even richer results. The neighboring field of medicine has amply demonstrated the worth of indigenous approaches: Chinese traditional medicine, herbal therapies, or acupuncture have expanded medical knowledge and therapeutic repertoires all over the world. They are being studied internationally, tested for results and integrated into therapeutic schemes. The investigation of indigenous psychology could likewise enlarge the international knowledge base and prove fruitful for developing new concepts, theories, or methods. Chinese indigenous psychology holds potential for enriching the social sciences in the following ways:

- By relying on indigenous theories, concepts, and methods, Chinese indigenous psychology would offer better insight into Chinese behavior, cognition, and emotion. In times of globalization, unprejudiced, nonstereotypical knowledge about non-Western societies is urgently needed.

- Indigenous psychologies would raise attention to the fact that psychology is always and unavoidably culture bound. Discussions about foundations laid by culture and language could then be carried out from a better informed metaperspective that would not define one model as the central reference point, and all others as "deviations" but that would initiate a polycentric dialogue (also see Weidemann 2010).

- As a result, indigenous psychologies would serve to overcome the implicit understanding that Euro-American societies constitute the norm. Interestingly, this idea is even traceable in contributions by authors with a longstanding interest in the promotion of indigenous psychology: Writing about the "role of indigenous theorizing" Bond (2010: 713) argues: "Non-mainstream cultural groups like the Chinese can enlarge our conceptual ambit, and ground psychology in the whole of human reality, not just their Western, usually American, versions." While the expansion of knowledge is certainly desirable, the reader is left to wonder where the "mainstream" collective is to be located if "the Chinese" who amount to 20 percent of the world population are considered a "non-mainstream cultural group." Indigenous psychology could invite perspective change and overcome the idea that Western societies are the standard reference point.

- By raising new questions, addressing different topics, and formulating alternative concepts and theories, indigenous psychologies could expand psychological knowledge in general.

- Finally, indigenous psychologies would provoke questions about the kind of psychology we consider adequate and useful. Discussions about the direction, necessity, and worth of academic psychology should not be restricted to "peripheral" science communities that struggle to find mainstream theories "useful" or "applicable." They should remain at the core of the academic enterprise itself.

While many questions about the feasibility of indigenous psychologies still remain to be answered (Is ethnocentrism in science cured by developing alternative ethnocentrisms? How many indigenous psychologies would we need [Poortinga 1999] How would we approach translation of truly different science approaches; etc.), the option for indigenized rather than indigenous Chinese psychology still seems to forego chances of enlarging psychological knowledge beyond the boundaries defined by current international academic standards. As has been shown, Chinese indigenized psychology still operates largely within the hegemonic system of Western dominated science. On the other hand, if it is true that academic "hegemony" follows economic, political, and military power, global shifts in power structures may eventually lead to changes in academic structures, standards, topics, and research conventions and establish new forms of international dialogue unanticipated today.

References

Adair, J. G. (2006) Creating Indigenous Psychologies: Insights from Empirical Social Studies of the Science of Psychology, in U. Kim, K. Yang und K. Hwang (eds.), Indigenous and Cultural Psychology: Understanding People in Context. New York: Springer, pp.467–485.

Alatas, S. F. (2003) Academic Dependency and the Global Division of Labour in the Social Sciences, in Current Sociology 51 (6), 599–613.

Allwood, C. M. and J. W. Berry (2006) Origins and development of indigenous psychologies. An international analysis, in C. M. Allwood und J. W. Berry (Hg.) Special Issue on the Indigenous Psychologies, in International Journal of Psychology 41 (4), S. 243–268.

Bond, M. H. (ed.) (1996) The Handbook of Chinese Psychology. Hong Kong: Oxford University Press.

――― (2010) Moving the scientific study of Chinese psychology into our twenty-first century: some ways forword, in M. H. Bond (Hg.) The Oxford Handbook of Chinese Psychology. New York: Oxford University Press, pp.711–715.

―――(ed.) (2010) The Oxford Handbook of Chinese Psychology. New York: Oxford University Press.

Chakkarath, P. (2004) What Can Western Psychology Learn from Indigenous Psychologies? Lessons from Hindu Psychology, in W. Friedlmeier, P. Chakkarath, and B. Schwarz (eds.), Culture and Human Development: The Importance of Cross-Cultural Research for the Social Sciences. Hove, New York: Psychology Press, pp.31–51.

―――(2007) Kulturpsychologie und indigene Psychologie, in J. Straub, A. Weidemann und D. Weidemann (Hg.) Handbuch interkulturelle Kommunikation und Kompetenz. Grundbegriffe—Theorien—Anwendungsfelder. Stuttgart: Metzler, S. 237–249.

Danziger, K. (2009) Universalism and Indigenization in the History of Modern Psychology, in A. C. Brock (ed.), Internationalizing the History of Psychology. New York: New York University Press, pp.208–225.

Gild, G. (2010) Die Indigene Psychologie in China, in K. Tschuggnall and L. Allolio-Näcke (eds.), Indigene Psychologie (Psychologie & Gesellschaftskritik) 34 (2), No. 134, 55–81.

Higgins, L. and M. Zheng (2002) An Introduction to Chinese Psychology—its Historical Roots until the Present Day, in Journal of Psychology 136 (2), 225–238.

Ho, D. Y. (1993) Relational Orientation in Asian Social Psychology, in U. Kim and J. W. Berry (eds.), Indigenous Psychologies: Research and Experience in Cultural Context. London: Sage, 240–259

――― (1998) Indigenous Psychologies: Asian Perspectives, in Journal of Cross-Cultural Psychology 29, 1, 88–103.

Hofstede, G. (1980) Culture's Consequences: International Differences in Work-Related Values. Beverly Hills, CA: Sage.

―――(2001) Culture's Consequences: Comparing Values, Behaviors, Institutions and Organizations Across Nations. 2d ed. Thousand Oaks, CA: Sage.

Hwang, K. (2005) From Anticolonialism to Postcolonialism: The Emergence of Chinese Indigenous Psychology in Taiwan, in International Journal of Psychology 40 (4), 228–238.

———(2012) Foundations of Chinese Psychology: Confucian Social Relations. New York: Springer.

Jing, Q. and X. Fu (2001) Modern Chinese Psychology: Its Indigenous Roots and International Influences, in International Journal of Psychology 36 (6), 408–418.

Kim, U., K. Yang, and K. Hwang (2006) Indigenous and Cultural Psychology: Understanding People in Context. New York: Springer.

Kim, U. and J. W. Berry (eds.) (1993) Indigenous Psychologies: Research and Experience in Cultural Context. Newbury Park: Sage.

Kuhn, M. and D. Weidemann (eds.) (2010) Internationalization of the Social Sciences: Asia—Latin America—Middle East—Africa—Eurasia. Bielefeld: transcript.

Markus, H. R. and S. Kitayama (1991) Culture and the Self: Implications for Cognition, Emotion, and Motivation, in Psychological Review 98, 224–253.

Moghaddam, F. M. and N. Lee (2009) Double Reification: The Process of Universalizing Psychology in the Three Worlds, in A. C. Brock (ed.), Internationalizing the History of Psychology. New York: New York University Press, pp.163–182.

Nisbett, R. E. (2005) The Geography of Thought: How Asians and Westerners Think Differently—And Why. London: Brealy.

Oommen, T. K. (1991) Internationalization of Sociology. A View from Developing Countries, in Current Sociology 39 (1), 67–84.

Peng, K. et al. (2006) Naive Dialecticism and the Tao of Chinese Thought, in U. Kim, K. Yang and K. Hwang (eds.), Indigenous and Cultural Psychology: Understanding People in Context. New York: Springer, pp.249–262.

Poortinga, Y. H. (1996) Indigenous Psychology: Scientific Ethnocentrism in a New Guise? in J. Pandey, D. P. S. Bhawuk and D. Sinha (eds.), Asian Contributions to Cross-Cultural Psychology. Thousand Oaks, CA: Sage, pp.59–71.

——(1999) Do Differences in Behaviour Imply a Need for Different Psychologies, in Applied Psychology: An International Review 48 (4), 419–432.

Wang, F. and Z. Hong (2008) Zhongguo Wenhua Xinlixue [Chinese Cultural Psychology]. Guangzhou: Jinan University Press.

Weidemann, D. (2010) Challenges of International Collaboration in the Social Sciences, in M. Kuhn and D. Weidemann (eds.), Internationalization of the Social Sciences. Bielefeld: transcript, pp.353–378.

Yang, K. (2006) Indigenized conceptual and empirical analyses of selected Chinese psychological characteristics, in International Journal of Psychology 41 (4), 298–303.

Towards Internationalism: Beyond Colonial and Nationalist Sociologies

Sujata Patel

Introduction

In this paper I ask two sets of questions. First, given the organic links between power-knowledge, what frames of hegemonic social sciences organize global/international knowledge? Second, what are the protocols to be mobilised in order to displace these hegemonic trends in global/international social sciences?

Before I answer these questions, I feel it is important to recall a principle guiding the history of the growth of social sciences in the world. Since its emergence in the nineteenth century Europe, social science theories and perspectives have been constantly confronted and challenged by those who have questioned its hegemonic orientation and thus its conservative and establishment oriented approach. Such challenges have not only presented a new approach to the study of change and transition to modernity but also attempted to map out theories that grasp the intimate and organic link between knowledge and power.

Marxism inaugurated this project when on one hand it presented an analysis of capitalism as a mode of exploitation and opened up for debate the nature of capitalist modernity and on the other hand elaborated a theory that explored the links between class knowledge and bourgeois power. In the mid twentieth century, similar roles were played by feminism and racism as it restructured Marxist and non-Marxist perspectives to assess and examine how gender and race organised inequalities. These perspectives deconstructed the "male" and the "white" representations of power within social sciences in order to make visible the presence of the many "other(s)" as oppressed groups. In this endeavour, structuralist and post structuralist perspectives have played a seminal role.

A new trend in this legacy has articulated itself as social sciences found its presence in different parts of the world. Its incipient formulations have been aided by anti-colonial nationalist ideas. The latter planted a seed of a new analysis when it argued that colonialism and now contemporary global geopolitics has structured the corpus of social science knowledge. This developing idea has found its professional expression and language with the linkages it has established between Marxist and structuralist perspectives of power. These linkages have elaborated two theories, that of Eurocentrism and Orientalism as the definitive modes that are organising the frames of hegemonic social sciences.

The first part of the paper elaborates how Eurocentrism and Orientalism have framed social science language globally. In its discussion of these theories, it highlights how the binaries of the universal-particular have been organised in context to the geopolitics of global/international-national.

The second part of the paper shifts the focus to methodological nationalism and maps out its two avatars-the first in the North and the second in ex-colonial nation states. In this section I indicate how methodological nationalism's positive orientation as an articulation of the project of new nation-states helped to destabilise (to some extent) the hegemonic orientation of Northern/global social science. In both these sections, I use the case of India to illustrate the issues. I also elaborate some of the problems in this strategy.

The last section develops the ideas elaborated in section two to indicate how the strategies developed by methodological nationalism in ex-colonial countries (such as India) can be used as a guidepost for evolving the protocols necessary for displacing hegemonic global social sciences. In the course of this discussion I indicate the reasons for using diverse instead of universal and international instead of global as key concepts in this project.

Colonialism and the Episteme of the Universal-Particular

Eurocentrism and Orientalism are inter-connected cultural and epistemic logics of capitalist imperialism. They incorporated themselves in the disciplines of history and sociology to make Europe the central point of narrative of the analysis of the growth of modernity. Not only did these argue that Europe's superiority and its control of the world had provided the conditions for Europe's ascendance, but these created a scientific language that justified and legitimized this perspective and made it a universal truth (Amin 1989).

European modernity analysed its own birth (through a linear conception of time) and suggested it was produced through the values and institutional system that were universalised in Europe in the last five hundred years, in its own backyard. It incorporated two master narratives: the superiority of Western civilisation (through progress and reason) and the belief in the continuous growth of capitalism (through modernisation, development and the creations of new markets). These master narratives, which Charles Taylor (1995) calls a culturist approach, is recognized now, as ethnocentric in nature. This ethnocentrism assessed its own growth in terms of itself (Europe) rather than in terms of the other (the rest of the colonised world) which was its object of control and through which it became modern. It was a theory of interiority—that is, a perspective that perceived itself from within rather than from the outside (Dussel 1993).

Dussel (ibid.: 65) has said:

> Modernity appears when Europe affirms itself as the 'centre' of a *World History* that it inaugurates; the "periphery" that surrounds this centre is consequently part of its self-definition. The occlusion of this periphery ….leads the major thinkers of the 'center' into a Eurocentric fallacy in their understanding of modernity. If their understanding of the genealogy of modernity is thus partial and provincial, their attempts at a critique or defence of it are likewise unilateral, and in part, false.

A notion of linear time affirmed a belief that social life and its institutions, emerging in Europe from around fourteen century onwards would now influence the making of the new world. In doing so, it silenced its own imperial experience and the violence, without which it could not have become modern. These assumptions framed the ideas elaborated by Hegel, Kant and the Encyclopaedists and were incorporated in the sociologies of Durkheim, Weber and Marx. No wonder these theories legitimized the control and domination of the rest of the world through the episteme of coloniality (Quijano 2000).

This discourse of modernity presented a universal set of axioms in which time as historicity defined its relationship to space. To put it differently, because it saw its own growth in terms of itself and defined it through its own history, that which was outside itself (the place) was perceived in terms of its opposite: lack of history, particular and thus inferior. Henceforth all knowledge was structured in terms of the master binary of the West (which had history, culture, reason, and science, all of which were universals) and the East (which was enclosed in space, nature, religion and spirituality and were particular). This binary linked the division and subsequent hierarchisation of groups of the globe within geo-spatial territories in the world in terms of a theory of temporal linearity: the West was modern because it had evolved to articulate the key features of modernity as against the East which was traditional (Lander 2002).

These binary oppositions constructed the knowledge of the two worlds, the West and the East and placed these as oppositions, creating hierarchies between them and thereby dividing them in terms of I and the other; positing an universality for I and particularities for the other. "Maintaining a difference under the assumption that we are all human" (Mignolo 2002: 71) was part of the normative project of modernity and subsequently of its sociological theory. These were the truths of modernity and the modern world; these truths were considered objective and universal.

These seminal assumptions of Eurocentrism-Orientalism were embodied in the framing of the disciplines of sociology and anthropology in late eighteenth century. Sociology became the study of modern (European-later to be extended to Western) society while anthropology was the study of the Orient (the non-European and non-Western) traditional societies. Thus sociologists studied how the new societies evolved from the deadwood of the old; a notion of time and history were embedded in its discourse. Contrarily anthropologists studied how space/place organised "static" culture that could not transcend its internal structures to be and become modern (Patel 2006; 2011a).

I now take the case of India to indicate how the particular were organised by colonial anthropologists and administrators as academic knowledge in the context of colonialism. They used the same binaries to further divide the East that they were studying in separate geo-spatial territories with each territory given an overarching cultural value. In the case of India, it was religion: Hinduism. The discourse of coloniality collapsed India and Hinduism into each other. The collapse of India into Hindu India is not new. The genealogy of the collapse goes back to the nineteenth century colonial constructs which assumed two principles. The first assumption was geographical and distinguished between groups living in the subcontinent from the spatial-cultural structures of the West, thereby creating the master binary of the West and the East. Later those living in the subcontinent were further classified geographically in spatial-cultural zones and regionally sub-divided (Patel 2007).

The second assumption related to the internal division and relationship between these groups within India. All groups living in the subcontinent were defined by its relationship with Hinduism. Those that were directly related to Hinduism, such as castes and tribes were termed the majority and organized in terms of distinct hierarchies (castes were considered more superior than tribes who were thought to be primitive), while those, that were not, were conceived as minorities, these being mainly groups who practiced Islam and Christianity. Evolutionist theories were used to make Hinduism the Great tradition and anchored into a timeless civilization and its margins, the folk cultures, and the little traditions (Patel 2007).

Anthropologists/sociologists researching on South Asian religions have oftentimes uncritically accepted this logic, and thereby become trapped in this discourse. No wonder Dirks (2001: 13) has argued that the colonial conquest was sustained not only by superior arms and military organization, nor by political power and economic wealth, but also through cultural technology of rule. Colonial conquest and knowledge both enabled ways to rule and to construct what colonialism was all about—its own self knowledge. The British played a major role in identifying and producing Indian tradition that is the belief and customs, of those living in the region. Thus Cohn states that:

> In the conceptual scheme which the British created to understand and to act in India, they constantly followed the same logic; they reduced vastly complex codes and associated meaning to a few metonyms. . . . [This process allowed them] to save themselves the effort of understanding or adequately explaining subtle or not-so-subtle meanings attached to the actions of their subjects. Once the British had defined something as an Indian custom, or traditional dress, or the proper form of salutation, any deviations from it was defined as a rebellion or an act to be punished. India was redefined by the British to be a place of rules and order; once the British had defined to their own satisfaction what they constructed as Indian rules and customs, then the Indians had to conform to these constructions. (Cohn 1997: 162)

The geographically vast subcontinent of South Asia with its thousands of communities having distinct cultural practices and ideas have lived and experienced existence in various forms of unequal and subordinate relationships with each other. In fact, ancient and medieval historiographers now inform us that those whom we identify as castes and tribes were groups that were shaped by political struggles and processes over material resources. In precolonial India, multiple markers of identity defined relationship between groups and were contingent on complex processes, which were constantly changing and were related to political power. Thus we had temple communities, territorial groups, lineage segments, family units, royal retinues, warrior subcastes, little as opposed to large kingdoms, occupational reference groups, agricultural and trading associations, networks of devotional and sectarian religious communities, and priestly cables. Those who came under the name caste as defined by the colonial powers were just one category among many and one way of representing and organizing identity (Dirks 2001).

In the nineteenth century, anthropological/sociological knowledge dissolved these distinctions and re-categorised them into four or five major religious traditions thereby constructing a master narrative of the majority and minority. This logic homogenised distinctions between groups but it also naturalised the Orientalist-Eurocentric language as the only language to comprehend the unequal distribution of power and resources. To this end, they mobilised Orientalist theories of race and linguistic classification (Patel 2006).

Henceforth Orientalist theories of race and linguistic classification were used to produce hierarchical divisions between groups white, superior Aryan races called castes and black, inferior non-Aryan races, now termed tribes. What is of interest is the fact that while castes were defined in the context of Hinduism, as groups who cultivated land, had better technology and a high civilizational attribute, tribes were defined in contrast to castes, who practised primitive technology, lived in interior jungles and were animistic in religious practices. Such classifications and categorization were not peculiar to India. They also found manifestation in the African continent, as British officials used this knowledge to construct categories of social groups in Africa and retransferred these newly constructed classifications back again to India, as happened in the case of the term tribe as a lineage group based on a segmentary state. It is no wonder that these colonial categories helped to legitimise the power of the existing internal elites, in this case of the upper castes and particularly the Brahmins (Patel 2006; 2011a). In the next section I elaborate the ways and means through which anticolonial nationalism aided to dismember this colonial episteme.

The Two Avatars of Methodological Nationalisms

In the context of creating a global cosmopolitan theory, social theorists have critically examined the methodological assumptions of the first wave of sociological theory. Calling this critique, methodological nationalism, they have deliberated the ways on which it has framed and organized sociological knowledge and carried with it assumptions which work to structure sociological inquiry. They argue that though sociology was structured through the prism of the nation, nation-state and that of nationalism, (European) sociological theories ignored these intellectual moorings and universalized its language disregarding this history (Beck 2000).

In its most straightforward usage, methodological nationalism implies coevalness between society and the nation-state i.e., it argues that a discussion on modern society (which sociology does) entails an implicit understanding of the nation. Or, in other words, the nation is treated as the natural and necessary representation of the modern society (Chernillo 2006). Methodological nationalism is the taken-for-granted belief that nation-state boundaries are natural boundaries within which societies are contained. This ignorance and/or blindness is reinforced through a mode of naturalisation; sociological theories take for granted official discourses, agendas, loyalties and histories without problematising these. Ultimately this error leads sociologists to territorialise social science language and reduce it to the boundaries of the nation-state. Methodological nationalism recognizes that it is embedded in Eurocentric positions (Rodríguez, Boatcâ, and Costa 2010).

It is my argument that what were considered as methodological errors by European sociologists became in the case of ex-colonial countries an advantage in the historical moment that defines the decades of post-independence epoch. Thus, in the case of India, as in other ex-colonial countries, methodological nationalism was a self-conscious embrace of a place/territory to create a set of guidelines to confront colonial discourses of social sciences. Identification with the place allowed national intellectuals to build intellectual solidarity against dominant colonial knowledge. Second, the recognition of this place-bound solidarity facilitated the growth of an alternate discourse. This then became the principle for organizing the institutionalization of knowledge systems through a gamut of policies and regulations. These policies determined the protocols and practices of teaching and learning processes, establishment and practices of research within research institutes, distribution of grants for research, language of reflection, organization of the profession and definitions of scholars and scholarship (Patel 2011d).

For example the initiation of sociology as a discipline (against anthropology) allowed some departments in India to inaugurate the teaching, learning and research of a modern Indian society rather than as a traditional one. In this it was aided by the legacy of nationalist ideologies which wished to see India as a modern nation-state. This advantage got a further fillip with the initiation of a nationalist modernist project, by the post-independence state and its use of higher education for creating a new India (Patel 2011a).

No wonder, this sociological knowledge discussed, debated and represented social changes occurring within one nation and territory—India. Sociologists saw their project as that which analyses one's own society (India) in one's (indigenous) own terms, without colonial and now neo-colonial tutelage. This project allowed for the institutionalisation of a particularistic problematique in a new way—an assessment of how modernity and modernization were changing India's characteristic institutions—caste, kinship, family, and religion. This particularistic problematique also influenced Marxist perspectives as radical sociologists interrogated and set aside revisionist Orientalist theories and elaborated the distinct nature of class and class relations in India and theorised its differential modes of production (Patel 2011b).

These developments took place in a context wherein social sciences were engendered to play a critical role in conceptualizing development and planned change. This agenda entailed a need to professionalise the discipline and organize it within the territory of the nation-state. In this context, two strands of methodological nationalism mentioned above, that of territorialisation and naturalisation became in new ways, symbiotically linked with each other to become an integral part of the traditions of sociological thinking in India. Sociology not only interrogated (even if partially) the received inheritance of colonial theories and methodologies, but also promoted a new language with new perspectives and methodologies that defined itself as Indian sociology (Patel 2011a).

Rather than restricting an understanding of international sociology, nationalist sociologies from ex-colonial countries have enlarged it. On one hand, these have asserted alternate ways of assessing contextual processes thereby underlining the many particularities that have structured the world and on the other, have highlighted the inequalities that structures international sociology. This heritage has relevance today and cannot be washed away (Patel 2011c).

However both Syed Hussein Alatas (1972) and Paulin Hountondji (1997) have also raised cautionary arguments about these nationalist projects and have suggested that these have not necessarily restructured social sciences in the ex-colonial countries nor have displaced the hegemony of global social science knowledge. There are two sets of arguments raised here and these relate to two strategies that have evolved for displacing hegemonic tendencies in global social science. These can be conveniently termed the strong version and the weaker version. While the first strategy of nationalist social science would postulate a need to create an alternative national sociology based on indigenous and national cultural and philosophical positions, the weaker version would argue that there are some experiences historically distinctive to the nation state and its culture which needs to be analysed and examined in its distinctive attributes. In order to do so, one need not create a separate social science for a nation-state or for that matter for the South. Hountondji (1997) would argue that such culturist projects which he calls ethnoscience remain part of the colonial and neo-colonial binaries of the universal-particular and the global-national. Rather there is a need to evolve a strategy displace these binaries.

How can one do so? I would argue that we have to look towards the weaker strategy to answer this question. This strategy incorporates two steps: First, a need to deconstruct the provincialism of European universalisms and locate it in its own cultural and national contexts. Second a need to go beyond the "content" of the social sciences (the explanations they offer, the narratives they construct) shaped as it is by a genealogy that is both European and colonial. Rather we need to analyse their very "form" (the concepts through which explanations become possible, including the very idea of what counts as an explanation). We cannot argue that the social sciences are purely and simply European and are therefore "wrong." We cannot dispense with these categories, but that they often provide only partial and flawed understanding (Seth 2009: 335).

Alatas and Hountondji have discussed these as the captive mind syndrome and extroversion respectively. These relates to the culture of doing social science globally. This culture has been defined by Northern social science and is held out as a model for the rest of the world. It is backed by sheer size of its, intellectual, human, physical and capital resources together with the infrastructure that is necessary for its reproduction. This includes not only equipment, but archives, libraries, publishing houses, and journals; an evolution of a professional culture of intellectual commitment and engagement which connects the producers and consumers of knowledge; institutions such as universities and students having links with others based in Northern nation-states and global knowledge production agencies.

Behind these cultures and practices are the unequal political economic processes that organise the production and reproduction of international social sciences. In the fifties and the sixties intellectuals in the ex-colonial nation-states used a nationalist strategy to confront colonial dependencies. Today there is a need for a multi-dimensional strategy for displacing such hegemonic social sciences. There is a need to ask whether the above mentioned nationalist strategy remains significant and if so in what form. For, the nationalist strategy dominated and universalised its local subalterns and muted their voices. In these circumstances, can the nation-state be the site for creating knowledge that organises particularities against its binary opposite, the universal? Can it become a location to consolidate the many particulars within the nation-state and thereby attempt to displace hegemonic knowledges? In the next section I discuss some of the complexities that organise our interventions and suggest that the journey has to surmount many obstacles.

Challenges and Pathways

The paper has argued that the reduction of society to national territory within nationalist sociologies of the ex-colonial countries, have created methodological and theoretical problems. It is clear that nationalist sociologies have made invisible and/or discounted the place bound voices and experiences of the local, weak, and the marginal subalterns within their territory. Over time, social sciences have also become closely associated with the official discourses and methods of understanding the relationship between nation, nation-state and modernity. If sociologies of the end of the twentieth century questioned the supra national, it also dominated and universalized its own infra local. The moot question is: What kinds of frames are needed to create an international sociology that can include in its analysis these conflictual and contradictory processes of dominance-subordination that have organised its differential epistemes and silenced the many others in the world? A need for a comparative framework outside the universal-particular and global-national is necessary.

Sociologists across the world are trying to theorise a way to combine the global demands without neglecting the many local and subaltern voices. Some have it called this theory global modernity (Dirlik 2007), others have termed it entangled one (Therborn 2003) and yet others have called it cosmopolitanism (Beck 2000). They have highlighted that since the seventies and particularly after the nineties the dynamics of the world has changed.

Though it is difficult to come to an agreement as to what globalisation implies, most would agree that the openness inherent in this process subsumes a free flow of ideas, information and knowledge, goods, services, finance, technology and even diseases, drugs and arms. Contemporary globalisation has opened up possibilities of diverse kinds of transborder movements, widened the arenas of likely projects of cooperation and that of conflicts and brought about change in the way power is conceived and consolidated. Inequalities and hierarchies are no longer a characteristic of colonial and ex-colonial countries. These are being reproduced the world over and are being differently organized in uneven ways by the global dominant form of modernity. Lack of access to livelihoods, infrastructure and political citizenship now blends with exclusions relating to cultural and group identity in distinct spatial locations. This process is and has challenged the constitution of agency of actors and groups of actors (Patel 2010).

However, it is clear to keep in mind that globalisation entails multiple, complex and contradictory processes that incessantly continue to unfold with the passage of time. For example, while it encourages trends towards global integration of the erstwhile nation states to become a region, such as ASEAN and BRICS, it also promotes trends towards regional and nation-state disintegration, such as that of the erstwhile federations former Soviet Union and Yugoslavia. Also in some regions the nation state, which was the crux of all political theory, has witnessed a political and an existential crisis. On one hand these nation-states are being pressurized from above by international regimes such as World Trade Organisation and on the other hand they are also been afflicted by sub-nationalist processes inspired by ethno nationalist movements. This is not true in the case of the USA wherein the ideology and politics of insularity has increasingly privileged it against internationalism.

It thus needs to be recognised that globalisation creates trends that are unevenly organised across the world and that its impact with the many local and regional processes are distinct, different and various. And in some rare cases, the contemporary global process has not even imprinted itself across the world either economically politically and/or culturally. These developments create challenges to connect the global/international with the national regional and local without embedding them in the binaries of universal and particular inherited from the nineteenth century sociology.

I had argued earlier that social theory needs to assert the principle of diversities. I use the concept of diversities because it connotes more meanings than other concepts in use, such alternate, multiple and cosmopolitan. In many languages within ex-colonial countries (including colonial ones such as English), the term diverse has had multivariate usage and its meanings range from a simple assertion of difference to an elaboration of an ontological theory of difference that recognizes power as a central concept in the creation of epistemes. Symbolically it also implies a dispersal rather than homogenization. They present and define their own theories to assess their distinct and different perspectives of sociologies and its theories and practices. Individually these manifestations are neither superior nor inferior and collectively they remain distinct, variate, universal but interconnected. Its usage exhorts them to consider these interconnections not as equal but distinct having its own histories of mutualities. Also, in its effects, (as an ontological theory), its usage allows its practitioners not to place the many manifestations that they are outlining in a single (linear) line.

The term diversity suggests a need to access the ways knowledge is organised and structured by various levels of space/place dynamics within a matrix of power. There is a necessity to give an epistemic location to the constantly evolving dynamics of space/place and voice that is organising the contemporary world in order to integrate the social science disciplines to new actors, institutions and processes. Given the received vertical linkages of dependencies (organised during colonialism and continued after through the systematic inequalities that organise the North against the South) it is important to link and interface space/place-voice articulations at horizontal levels (South-South). For if we agree that the colonial and post colonial dependencies of domination and control need to be combated these have to be done politically.

Thus, social sciences need to promote the many voices of sociological traditions-infra local and supra national with its own culturist oeuvres, epistemologies, and theoretical frames, cultures of science and languages of reflection, sites of knowledge production and its transmission across the many Souths. In order to do so, social theory, needs to ontologically assert the necessity of combining space/place with a voice (Patel, 2010, 2011d). The challenge today is in creating a political language and the intellectual infrastructure that can interface the many Souths, dissolve the markers of distinction between and within them and made their various voices recognize the matrix of power that has organised these divisions.

There are many sites wherein these dialogues can take place: classrooms and departments and within campaigns, movements and advocacies. Such a dialogue would entail academic exchange and joint research programmes, joint formulations of syllabi and evolving South-South protocols of professional codes. This project needs to involve actors of various kinds: scholars and researchers, publishers and publishing houses and the larger epistemic communities together with activists and political interlocutors. They need to assess, reflect and elucidate issues that define the teaching and learning and the research processes so that an effort is made to organize and systematize knowledge that is outside the heritage of earlier and received dependencies.

Can we accept this strategy to countervail hegemonic tendencies of the nineteenth century social sciences which continue even today?

References

Alatas, S. H. (1972) The captive mind in development studies International Social Science Journal 24(1): 9–25.

Amin, S. (1989) Eurocentrism. London: Zed Books.

Beck, U. (2000) The cosmopolitan perspective: Sociology in the second age of modernity British Journal of Sociology 151: 79–106.

Chernilo, D. (2006) Social theory's methodological nationalism: Myth and reality European Journal of Social Theory 9 (1): 5–22.

Cohn, B. S. (1997) Colonialism and its Forms of Knowledge: The British in India. New Delhi: Oxford University Press.

Dirks, N. (2001) Castes of Mind: Colonialism and the Making of Modern India. Princeton: Princeton University Press.

Dirlik, A. (2007) Global Modernity: Modernity in the Age of Global Capitalism. London: Paradigm.

Dussel, E. (1993) Eurocentrism and modernity, in Boundary 2 (3): 65–76.

Hountondji, P. (1997) Endogenous Knowledge: Research Trails. Dakar: Codesria

Lander E. (2002) Eurocentrism, modern knowledges, and the "natural" order of global capital, in Nepantla: Views from South 3 (2): 249–268.

Mignolo, W. D. (2002) The geopolitics of knowledge and the colonial difference, in The South AtlanticQuarterly 101 (1): 57–96.

Patel, S. (2006) Beyond binaries: A case for self-reflexive sociologies, in Current Sociology 54 (3): 381–395.

———(2007) Sociological study of Religion: Colonial modernity and nineteenth century majoritarianism, in Economic and Political Weekly 42 (13): 1089–1094.

―――(2010) Introduction: Diversities of sociological traditions, in S. Patel (ed.), The ISA Handbook of Diverse Sociological Traditions. London: Sage, 1–18.

―――(2011a) Ruminating on sociological traditions in India, in S. Patel (ed.), Doing Sociology in India: Genealogies, Locations, and Practices. New Delhi: Oxford University Press, xi-xxxviii.

―――(2011b) Social anthropology or Marxist Sociology?, Assessing the contesting sociological visions of M. N. Srinivas and A. R. Desai in S. Patel (ed.), Doing Sociology in India: Genealogies, Locations, and Practices. New Delhi: Oxford University Press, 72–99.

―――(2011c) Lineages, trajectories and challenges to sociology, in India Footnotes, American Sociological Association, March Retrieved from http://www.asanet.org/footnotes/mar11/intl_persp_0311.html (Last access on 18 December 2012)

―――(2011 d) Against Cosmopolitanism, in Global Dialogue, Issue No 4, International Sociological Association, 2 (3) Retrieved from http://www.isa-sociology.org/global-dialogue/2011/05/challenging-cosmopolitanism/ (Last access on 18 December 2012)

Quijano, A. (2000) Coloniality of power, Eurocentrism and Latin America, in Nepantla 1 (3): 533–580.

Rodriguez, E.G, M. Boatca and S. Costa (eds.) (2010) Decolonising European Sociology: Transdisciplinary Approaches. London: Ashgate.

Seth, S. (2009) Historical sociology and Postcolonial theory: Two strategies for challenging Eurocentrism, in International Political Sociology 3: 334–338.

Taylor, C. (1995) Two theories of modernity,in The Hastings Centre Report 25 (2): 24–33.

Therborn, G. (2003) Entangled Modernities, in European Journal of Social Theory 7(3): 293–305.

Who is the Social Scientist in the Twenty-First Century? Commentaries from Academic and Applied Contexts in the Mainstream and the Periphery

Hebe Vessuri

Introduction

Science and its social and historical reconstructions face particular problems in terms of their relationship with the public and policy-makers. Embedded in universities, industry and government, science is a powerful cultural and ideological force, with relatively autonomous and fairly atypical governance structures. An explanation for this situation is the specialized nature of scientific expertise and a strongly perceived need to protect scientific work from outside direction or "interference." Structures from peer-review to policy-making supposedly linked to those broader domains have often been much more in the control of practitioners—that is, scientists—than is the case in other areas of public policy. Hence, policy and the public discourse about science have been largely shaped by scientists and other writers from within a relatively closed community, producing a radically simplified version of reality that emphasizes linearity, progress, and the intellectual and material products of science. This form of reconstruction has served a powerful ideological purpose, helping to maintain scientists' control over public and private representations of their enterprise (Hughes, 2004).

With specificities of its own, social science has broadly shared the same form of social and historical reconstruction. In this paper, I briefly review the evolution of this general self-legitimating aspect of social scientists' outlook in their social-historical reconstruction and speculate on some of the consequences of this. l complement this brief analysis by making reference to development studies and approaches. Today the long-delayed analysis of these different intellectual traditions within concrete dialogue spaces seems to be making some progress. Finally I consider the world expansion of social science in recent decades and its implications for the notion of international science. Indeed I make my argument in terms of three stories about the following: (1) the identity of academic social science; (2) the evolution of the development problematic that has existed since the early twentieth century; and (3) international social science in the era of globalization. I pose several questions that I mention briefly here but are part of a more ambitious endeavor in which I am engaged at present about the social sciences in the global era. What determines the degree of segregation or integration of academic social science and social problems? What conditions the relative dominance of one or the other? What kind of description results from Development/Dependence studies? What difference do these variable configurations make to the understanding of social reality in different contexts? What organizational changes will social sciences have to undergo to contribute more effectively to public debate and informed policy? Or will they become more marginal to society and social change?

The Identity of Academic Social Science

The first story is a commentary on the powerful socialization characteristic of the social sciences into the unique set of scientific values that grew closely linked to the university in the twentieth century. I call its sources the academic commentary. In the transition from traditional to modern societies a criterion of interpretation was used based on the norms and trends of the social values observed in the most advanced societies of Europe and North America. Since the mid-century there was a search for differentiation between "sociological" and "social" problems, by means of which social science would strategically distance itself from the turmoil of social reality to safeguard its "scientific quality." This was to a large extent the basis for the "ivory tower" legend that views academia as aloof and removed from the heat of the struggles for power and resistance. Although such distance was contested at different times and places, on the whole it has been at the root of the ideology of the university teacher and researcher in both the global North and the global South.

The institutional and intellectual structuring force of science was so strong that in the early 1970s it was conceived as an activity carried out by a human group (the scientific community or better communities specialized by disciplines), and a well-known social scientist could say that this group was "so totally isolated from the external world that to all practical effects it is not necessary to take into consideration the idiosyncrasy of different societies in which scientists live and work" (Ben-David, 1970). In the 1970s interest in the social study of science was concentrated in the social conditions of academic work. Often a comparative vision was adopted in the study of the constitution of professional teams in laboratories, organizations structured on the basis of disciplines, national plans, and scientific research institutes, as well as communication networks among scientists.

Scientific disciplines represent cognitive frameworks determining legitimate sets of problems for canonical scientific research and the methods, concepts and traditions to solve them. Social sciences present special features. Their disciplinary structure is a constraint for professors, scientists and students, while it is also a guide for learning and research. To some observers, however, recent trends suggest that social science will soon enter a post-disciplinary age. At different times and institutional locations, domains and objects of analysis have been reconfigured, which has led to moving some issues into the foreground while others seem to have receded. Depending on the author considered, current changes may trigger a new integration of the social sciences and the hard sciences, which have been separated for over a century; however, they may result in a new truly universal profile of social science. Yet this trend may mean that knowledge will be oriented increasingly towards local, context-dependent, problem-solving efforts integrated into epistemic "communities" with actors originating from different social activities outside science.

In academic social science disciplines, academic institutions, scientific societies, journals, funding mechanisms, and peer-review are all elements that help to structure the space and world of the academic scientist and serve in the global distribution of knowledge and values. In institutional and also in cognitive terms, there is no doubt that several countries, universities and disciplines have served as models to be emulated. A common intellectual matrix is recognized, which is reflected in national disciplinary research styles. Knowledge production is usually defined by the distance between the knowledge seeker and the object of knowledge, in constant tension to achieve the appropriate balance between "distance and commitment". The topic of the adequacy of forms involving a greater distance or more engaged forms of social and human knowledge continues to be controversial and varies with time. The social sciences provide tools allowing practitioners and critics to question the interpretations of social reality, the legitimacy of policies and the terms used by scientists themselves. Many recent academic and political debates share precisely those critical features that render the social sciences an important element in current tensions and antinomies.

Social scientists are changing their attitudes towards the hegemony of disciplinary departments and disciplinary research. Although disciplinary institutions continue to be important for undergraduate and graduate education, as well as for focalized research projects and new scientific hypotheses, traditional disciplines in the future will have to compete with interdisciplinary research and educational projects. Besides, the gaps between social sciences and other forms of knowledge are currently being challenged, as will become apparent below. In addition transdisciplinarity or interdisciplinarity are sought to handle complex problems.

Although it has been easier for natural and physical scientists than for social scientists to build a scheme of academic professionalization of research, social science has also become highly professionalized, exhibiting a steep ranking system. This first story asserts that the social scientist who did not stay within academia was second-rate, academically "impure."

A profoundly hierarchical view arose in which the most valued position was that of the academic scientist in the university context pursuing disciplinary research and teaching. The idea was that a young person took governmental or nongovernment organization (NGO) employment only because suitable academic careers were in short supply or too low-paid, or perhaps because he was not talented enough to pursue a life devoted to research and intellectual endeavor. This is, in fact, a story about "hierarchy" and "competition" between the academic values of free research and those of oriented, applied work, which has often been even denied the quality of research, being clearly debased in terms of prestige. The notion of the ethos of science and by implication social science was expressed by Robert Merton for the United States in early 1940s essays and was modified and developed by such students and colleagues as Bernard Barber (1952), Norman Storer (1966), and Warren Hagstrom (1965). It became institutionalized in the canon of American sociology of science as a "norm of science." In its expansion into the different regions of the world, the newly institutionalized social science adopted many such normative prescriptions as revealed in the formal programs through which it was integrated into the world's universities.

Among the social scientist's basic academic activities, publishing stands out. Its international dimension has grown considerably in the different regions, showing that regional social science is not exclusively oriented to local consumption; if we add to this the scientific literature that is translated into languages other than English, we get a glimpse of the importance that the international cognitive orientation has for the reproduction of the social sciences in the world at large. This dependence becomes evident with regard to thematic repertoires. These are key to insure a meaningful exchange between the academic world and the nonacademic one. A frequent source of anxiety for the researcher is how to approach a public audience when not thinking priority-wise about one's colleagues, feeling "vertigo" in the confrontation with the general public. From the vision constructed by academic social science of applied work in public agencies and NGOs, a prediction resulted that would confirm a matter-of-course state of affairs: scientists socialized into the academic value system would suffer the "pain of psychological conflict" when presented with situations that required or encouraged them to behave in ways that violated the norms they had acquired. These notably included the notion of distance from social reality and its entanglements, powerfully presented by Max Weber in his celebrated work in The Politician and the Scientist (2003). To avoid or free themselves of this "pain," it was "in the social scientist's interest" to conform to the ethos in which he had been socialized. Contrasting with political pressures, moral dilemmas and commercial temptations, the academic world offered intellectual and normative security, away from the complications of real life. In this first story, the scientist in a Development Program or institution or in a NGO is a frustrated, anxious and possibly awkward character who is in constant conflict with political or commercial values and organizational structures. By contrast, as a result of the academic scientists' unique pattern of socialization, their personalities are depicted as intolerant of organizational or political constraints: scientists are said to be quite independent and mindful of their individual integrity, too sceptical, too hostile to authority structures, too loyal to science and disdainful of local organizational values. Such persons are supposed to pose a major problem for the smooth running of development or entrepreneurial organizations.[1]

---

[1] An example of the kind of perception of the stratification and hierarchy induced by the academic community and its powerful values is the Chil-ean arrangement of traditional prestigious universities compared with public institutes of technological research (IPTs in the Spanish acronym), even though the latter fulfil important socioeconomic functions in society such as the fol-

The current double movement in which a research community becomes more internationalized while specific local claims also gain status is not as paradoxical as it might seem. In a recent revisit to this problem Keim (2010) comments that the tensions between local and general sociologies may be considered a direct consequence of growing international communication. In her view the more frequent access of "peripheral" academic scientists to the "central" forums confronts researchers who regard themselves as contributing to universally valid theory, with a situation in which

> lowing: "1) A solid administration of natural resources and environment; 2) Infrastructural provision for a modern economy; 3) Establishment of conditions for an innovating economy and 4) Promotion of development of key elements of the national economy" (Mullin et al., 2000). One of the problems inhibiting a more constructive and fruitful dialogue between researchers in both settings has been the difference in social value of the two different kinds of institutional settings for career making in research. University scientists are better appreciated socially than their counterparts in the public institutes of technology. Despite their obvious achievements, a certain public image of IPTs has depicted them as costly and inefficient, quite disconnected from the sectors they are expected to serve. In addition, the research done is often judged as not of the best quality nor useful, with insufficient contact with international trends, obsolete equipment and libraries, underpaid poorly man-aged and unmotivated staff. Even the provision of services was perceived by some as being ill managed and with staff insufficiencies. The negative social perception of the technology institutes contributed to reinforce the vicious circle in which the valuable IPTs had to function.

they are placed by the dominant Northern establishment in a position as specialists in developing peripheral regions, and their knowledge not being acknowledged as of universal value but only of regional or local validity and scope. This is part and parcel of the division of labor by which global Southern scientists continue to be relegated to data collection and empirical studies, while Northern scientists work out the theoretical implications.

The Development Turn

My second story refers to Development as a field of social inquiry and activity. Sources for it can be found in a wide variety of places. From early development programs and advocates in the aftermath of World War II we find arguments for the setting up of programs for the support of countries considered to be underdeveloped, working on the transfer of resources, technology and knowledge from the wealthy portion of the world to those lagging behind. The postwar years of progress were in more than one sense the culmination of a "modernization" process started in the mid-nineteenth century, by means of which a whole miscellany of cultures gave rise to the happy common world of modernity, conceived as a unique and homogeneous continuum.

A typical definition is found in The South Commission Report of 1990:

> Development is a process which enables human beings to realize their potential, build self-confidence, and lead lives of dignity and fulfillment. It is a process which frees people from the fear of want and exploitation. It is a movement away from political, economic or social oppression. Through development, political independence acquires its true significance. And it is a process of growth, a movement essentially springing from within the society that is developing...The base for a nation's development must be its own resources, both human and material, fully used to meet its own needs...Development has therefore to be an effort of, by, and for the people. True development has to be people-centered (The Challenge...1990).

The field of Development has been a powerful tool of social science, or better of social "engineering," particularly with regard to decolonization and the South, promising to solve the problems of poverty and stagnation, although the solution has always appeared to recede like the horizon just as one thought to be approaching it. It has maintained an uneasy relationship with academic social science. Sometimes it was considered as being part of the social science platform of theoretical construction while on other occasions was deemed to be an inferior kind of social thinking and action. By the 1970s research had become an important tool for military and industrial technology. It was no longer necessary to convince states or big industry of the relevance of science to them; the issue was how to foster and use it for their own ends. In the United States and other countries specific agencies were created to support and stimulate it. The problems related to human and financial resources of science, including science for development, acquired as much importance as those of organization. Science and scientists enjoyed social prestige.

At different times a number of the most thoughtful social researchers, particularly in the non-Western world, have published books and articles on the subject of organizing development research facilities and administering development programs. These sources constitute the "development/ist" commentary. In marked, if unsurprising, contrast to the academic commentary in our first story, "development" writing displayed no interest in making points of general disciplinary interest or in using the theoretical social science literature for any other purpose than coming to robust findings about recurring problems in and about the development program at hand and proffering some fairly plausible practical solutions to the problems in question. This, for example, comes out from the work by Calcagno (1990) in Latin America, when revising and updating development styles in the region (see also Frank, 1970; Rodriguez, 1983).

Despite a common origin in the social sciences, the two research communities remained largely separate. Curiously, the persistent and consequential problem of socialization so repeatedly identified in the academic literature is not found in the development commentary. Indeed, there are important and pervasive strands of such commentary that portray the daily realities of development work in ways that make the academically predicated role-conflict highly problematic. Although in government programs and in nongovernmental institutions, development social scientists may not be fully free since they are often "officers" in larger bureaucratic organizations, they frequently feel free from heavy teaching loads and from their academic colleagues' lack of interest in research. They also tend to express a sociopolitical and/or moral satisfaction from participating in the improvement of the social conditions of people.

Freedom in the science context is linked to the notion of autonomy, historically a highly appreciated feature in the academic narrative. However, what does autonomy mean for a social scientist? It does not mean much—in the past or now—if you cannot get the time or the funds to do the research you want to do. The issue whether a development researcher has relative time and freedom (autonomy) to define his own research has been there since an early stage. Participatory research (Fals Borda, 1978; Chambers, 2007) illustrates the kinds of arguments and debates social commitment fostered, involving different ideas of autonomy and social responsibility.

We may distinguish between the function of research for Development over a certain period—that is, the organizing commitment to it and its place in social activities—and planning the actual "act" or "conduct" of research, in which considerable freedom of action is simply deemed necessary. The inadequacies often experienced by academic social scientists when dealing with concrete problems related to development can be illustrated with an example. From the beginning, ecological societies in the United Kingdom and the United States acknowledged the importance of relating ecological studies with practical applications, mainly with productive activities such as agriculture, cattle-raising, and the management of natural resources (water, soils, and forest resources), all basic ingredients of development work. In this spirit, The Journal of Applied Ecology came into being in 1964. However, thirty years later, taking stock of what occurred in the journal during the three previous decades, the editors observed that the majority of the articles lacked indicators about practical applications of research and did not provide clear recommendations for management (Pienkowsky and Watkinson, 1996, in Castillo, 2011). In more recent years the journal has experienced an enormous increase both in the number of articles and their impact from a scientific point of view. Nevertheless, the editors also remarked the need that information reaches specific audiences, particularly those related to the management of ecosystems and forest resources, decision-makers and the public in general, through approaches more oriented to users (Freckleton et al., 2005). In this story we notice that academic scientists find great difficulty in conducting research in a manner that is appropriate to their expressed development aims, even though they may be free to formulate their projects in those terms.

On the other hand, there is also the issue of development specialists publishing technical reports (gray literature), not publishing at all, or publishing in academic journals. Many development experts have vigorously endorsed a free academic publishing policy and have argued for the barest minimum of internal in-house documents, as a way to foster quality as a consequence of public exposure to peer criticism. The free flow of technical information, or at least the freest flow compatible with the kind of literature produced, was for a long time widely accepted if not universally acknowledged in these circles as a net benefit to all parties. Indeed, some of the best social literature emerging from Latin American social science has been on development theory and problems, as shown by ECLAC publications on development and the critical responses of dependency theorists (ECLAC, 1969; Cardoso and Faletto, 1972). It may be noted that by the 1960s the Development challenge was perceived to be so great that academic social scientists were already producing extended quasi-empirical studies of "development research," defining a research agenda and methodological approaches from within the academic world itself (Cooper, 1973; Pavitt, 1984; Herrera, 1971).[2]

---

[2] The Science Policy Research Unit (SPRU) in Sussex University, United Kingdom, became a hotspot for committed university scholars who wished to contribute to the new challenges of Development and social change. Forty years ago its Sussex Manifesto focused on the scale and location of scientific and technological activity becoming very influential. This earlier manifesto was of its time; it distinguished between so-called "developing" and "advanced" nations in a way that today is problematic. It argued that research agendas needed to focus on the world's "develop-ing" countries and their needs, urging "advanced" nations to devote 5% of their own expenditure on research and development problems in "devel-oping" countries...Recognizing that it would "be folly if there was no reform of the institutions for carrying out these activi-

In Latin America, The Center of Development Studies (CENDES) of the Central University of Venezuela became an attraction pole in the region at the crossroad of social science disciplines and sociopolitical concerns. With a research scope that extended from national planning to agrarian reform through science and technology, it kept a *sui generis competitive* relationship with the Social Science Faculty within the same university, which cultivated and defended the disciplinary boundaries in separate schools for sociology, anthropology, and economics. CENDES was closely connected to the education of several generations of planning experts and officials in government agencies and NGOs (Darwich, 2005). When CENDES emerged, it did so accompanying the construction of the modern Venezuelan state in the incipient democracy installed in 1958. The origin of CENDES may be seen as deeply imbricated in that process of social construction, and CENDES saw itself as the provider of technical knowledge to the State in its rationalizing role of society. This optimistic rationalist ideology promoted a particular view of the social sciences. Being located in a university context and not being a government unit, afforded it a larger margin of autonomy than it would have had as a school of cadres in the Ministry of Planning. In addition, this location allowed the emergence of social thought linked to the management and development of the dependency approach as well as to rethinking the need of the State's and society's transformation to

---

ties," the Sussex Manifesto highlighted the importance of organizational reform (STEPS 2010).

produce the social changes perceived as necessary for reaching more equitable societies, with greater margins of freedom (Vessuri, 2005).

Of course, the rank-and-file development researcher combines a different menu of activities from that of his academic counterpart. Publishing in internationally refereed journals is not necessarily his target since he addresses his work preferably to local audiences, policy-makers, or decision-makers. Having said this, however, we must acknowledge that publishing is only one of his tasks, while there is a very rich variety of activities he engages in but fall outside the range of recognized publishing activities related to academic performance evaluation, such as inventories of biotic resources, community forest management planning, as well as different dimensions of participatory research.

In terms of values distinguishing development from academic research, it has been argued that academic values cluster around disinterestedness, autonomy, spontaneity, and openness, while development values center on concrete development outcomes, organization, planning, and the control of social goals. In academic institutions, it might plausibly be said that the "Mertonian" values (Merton, 1973 [1942]) can be publicly celebrated as institutional essence, while in development organizations values are more often asserted tactically as reminders to the uninformed that research is, to a great extent, an uncertain business, not to be subjected to the accountability regimes of other social activities. Yet, a theory of ideal-type differences between institutional cultures is one thing, and a description of daily realities in complex institutional environments is quite another. Those in the practical business of managing research enterprises have tended to acknowledge the intractable problems of distinguishing between these institutional environments, since theorizing essential differences has been of little concern to them.

For all that, certain obstinate facts remain:

1) In the second half of the twentieth century institutionalized social science underwent important changes that were identified under the banner of professionalization and mainstreaming. The new model was extended to the non-Western world through the expansion of the "international" curriculum, which served as a blueprint for new social science institutions and programs all over the world. However, one thing was the theory and a different one the practice of social science. The truth is that in many places in the global South the majority of academically-trained social scientists have not worked (full-time) in universities, while neither development nor government programs have had problems recruiting as many as they wanted, even with perpetual competition for the best and brightest.

2) Universities have not been universally regarded as natural homes for research: most have been under-resourced and have had a primary commitment to teaching. Furthermore, many have experienced cultural, political, and religious pressures that

seriously compromised any notion that universities, as such, were communities of free and suitably resourced inquiries.

Social Knowledge in the Era of Globalization

The third story concerns the emergence of a new player in the social science field, social science in the non-Western world, with an increasingly stronger voice and presence through its sheer numbers. The World Social Science Report published by the ISSC and UNESCO in 2010 offered a comprehensive review of the state of the art of social science in the world, analyzing its dynamics, geography, and the institutional, material, and social structures that influence its production and circulation. The review also examined the gaps that reduce social science's ability to analyze trends in human societies and effectively face global challenges. The greatest efforts of the report were to show figures, magnitudes and forms, and mechanisms of organization including the Shanghai and similar university rankings in addition to the main bibliometric databases. Clearly a report of this kind could not cover all possibilities in a single volume. Important dimensions remained unconsidered, as is the case of the capacity of social science to interpret the reality of the heterogeneous sociocultural units that make up the world.

However, today there are significant research communities in countries like China, India, Brazil, South Africa, Korea, and Mexico, which include individuals who are critically rethinking the relationships between knowledge and power in the Third World, thus contributing to change the architecture of world social science and the structures of scientific power. Globalization begins to undermine the prestige of social theories developed in Europe and North America and helps to raise the relevance of intellectual thinking from other regions while generating anomalies with regard to classical social science concepts and theories in the West. More mature and ubiquitous, social science in different contexts begins to ask questions more frequently and systematically about social categories and thought traditions that until the recent past were ignored or relegated under the weight of canonical forms of social scientific knowledge created in the West, resuming the exploration of different concepts and methodological approaches.

Growing numbers of scientists, mainly from the non-Western world, argue that Western theories pretend universal validity although they do not adequately interpret phenomena in other contexts. In turn they question that in pretending to interpret reality through the lenses of the Western model the theories produced by social science in the rest of the world also fail to fully understand what happens. Despite these limitations, the notion of science widened with its growing diffusion and also suffered deeper changes. Emphasizing the permeability of science to the external world became more common through the "market," funding opportunities, demands from civil society or, more concretely, from anonymous or limited societies, private clients, etc. Far from being isolated, in this new narrative social science came to be perceived as being closely interconnected with the economic, political, and social structures. This implied a whole new series of limitations and possibilities. In the last quarter of the twentieth century there was an explosion of institutional studies about scientific activity in different countries. Never before had national and international science policy been so stimulated, nor had such large numbers of social researchers assessed scientific production and participated in the elaboration of indicators about science, technology, and innovation in the midst of a growing globalization.

In the 1960s and 1970s the dependency approach had offered an opportunity to critically examine the hegemony of the theory of modernization and its outgrowth of development theory. This was a time when Latin American social and "hard" scientists began to challenge the social theories developed in the West critically recognizing the economic and social reality of Latin America. The 1990s witnessed the explorations by East Asian social scientists keen to reconsider the validity of social theories based on European or North American experiences (Chakrabarty, 2000). While the classic social sciences in nineteenth century Europe had reflected European social changes, now Asian, African, and Latin American social scientists are rethinking social theories based on the social changes in East Asia, Sub-Saharan Africa, and South America. Although the research groups are not as large or as powerful in resources, they might come to challenge the strong influence of the West in the social sciences.

In 2001 in a special issue of UNESCO's International Social Science Journal, of which I was guest editor about science and its cultures, I noticed that there were many signals that science and technology were already facing new challenges, this time of a global character. While academic imperialism had waned with the end of the colonial system, as we have seen in our first story a weak although penetrating version of the academic hegemony of the West persisted in several forms after the Cold War and in what already presented itself as the era of globalization.

Theories such as comparative research (Mahoney and Rueschemeyer, 2003), the indigenization of knowledge (Sillitoe, 1998; ICSU-UNESCO, 2002), subaltern knowledge (Chakrabarty, 1993), coloniality of power (Quijano, 1997), Southern theory (Connell, 2007), cognitive and moral relativism (Lukes, 2008), multiculturalism (Inglis, 1995), and similar approaches question the validity of hegemonic science. It needs be explored, however, whether they afford paths towards a non-hegemonic scientific world and in such a case how. Whether these criticisms question the Western epistemological bases of theorizing and whether they help build non-hegemonic sciences is not at all clear. There are no sufficiently deep contributions in the theoretical dimension, especially in the construction of models by which world knowledge and globalization are conceived, as reflected by the World Social Science Report 2010 (WSSR, 2010).As soon as these views are expressed, one must admit the institutional weakness of social research outside the West. In general the social sciences in postcolonial contexts dissociated themselves from the nonformal and noninstitutional epistemological foundations of other cultured and popular wisdom. If the social sciences were ever related to those other knowledge forms, it was only to learn about them but never to learn from them (Rajagopal, 2012). In this they were part and parcel of the mistrust induced by those with power relative to other, foreign, or popular consciousness, customs, and mores that were perceived as being unscientific, "contrary to progress," always confined to the "barbarian" and uncivilized pole. Eurocentrism and orientalism are cultural and epistemic logics interconnected with capitalist imperialism and embedded in the social disciplines to make Europe the central point of a narrative for the analysis of the development of modernity, silencing its imperial experience and its violence.

Nationalism, and particularly methodological nationalism in connection to social science in postcolonial countries, was a conscious embracing of a place/territory for creating a set of orientations wherefrom to confront colonial discourses in the social sciences. Identification with a place allowed "national" intellectuals in different countries to build intellectual solidarities against the dominant colonial/postcolonial knowledge (Patel, 2012). Nationalist modernist projects were started by the new modern states using among other things higher education to create the new India, Brazil, Korea, Argentina, Egypt, Taiwan, etc. Social knowledge came to discuss and represent the social change occurring within a particular nation and territory, the nation-state, and to allow the institutionalization of a particularistic problem agenda in a new manner: an assessment of how modernity changed the institutions (kinship, family, caste, and religion) that were characteristic to a particular country. Social knowledge also participated in the social planning of the new societies. In doing this, though, the new "national" social sciences structured themselves within the frame of so-called international social sciences, increasing the latter's relevance.

However, looking back into the history of social knowledge and arguing that national social sciences are purely European copies, and therefore "erroneous," is not valid. We cannot dispense with analytic categories because of their Eurocentric and colonial genealogy, although they may on occasions afford only a partial and defective understanding. Clearly we need a multidimensional strategy to displace hegemonic science, including basic components of the institutional setup. On the other hand, in this new strategy the nation state seems to remain significant, although not as a site for creating "particularities" but for an intervention that displaces unlawful hegemonic knowledge pretensions. Reducing "society" to the national territory in nationalist sociologies from former colonial countries has created methodological and theoretical problems which render the voices and experiences of the "local weak" and "marginal" subalterns in their territory invisible and inaudible. With time disciplines in non-western contexts have also associated themselves too closely with the official discourses and methods of understanding the relationship between the nation, the nation-state, and modernity, which was carefully avoided in the first story through the mechanisms of "distancing." However, the nation-state remains the site for making politics and defining identities. Thus it is a key site of intervention.

Discussion

The three stories sketched above involve descriptions of intellectual fields and the roles of individuals and collectives as subjects and agents of change both in science and in social reality. The three reflect particular ways of establishing boundaries and manners of social intervention. By means of the three stories, I have presented some elements of an analytical framework that aims to aid comprehension of how social science is part of the differentiations and transformations of society through its theoretical expressions and practices.

We have seen that there are problems with the empirical adequacy of the academic story, problems similar to those articulated in the late 1960s and early 1970s by such sociologists of science as Barry Barnes (1971), and Steven Cotgrove and Stephen Box (1970). In this connection criticism of academic theorizing disengaged from empirical realities can be explained by a historical appreciation of the circumstances in which such a story emerged and secured credibility. In the 1960s some academic scientists, troubled by the changes accompanying the industrialization, commercialization, and politicization of science, nervously broached the idea that for the academic scientist it was dangerous to venture into the troubled waters of development, industry, or business, and that the academic context offered the best alternative of freedom, autonomy, and even social purity for some with progressive inclinations.

In our second story we have shown that a gap exists between the world seen by academic social scientists in the second half of the twentieth century when the professionalization of social research occurred in the university context and the same bit of the world observed by Development specialists with their lenses focused on economic and social dimensions. If the academic scientist tends to isolate himself by distancing himself from reality, the Development specialist tends to take technical truths for granted in packages elaborated without the significant participation of the subjects of Development. Although there is by no means a clear-cut division of labor, most of the latter are in the global South. Nonetheless, theoreticians or practitioners from northern and southern countries ultimately share the same academic culture, a common base of professional knowledge and a high formal educational level. These elements afford them a certain power and authority in the dialogue with others. Precisely many of the reactions and conflicts observed today against the dominance of mainstream social science involve scientists from the global South refusing to fulfill a role more linked to what they perceive as applied work, Development, or area studies than social science lato sensu.

The cultural and political junctures from which the academic commentary emerged had characteristics that made the story about role-conflict especially appealing to social scientists. Different from development and other applied specialists, the majority of social science researchers did not take the chance to leap from the university into other contexts; the university was their natural home. There they became entrenched and jealously guarded their intellectual disciplinary cultures and institutional bastions, sometimes against government interference with the proclaimed autonomy of academia. On other occasions, they demonstrated little interest in opening up even to collaborate with neighboring disciplines in the university context, while maintaining a feudal control of themes. Internal psychological barriers hindered a richer dialogue from transpiring in the construction of new knowledge and solutions.

The professionalization of social science research and full-time regimes took some time to become established. Once achieved, researchers were often inclined to build ideal-type differences between university life and other possible lives outside academia, which were supposed to be inferior and damaging to the work ethics of academic social science. However, the actual description of daily activities in complex institutional environments always turns out to be difficult and does not adjust to constructing essential differences between them. Thus, the fact that social science research was a clearly minor endeavor in universities did not matter. In Latin America, for example, even today 90% of higher education institutions are only engaged in teaching activities. Most social science research is performed at the postgraduate level, where some public universities play a major role (Vessuri & López, 2010), and others (the majority) prefer to divert as little energy as possible from the business of teaching, which they regard as the primary function of the university.

The third story takes us to a different setting where social sciences are deeply involved in instrumentalized rational operations by states, corporations, and NGOs. In this new setting, consultancy work represents a new model of knowledge production, supported by mixed funding, which promotes interdisciplinary research and is sensitive to market demands; furthermore, projects of radical social transformation also make use of social science knowledge. The world expansion of social sciences means an enormous increase in the number of graduate and postgraduate students in social sciences. The sheer growth in the size of the social science community implies a great variety of visions and perspectives. The same global trend is seen differently in various societies, with the implication that responses to change are adapted to context. Nevertheless, although the axiom of "context matters" is not contested in theory, it continues to be so in practice. This thus reflects some of the divides identified by the WSSR 2010. Even though the report clearly supports the mainstream view of social science, it admits the existence of inequalities and asymmetries, which in its view undermine the capacity of social sciences to contribute answers to global challenges and to analyze trends affecting human societies.

Its concluding argument puts the emphasis on the persistent disparities in research capacities in the world at large and knowledge fragmentation. With regard to the former, the internationalization of knowledge seems to have strengthened the existing big players. There are huge differences in funding for higher education and research that increase the gap. Consultancy work unduly politicizes knowledge production and lowers institutional and individual quality. The predominance of quantitative evaluation methods, particularly as concerns bibliometrics and university rankings, enlarge the divide. In addition, the brain drain and professional migration, present everywhere, have very deleterious effects on weaker countries. Other issues the report touches on concern theoretical and epistemological problems like the meaning and limits of the internationalization of social science knowledge, and whether or not it contributes to improving the quality and relevance of social science, as well as the multiplication of disciplines and their presumed lack of collaboration that might undermine their ability to respond to today's problems. But the report scarcely touches on the many attempts at exploration of the social on different epistemological and theoretical foundations.

The conditions of applying hegemonic social science to non-Western societies need to be revised, as well as the modalities of adaptation of the latter to the former. There are already attempts in the most disparate contexts, starting from indigenous objects that had been privileged through their appropriation by Western social science. By examining the modalities of choice of these objects, the logic presiding the delimitation of their boundaries and the logical and methodological forms that participate in the collection and treatment of data, we may reveal how Western social sciences have omitted dimensions that might be reinterpreted extending the explanatory power of the phenomena studied, phenomena that were distorted, taken up only partially, in a fragmented way, amputated. The resultant completed, reconstituted objects would be a way to begin to reconfigure the field of social science aiming at a better, more relevant, and truly international scope.

Conclusion

What kinds of frameworks are needed to create an international social science that may include in its analysis the conflictive and contradictory processes of domination-subordination that have organized its differential epistemes and silenced so many others in the world? It seems that we need a comparative frame beyond the universal/particular and the global/national. To assert the need of combining place (and not only that of the nation-state) with multiple voices in the process of becoming organically interconnected among themselves is vital. A current challenge is to create a language and intellectual infrastructure that may recognize this complex matrix when promoting the many voices of infra-local and supranational traditions with their own cultural works, epistemologies and theoretical frameworks, cultures of science and reflexion languages, as well as sites of production and transmission of knowledge.

Social scientists have begun to conceptualize this perspective in many ways. Some have called it global modernity, others speak of "entanglements," and still others of cosmopolitism. Some speak of diversities, for what it suggests of dispersal, of difference, of de-homogenization. Since we cannot forget the power dimension, it is obviously not the case that all the "others," the different ones, are in a same line and are equal in reciprocal terms. They remain in mutual relationships among themselves organized by the conditions of that mutuality. These conditions are structured at various levels of a space/time dynamic matrix.

The separation and autonomy characteristic of academic science that initially was a useful barrier against the threats to the curiosity-driven, free-knowledge search will be increasingly challenged by the consequences of knowledge policy for the scientific endeavor. Public debate already shows that in increasingly larger numbers scientists leave their laboratories and offices to participate in public debates about the future of science and the social consequences of scientific development. At the same time, more and more varied audiences in Western and non-Western societies alike discuss the social roles of formal science and of other forms of knowledge for their desired futures.

It is not a question of the economic experience, nor of the psychological or religious one, being cut into segments and studied in a separate manner, but of the whole human experience understood as life experience. As early as the 1960s, Eric Wolf (1964) stated that each segmented argument of man is a straitjacket for human understanding. He reminded us that the economist that uses a segmented model of Homo Economicus not only describes men as economic men; it also tells them how to be economic men. The psychologist who studies humans as a set of responses detonated by an appropriate stimulus, teaches his subjects to act as the experiment requires. These schemes have a simplicity, which makes them praiseworthy, and maybe we manage to redefine men to their image thus increasing predictability and order in human society. However, given the range of possibilities, we can more likely think of an affirmative image of the variability and complexity of human life.

It would seem that so far the variants of criticism of a world hegemonic science based on the universalization of the Western model of science have remained within the premises of this science model and are not, therefore, true criticisms, but only variants of that science model (Kuhn, 2012). In the process of creating the science of mankind, social science might change significantly. Some of those changes are already under way.

References

Barber, B. (1952) Science and the Social Order. New York: Collier Books.

Barnes, B. (1971) Making Out in Industrial Research, in Science Studies 1, pp.157–175.

Ben-David, J. (1970) Sociology of science: Introduction, in International Social Science Journal XXII, Paris: ISSC-UNESCO, pp.7–27.

Calcagno, E. (1990) Evolución y actualización de los estilos de desarrollo, in Revista de la CEPAL Nr. 42, December, Santiago de Chile, pp.55–67.

Cardoso, F. H. and E. Faletto. (1972) Dependencia y desarrollo en América Latina, Siglo XXI Editores, Mexico.

Castillo, A. (2011) Comunicación e interacciones entre las ciencias ambientales (socio-ecológicas) y distintos sectores de la sociedad, in A. Argueta-Villamar, E. Corona M. y P. Hersch (coordinadores), Saberes colectivos y diálogos de saberes en México. Cuernavaca, Morelos: UNAM (CRIM)/Universidad Iberoamericana-Puebla.

Chakrabarty, D. (1993) Marx after Marxism: History, Subalternity and Difference, in Meanjin 52 Nr.3, pp.421-434.

——(2000) Provincializing Europe. Postcolonial Thought and Historical Difference. Princeton University Press.

Chambers, R. (2007) Out of the Closet, Into the Open: Professionalism, Power, and the Personal in Development, in World Review of Science, Technology and Sustainable Development 4.4,11, Oct, pp.385-394.

Connell, R. (2007) Southern Theory: The global dynamics of knowledge in social science. Polity, Malden, MA.

Cooper, C. (1973) Science, Technology and Development: The Political Economy of Technical Advance in Underdeveloped Countries. London: F. Cass.

Cotgrove, S. and S. Box. (1970) Science, Industry and Society: Studies in the Sociology of Science. London: George Allen and Unwin, London and New York: Barnes & Noble.

Darwich, G. (2005) Pensamientos plurales. Orígenes de los Estudios del Desarrollo en Venezuela. Caracas: CENDES-UCV.

ECLA [CEPAL]. (1969) El pensamiento de la CEPAL. Collection directed by F.H. Cardoso, A. Pinto and O. Sunkel. Santiago de Chile: Editorial Universitaria.

Fals Borda, O. (1978) Por la praxis: el problema de cómo investigar la realidad para transformarla, in Simposio Mundial de Cartagena, Crítica y política en ciencias sociales, Bogotá, Punta de Lanza-Universidad de Los Andes, Vol. I, pp.209-249.

Frank, A. G. (1970) Sociología del desarrollo y subdesarrollo de la sociología, in Economía política del subdesarrollo en América Latina. Biblioteca El Pensamiento Crítico, Buenos Aires:Ediciones Signos.

Freckleton, R.P., P. Hulme, P. Giller and G. Kerby (2005) The Changing Face of Applied Ecology, in Journal of Applied Ecology Nr.42, pp.1-3.

Green, J. F. and W. B. Chambers (eds.) (2006) The Politics of Participation in Sustainable Development Governance. Tokyo: United Nations University Press.

Hagstrom, W. (1965) The Scientific Community. Carbondale: Southern Illinois University Press.

Herrera, A. (1971) Ciencia y política en América Latina. Buenos Aires: Fundación Bariloche.

Hughes, J. (2004) The History of Science, the Public, and the "Problem" of Policy, in K. Grandin, N. Wormbs, and S. Widmalm (eds.), The Science-Industry Nexus. History, Policy, Implications. Nobel Symposium 123, Science History Publications/USA, pp.365-386.

ICSU-UNESCO (2002) Science, Traditional Knowledge, and Sustainable Development. IC SU Series or Sustainable Development Nr. 4, Paris.

Inglis, C. (1995) Multiculturalism. New Policy Responses to Diversity. Policy Paper Nr. 4, Management of Social Transformations (MOST), Paris: UNESCO), pp.47.

Keim, W. (2010) The Internationalization of Social Sciences: Distortions, Dominations and Prospects, in World Social Science Report 2010. Paris: ISSC-UNESCO., pp.169–170.

Kuhn, M. (2012) Hegemonic Science: Critique Strands, Counter-Strategies and their Paradigmatic Premises, Paper presented at the International Thinkshop Theories about and Strategies against Hegemonic Social Sciences. Center for Global Studies, Tokyo: Seijo University.

Lukes, S. (2008) Moral Relativism. London: Profile Books, Ltd.

Mahoney, J. and D. Rueschemeyer(eds.) (2003) Comparative Historical Analysis in the Social Sciences. Cambridge University Press.

Merton, R. (1973 [1942]) The Normative Structure of Science, in idem, The Sociology of Science, N. W. Storer (ed.), Chicago: Chicago University Press.

Mullin, J. et al. (2000) Evaluación de los Institutos Científicos y Tecnológicos Públicos de Chile. Corfo-Ministerio de Economía de Chile y IDRC.

Patel, S. (2012) Towards Internationalism: Beyond Colonial and Nationalist Sociologies. Paper presented at the International Thinkshop Theories about and Strategies against Hegemonic Social Sciences. Center for Global Studies, Tokyo: Seijo University.

Pavitt, K. (1984) Sectoral Patterns of Technical Change: Towards a Taxonomy and a Theory, in Research Policy Volume 13, Issue 6, December 1984.

Pienkowsky, M. W. and A. R. Watkinson. (1996) The Applications of Ecology, in The Journal of Applied Ecology Nr. 33, pp.1–4.

Quijano, A. (1997) Colonialidad del poder, cultura y conocimiento en América Latina, in Anuario Mariateguiano 9, Nr. 9, pp.113–121.

Rajagopal, K. (2012) Making Social Knowledge One-step Outside Modern Science: Some Cases of Social Knowledge-making Strategies from Peripheries. Paper presented at the International Thinkshop Theories about and Strategies against Hegemonic Social Sciences. Center for Global Studies, Tokyo: Seijo University.

Rodriguez, A. (1983) Los científicos sociales latinoamericanos como nuevo grupo de intelectuales, in Revista El Trimestre Económico Vol. L (2), México: April-June, pp.939–962.

Sillitoe, P. (1998) The Development of Indigenous Knowledge: A New Applied Anthropology, in Current Anthropology 39 (2), pp.223–251.

South Commission (1990) The Challenge to the South: The Report of the South Commission, under the chairmanship of Julius Nyerere. 1990. Oxford: Oxford University Press.

STEPS. (2010) Innovation, Sustainability, Development: A New Manifesto. The STEPS Centre, Brighton: Sussex University.

Storer, N. W. (1966) The Social System of Science. Holt, New York: Rhinehart & Winston.

Vessuri, H. (2005) Prólogo, in G. Darwich, Pensamientos plurales. Orígenes de los estudios del desarrollo en Venezuela. Caracas: CENDES.

Vessuri, H. and M. S. López. (2010) Institutional Aspects of the Social Sciences in Latin America, World Social Report 2010. Paris: ISSC-UNESCO, pp.59–62.

Weber, M. (2003) El politico y el científico. Buenos Aires: Prometeo Libros.

Wolf, E.R. (1964) Anthropology. New Jersey: Prentice-Hall, Inc., Englewood Cliffs.

WSSR. (2010) World Social Science Report. Knowledge Divides. Paris: ISSC-UNESCO.

Making Social Knowledge One-Step Outside Modern Science: Some Cases of Social Knowledge-Making Strategies from Peripheries

Kumaran Rajagopal

Introduction

The hegemonic dominance of modern science and its worldview on a global scale needs no elaborating. Even in strong civilizational societies like India, which have long existed without anything even remotely akin to modern science for long stretch of time, the dominance of science and scientific worldview has been decisive ever since they came under colonial rules. This dominance is not so much the outcome of people voluntarily absorbing modern science and 'scientific temper' (as it is known here), but of the ideological alliance of science, state and global capitalism. Yet, the all-pervading reach of science into the everyday vocabulary, idioms and even the remote recesses of popular consciousness in civilizational societies is phenomenal. Thus, it is no wonder that in these societies formal social science knowledge production too assumed the value-system of modern science unquestioningly, as the post-colonial Indian state took upon itself the holy task of infusing scientific temper, not just into the intellectuals, who were always and already assumed to have gone the science way, but also into the general populace. In a backdrop like this, formal, institutional social science practitioners had no freedom to evolve validation methods and strategies for social science knowledge-making by stepping outside the value-systems of modern science. What is more, they have also been mandated by the post-colonial state to distrust popular conscience as unscientific and therefore spread scientific temper to it. Consequently, social sciences, in these contexts, had, perforce, set out to declare their dissociation from non-formal and non-institutional popular wisdom. If ever they related to them, it was only learning about them and never for learning from them.

But the triumph of science over the popular consciousness and its ways of making sense of the world has never been total, as they have somehow preserved their independence from, critical engagement with and resistance to hegemonic science in the crevices of everyday life, as well as in those public domains (still weakly monitored by science-promoting state), such as films, vernacular magazines and publications. In recent years these practices have acquired so much virulence and salience as to emerge as an organized movement and to pose a remarkable challenge to formal institutional social knowledge-making practices, around what is called Little Magazines and vernacular publications. There is a lot to learn from these groups, for all those who are concerned about producing and disseminating social knowledge outside modernity and modern science.

What is of crucial significance, here in the context of present conference, are their imaginations, value-orientations and knowledge validation forms outside modern science. Yet, their engagement with scientific worldview is not free from ambiguity. They have evolved their social knowledge-making strategies by structuring their responses to science in three different ways: (1) Spiritualizing science; (2) subverting science and (3) working outside science. This paper will be elaborating on these, particularly the third response, focusing on the following aspects that qualify themselves as evolved-outside-science; (a) what approach they adopt to reach truth and reality, (b) the way strategize their learning about social reality, and (c) their attitude toward the nature of social research.

Little Magazines of Tamil Nadu

Little magazine in Tamil Nadu has a history dating back to 1912, when Adi Dravidan (Indigenous Dravidian) magazine was started in that year. Since then more than 1600 such magazines have been published at different points in time in the last sixty years. These Little Magazines had taken different forms during their existence as handwritten magazines as printed books and recently as webzines or as blogs.

Most of these magazines have a short life span in that they are not published regularly for a long period. Since they are started with meagre fund and solely depend on the subscription money. Without any revenue from advertisement they stutter to continue. Even the ones that have a wider subscription base fail to arrive on stands on the designated time. It is because more often than not these publications are managed by individuals who have other pursuits in life for their earning. For them publication of Little Magazines is more a passion than a profession. Thus they need to squeeze out time from their regular work life and spend that on publishing these magazines. This accounts for their fits and starts manner of arrival. Their longevity too is limited because of their non-institutionalized nature. Very often these founders of these Little Magazines do not find right successors when they die or have to move temporarily or permanently to faraway places for jobs or other pursuits. Most of these magazines do not have an office or secretariat to assist their publications nor do they find willing retail booksellers. They evolve from the desks of their respective editors and straightaway go to the subscribers through post. Pandian in his survey on Social Sciences in South India has this to say about the plight of Little Magazines: "Despite such intellectual vibrancy which animates these social science journals in local languages, they are, as a rule, the result of the efforts of a handful of enthusiasts without any institutional or financial support. Given this, they survive for a few years and disappear. Even when they are alive and kicking, the regularity of publication becomes difficult." (Pandian 2002: 3617)

These local social science magazines were largely limited to a small and exclusive reader base numbering some 100 at the lowest to 3000 at the highest. These magazines are normally started by individuals who are established writers themselves or by those who have a disagreement with existing literary or intellectual trends or tendencies. Some individuals start it also to initiate new forms of writing or to make a new view point. Very often those who are initiators and founders of one magazine may soon fall out with each other on ideological or intellectual grounds and start their own individual magazines. When they are not mere literary magazines, they are avenues for intellectual expressions by which those who would not find space within the entrenched institutional settings for producing knowledge would vent their views. In whichever forms they appear they can be called as 'magazines of dissent' or 'magazines of rebellion' by alluding to Max Gluckman's concept of rituals of rebellion. In recent years inspired by postmodern tendencies these magazines call themselves as 'counterculture magazines' (Sivagurunathan 2010).

Hence pickup any one of these magazines and you can sense palpable intensity of their dissent and anger. Their dissent takes on a variety of expressions: expression in forms, styles and issues. For example since they are not (not all of them) registered with any government regulatory agencies they are uncensored and free from any control they use even tabooed or 'bad language' not admissible in a sanitized registered magazines—this is however not incidental but deliberate as they pit themselves against the entrenched high culture. In terms of forms and size they show enormous amount of dissent and innovation by designing them in unconventional forms with one such magazine Chutty (Naughty) appearing in the size of a telephone diary. We shall have occasion to elaborate on the issues or content dimension later. I would rather turn my attention on their ideological orientation in the next section.

In the Tamil context most, if not all of these magazines are secular and modern in their outlook. However in recent years this space has been invaded by fundamentalist and communal forces. Even though their engagement with modernity is ridden with tensions and contradictions, their modern orientation cannot be questioned as the magazine itself is born of the desire to communicate and debate in the public sphere. The secular among them in a truly Western sense in that they aspire to rise above primordial loyalties and their stridently critical engagement with traditions. Very often this transcendence form primordial identities take on the form of the contributors assuming pseudonyms that do not reveal much about their caste religious or ethnic identities.

Even in terms of their ideological underpinning they demonstrate diversity. Simultaneously one can see three categories: (1) **art for art sake** pure literary magazines inspired by romanticism and humanism of the West, (2) **art for people** magazines which are Marxist in orientation that thrived in the cold war era but continue to be influential even today, and (3) **postmodern** magazines triggered by the spirit of counter culture and cultural turn. These three categories are crosscut by recent emergence of Dalit magazines (Dalits are the most oppressed caste in caste-ridden Indian society) which themselves are inspired by black movement of Afro-Americans. Another trend that crosscuts the three categories is that which is inspired by Dravidian movement (an ethnic movement built around imagined notion of Dravidian race). All these three categories continue to be influential in contemporary times even though historically there may be one trend swaying over the other.

For example in the beginning art for art sake type dominated the immediate postindependent phase of India. Once the honeymoon between newly independent Indian state and its people was over after the declaration of emergency in 1975, politicization of art began arguing for art for people's awakening. They took on strong Marxist character. This Marxist orientation continued to dominate until 1990. The phase after that is dominated by postmodern turn with Marxist orientation coming under strong attack. The linguistic, cultural and relativistic turn evident in the latest crop of Little Magazines has given voice to 'little' narratives as against the 'grand' narratives such as Marxism or humanism. Thus, as of today despite the dominance of postmodern turn other trends too demonstrate vibrancy.

Art for art sake

This category of magazines is intensely literary in character. They mainly publish poems and short stories. Fictional works dominate their content with very little room for analytical writings. Very infrequently they publish literary criticisms. Their discontent is normally with prevailing forms of art work and their high culture or classical or canonical nature. They have been highly influential in introducing "new poetry" Pudhu Kavidhai which is known as verse writing in other parts of the world.

Art for people sake

Magazines belonging to this category take inspiration from Marxism of Soviet Russia as well as China. Undergirded by Marxism, Leninism and Maoism they make a strong case for rejecting both high culture and art for art sake tendencies. Majority of the content between the cover of these magazines are essays critically evaluating and dismissing high culture and their forms. It is very common to see translated articles/essays of original writings of renowned Marxists such as Lenin, Mao, Gramsci and others. It is not uncommon to find short stories and film reviews in the pages of these magazines. Strongly polemical in their spirit, these magazines are highly critical of state, parliamentary form of government, elections and government policies.

Postmodern Magazines

Strongly cultural-political rather than just political, magazines of this kind have large number of pages devoted to translation of poststructuralist writings from Western countries or essays inspired by such methodologies. They also publish large amount of poems and short stories that are avant-garde in spirit. They are also highly responsive to socio-cultural-political issues affecting the immediate Tamil society. Very sporadically they comment on global issues such as American invasion of Iraq etc.

Little Magazine as Movement

In spite of their fragmented and discontinuous nature their long history and spread has enabled Little Magazines to evolve and breed a culture of its own. They have gradually acquired a movement like character generating their own figureheads, icons, cadres and followers. It has also created its own subculture of recruiting, apprenticing and socializing neophytes. It has formulated its own rules for defining insiders/outsiders and as to who are eligible to become members. There are entrenched processes of collaborating and interacting. Finally there are established ethos for reward and punishment. All these contribute to their strong movement like character. However, it must be cautioned that it is not a unified and consensual movement. It is acutely divided and often gossipy. Quite often, one magazine or the other becomes a school of thought or a subculture-centre, recruiting and training its votaries and litany of followers. At any point time one other group is deeply engaged in slinging mud at the other. Despite all these, their contribution to social science knowledge and tradition is immense but remains unacknowledged and even undocumented. Their bitchy nature apart, their dynamism, energy and swiftness to learn and adopt new intellectual currents, their extraordinary sensitivity to local cultural traditions, and their ever present readiness to respond to issues affecting the immediate social milieu have a lot to comment on and teach institutional social science practices.

When writing about these nonformal academics Pandian observes that Tamil Nadu, just as all other southern states "are marked by the presence of a vast sector of 'non-formal' academics who are not formally linked to academic institutions, but maintain a keen interest in scholarly writings and participate in debates of an academic nature. Most often this sector is a product of different social movements wherein social scientists too as public intellectuals participate. This intersection between the formal and 'non-formal' academics has given rise to a plethora of journals in local languages which deal with an array of social science themes. The papers published in them exhibit a high degree of theoretical sophistication while engaging with local problems" (Pandian 2002: 3617).

He cites two examples of such magazines. It is worth quoting him extensively.

> Aaraichi which is published from the provincial town of Thirunelveli was a product of the mainstream left movement, though its constituency both in terms of contributors and readers is ideologically inclusive. Founded in 1969 by Nellai Arivu Kuzhu (Nellai Research Group) under the leadership of late Na Vanamamalai, a Left intellectual, over 50 issues of Aaraichi has been published so far. The papers in the journal reflect a wide range of interests: sociology, history, anthropology, folkloristics and literary criticism. Nirappirigai is another social science journal which is a product of the Dalit literary movement. Nirappirigai carries, among other things, high quality literary criticism, local history with a subaltern perspective, and translations from English social science journals. The journal's engagement with contemporary debates in social sciences would be evident from the fact that it organised a two-day conference on

subaltern studies in 1996, and the set of papers discussed in the conference were subsequently published in a volume in Tamil. (Pandian 2002: 3617)

Little Magazine as Antithesis

In their very nature and spirit Little Magazines in Tamil Nadu have always pitted themselves against any form of institutionalized culture and practices. Their essential anti-establishment character has entailed a strong skeptical and critical stance towards institutional academics, particularly that of social science practices and practioners. Often accusing them of being hand maidens of the state apparatus on the one hand and as mouthpieces of Western superpowers on the other hand Little Magazines had always reserved contempt for institutional academics. Here is an example: "Universities have not produced any notable social critics. Instead they have converted knowledge and criticisms into 5 mark or 10 marks questions, thereby fragmenting the knowledge" (Ramakrishnan 2005). Although there are significant number of college and university in the rank and file of the Little Magazine fold and many such members from institutional cloister as T. Paramasivam, A.K Perumal, A. Marx, V. Arasu, Tamilavan, Nagarjunan, M.T Muthukumarasamy and S-Shanmugam do contribute articles to Little Magazines, they have to work very hard in the reverse to earn their place in the Little Magazines. Often working in the reverse means undergoing a reverse socialization and unlearning the culture of established academics. Only those who exhibit intense internal critical dissent and disown as well as distance themselves from rewarding entrenched practices followed in formal academic institutions are allowed entry into the portals of Little Magazine movement.

Apart from the hard-earned space given to the academics, very often the magazine themselves are started by non-academics and (as discussed above) more as a passion than as a livelihood option. These magazine founders are largely drawn from middle and lower middle class backgrounds and often have careers not connected to teaching and knowledge making—either as bank employee or as staff in postal-telegraph department, or as clerks of government/private sectors or as small business owners. It is not uncommon to find some of the founders of Little Magazines owning bookshops prior to starting the magazines. Many of them take recourse starting Little Magazines as a reaction to two things: first, because they are discontent with existing practices of knowledge-production and their ideological orientation; second, because they are finding it difficult to influence wider public opinion through established and institutionalized modes of knowledge dissemination. These institutionalized avenues are dominated by institutional academicians who have uncritically reproduced the academic culture and methods of knowledge-production and dissemination of the West. The fact these avenues are open only to those who fit into the eligibility criteria set by these institutional social science practitioners, with such criteria as possession of M. Phil. or PhD, formal position as academicians or qualifications of some exams or publications in refereed national or international journals are so resentful to these non-academic intellectuals. In protest to this rigid and purely colonial legacy, they have sought out their own media of knowledge dissemination and opinion-making (Arasu 1999: 39–44).

This interesting class background combined with the resentment against eligibility criterion, has engendered a unique character and intense energy and dynamism to this Little Magazines. Their own openness to accept and publish the writings of anyone with the courage and perspective, besides fulfilling certain ideological and value-commitment requirements, has given the Little Magazines great deal of diversity and synergy as many minds and hearts come together.

In the context of this Little Magazine movement in Tamil Nadu, it is very important to define its location in the larger debate on the academic dependency. While there has been a range of responses to the academic dependency accusations by evolving nationalist social sciences (e.g., Indian Sociology or Korean Sociology), indigenous sociology (e.g., Dalit Sociology, Tribal Sociology etc) or alternative sociologies (Black Sociology, Subaltern Sociology), the social science practices of the Little Magazines are best characterized as parallel 'sociologies'. It is by choice I describe as sociologies with a small's'. These sociologies of Little Magazines, are not necessarily consistent, there is not unity of methodology and theory. Their commonness lies in their non-reactionary style. They have not evolved in response to the hegemony of power center social sciences. They are independent and sui generis, in that they are more inward looking as they communicate with their intended audience drawn from outside the academic establishments of Tamil Nadu. Their writings are meant for internal circulation and not to the perceived or imagined hegemonies. Indeed there is no attempt to translate their writings to hegemonic languages such as English.

They demonstrate their parallelness in term so their adoption of new attitudes to truth and truth-seeking; organizing and disseminating knowledge and knowledge communities; choice of research topics, and forms of constructing their writing; evolving validating strategies. While these were formulated in highly proactive sense without necessarily pitching them against dominant power-center social sciences, they hold enormous significance as those falling outside modern, Western science.

There is no scope for delineating all the parallels, we shall elaborate on few that are methodologically significant. In the following section we shall elaborate on the parallel sociologies related to attitudes and strategies of approaching social realities and truth.

Listening to truths

Listening is an act of humility. It can be humbling too. However listening in the everyday life circumstances of the poor is a weak act, a practice condemned to be followed by the poor, marginalized and the oppressed. Normally it is women in relation to men, Dalits (the most oppressed caste in India) in relation to the non-Dalits and children in relation to adults who were forced to cultivate listening as a skill. In a scaled up version, even the larger social science research agendas only reiterated listening as a weak act or act of the weak by compelling the respondents in the research exercises to fit into the designs evolved in circumstances alien to the 'respondents'[1].

The commitment of Little Magazine writers to situate the act of listening at the heart of social science research exercises arises from the compelling necessity to transform the otherwise weak act of listening into a radical act. It is precisely because of this commitment they suggest that social researchers hold listening as a cardinal value in most of the social research exercises. By taking up the weak act of listening they want to humble themselves as well as to translate that into a radical act. In their understanding:

1. Listening is a radical act, primarily for it calls for repositioning of social actors. It presupposes altering and restructuring social relations and interaction patterns, first in the domain of research and later, by extension, in the domain of wider society.

2. Listening is a radical act in research exercise for it is done not so much for confirmations of the researchers' opinion, but for

---

[1] The choice of the word itself smacks of the arrogance of behavioural psy-chology which coined the word in fact. The 'respondents' have as much freedom only to respond to the stimuli from the scientist researcher, as the rats and other hapless animals had in the researches conducted in highly controlled environments. Instead of responding, if the researched being acts on its own, it would make no sense to the researcher or it would invite punishment, in the true behavioural psychological sense.

refutation. This has to be read in the background of how social research projects have been largely used by many researchers to confirm their frameworks rather than radically challenge them. In the context of poverty research, Kannan argues, "the boring uniformity of conclusions arrived at by many social research programmes about the perceptions of poverty across the globe, despite the expansive multidimensionality, only buttresses our argument that, if they had been conducted with listening as a value they would have led to the breakdown of many paradigms on poverty rather than presenting them as manageable data. If numerous studies on poor have merely confirmed that "here is one more poor person who is starving", that would be tantamount to an ornithologist declaring that she has found 'another crow that is black'" (Kannan 2011).

Only when the paradigm is held in doubt will we be engaged in refutations research. And only when we look for falsifying cases that would challenge our time-honoured paradigms, will we start listening to even the minutest of the noises. There commences a creative humane falsifying research. It is humane because the moment the existing paradigms are kept in doubt, the certainty and arrogance arising out of holding on to them steadfastly, disappear.

3.Listening is a radical act in another count too. When 'listening to' we witness the evolution of stories narrated with the desire for coherence, arguably for the first time in the lives of many we choose to study. Yet it is not a charitable admission of the story to take shape. It is a very natural outcome of listening, even when there is no conscious intention meant for it. This is very crucial because the act of listening subsumes or ought to be subsumed by different conception of humans as storying persons. Indeed it is a different ontological reality we posit to human being in line with many narrative analysts. It is to these aspects we turn our attention now.

I Tell Stories, Therefore I Am

The telling example of how parallel the discourse of these 'sociologies' comes from the way they conceive human beings as storying animals. This change in the very ontology of humans offers a lesson for other sociologies too. In the Western social sciences perspective humans are seen essentially as thinking and rational beings capable of processing and hierarchizing information which they will proffer for the social science research as data. In scientifically inclined social sciences, both the researcher and researched are seen as psychologically normal being possessing memory, learning and mental analytical capabilities. But these Little Magazines people are presenting and institutionalizing human as essentially storying animals, who operate more at the levels of hearts rather than mind. This we will elaborate below, but for now how the Little Magazine movements aspire to privilege listening to these storying animals will detain us here.

It is the contestation of the Little Magazines that human beings live storiable lives. It is in the act of storying they find their essence.

We can say "Humans are essentially storying animals." In many of their research endeavours too they argue that, more often than not, the evolution of these stories is a joint exercise between the researcher and the person listened to. The fact that a storiable life can be grasped by the people has a radical potential to transform people into humans. The arguments of Veena Das (1990), in her excellent essay on Bhopal Gas victims, that the absence of narration in the lives of the humans signifies the breakdown or disorganization of their personal selves are very relevant here. When trauma strikes, narratability is the casualty. And the return of the story to the persons is the moment of triumph of the person over the objective history, because by recuperating a story of ourselves we personalize the historical time and space as ours own. Listening can create those triumphant moments for others whose stories were never organized before. Yet, listening should not be construed as a charitable act by which the restoration of humanness in the poor through their recovery of storiability is a gift from the researcher to the poor. In contrast, listening has to herald an authentic meeting between authentic people as R.D.Laing (1990) would propose.

The astounding fact that listening ends up constituting the humanness in the other, is very important for it can radicalize social science research methods themselves. The extraordinary or proclaimed sensitivity to people's way of world-making notwithstanding, classical social science research methods have not seen the humans as storying persons inasmuch they saw them as speaking/answering persons. Even Participatory Rural Appraisal (PRA) which claimed an alternative status for itself has not been free from seeking fractured information from people. PRA's total reliance on the people's self-chosen modes and ways of revealing information could not still help PRA methodologies to overcome their obsession with information in whatever forms they came—be it stories, diagrams, or answers to interviews. This has not enabled the people to construct an ordered narration of themselves, as they only saw themselves as information-provides under whatever democratic or enabling environment it happened. The unintended breakdown of stories that was recurrently produced by even the sincerest application of PRA methods, failed to restore the essential human quality, namely as storying persons. It could also be attributed to the failure of the PRA to transfer the foundational values guiding them to the people it studied.

Thus by foregrounding listening as a value, Little Magazine movement aspires to turn social research exercise into a joint human enterprise. In this, humans emerge as storying individuals. Stories themselves can be an extraordinarily significant source of details in retrospect, because stories of humans are invariably enmeshed in history.

Researching/Learning through Heart

It was mentioned above that the Little Magazine members view humans as essentially heart driven beings. This can be juxtaposed to the Western scientific hierarchized vision that traces heart-driven existence to savagery and mind-driven existence as maturity and growth. Following from this, social research too detests and fears expression of savagery both from the researcher and the researched. In the name of preserving 'objectivity', it has evolved many checks and balances to preclude the intrusion of savagery of the researcher and the researched. Such a suspicion driven social research conveniently forgets the fact that social research essentially has to deal with human experiences in their original forms. Such experiences are lived in tier raw and savage forms and not as highly processed and neatly organized data. When doing such research we may rely on documents and texts that have recorded human experiences, however an authentic social research is done when it deals with human experiences directly.

It is the position of Little Magazine movement advocates that once we set upon ourselves the task of studying human experiences, it is incumbent upon the social researchers to refrain from engaging in mere collection of information. Writing about what is social research, Asif writes, "When doing social research, one has to bear in mind the changed background in which there is this refreshing understanding that any social research cannot be a mere fact-gathering exercise. In the social research we set out to do, there can only be points of entry—the points at which we, as researchers make the momentous decision to responsibly relate with the people we study. There are no exit points, much as we cannot have exit points from many of the relationships we have been born with—like our relationships as children to our parents, as parents to our children etc. This is because, research is no longer conducted in the orthodox sense of researchers comfortably walled by notions of objectivity and expertise. The wall has collapsed, as it were! If social research is a relationship exercise, then researchers have to relate with the subject of the research on equal footing. In other words, our attempts to explore the experiential universe of the people we study cannot happen without the active cooperation of the people themselves. In our endeavours to reconstruct the lived-reality of the social actors, the people are primary authors, as they continue to experience the reality much before we even attempt to study them. Hence, we have to recognize co-authorship of the people we study in the research project. In this sense they are our co-researchers, just as we are their co-researchers. We should indeed cease to use the word "subjects" to refer to 'respondents', in its stead we use the word co-researchers" (2003: 12).

It can be inferred from the above why the 'subjects' of the research have to become "co-researchers."

First and foremost, in most of the orthodox quantitatively oriented scientific social research exercises, it is the intentions of the researchers that dominate the research agenda, rather than the 'intentions' of the co-researchers. Given the options, the co-researchers would have shared what makes immediate sense and what holds deep relevance to their lives, rather than merely respond to that of researcher. Pradeep in another context demands, "In our research, we have to effect a non-conflictual interplay of intentions of researchers and co-researchers. To achieve this we have to imagine the very research exercise as that which generates right and enabling human/social processes, rather than that which limits itself to asking right questions. Essentially, social research is not asking right questions but is allowing right processes to emerge."(Pradeep 2004: 3)

Many among the Little Magazine practitioners, there is a deed urge to privilege heart over mind. In much of the conventional social research projects, the researchers expect deeply-felt and authentic answers and information from the co-researchers, even while the researchers aspire to remain authentic only to their research design and its structure, rather than to the co-researchers. In other words, while the researchers want the co-researches to speak from their hearts, the researchers themselves remain cerebral as they busy remembering sequences and structured answers. In their self-proclaimed radical understanding of social research, they demand a creative and authentic union of heart-to-heart dialogues and conversations, by turning the researchers into feeling and acting persons rather than as thinking persons. It is remarkable that there is such a demand as they foreground a completely radical revision of how the social research and researcher ought to be disciplined. In the established institutional academic social science research programmes there is an enormous premium placed on training the social researchers as objective and thinking social researchers. The courseworks in these programmes already assume the researchers as 'too much feeling persons' and such feelings are sought to be banished. For these institutional intellectuals in Tamil Nadu, the subjective researcher is an anathema to the good social research. But for the Little Magazine intellectuals, social research, foundationally, cannot be subject-object interaction, but a subject-to-subject dialogue. This necessitates immersion in the experiences we wish to explore in the company of co-researchers. All the research questions, if ought to emanate from the hearts of the researchers, have to be internalized in such a manner that they haunt the heart/mind of the researcher. Internalization has to happen in the form of imaginatively living and feeling the questions along with co-researchers. This cannot happen if the living universes of the researchers and co-researchers are thought to remain separated and irreconcilable. The researcher has to give up the outsider positions with reference to the universe he/she explores, but should imaginatively immerse in the universe he/she enquires into. Thus, the mechanical reproduction and reciting of questions by the researchers would mean that they will not have the right to elicit sensitive answers from the co-researchers. The questions the researchers choose to ask have to transform themselves into haunting issues that have a life of their own, as well as a form and intensity perfectly approximate to the inquisitiveness of the reflective members among the co-researchers. Put it differently, the researchers have to carry these questions in the heart and ask them in the manner in which one of the people we study would ask the other—not so much in the manner of getting answers but also collectively searching for them. It is here research turns into an illuminating humanist exercises, leadings both the researcher and co-researcher to a position of critical-self-awareness or critical subjectivity.

Word and Utterance as Action

Little Magazine authors often base their writings on the basis of not just what they read from books and articles and but more on the basis of what they have heard from others. They do not claim any element of objectivity or authenticity to these utterances and personal conversations. Their determination to use personal utterance and conversations as sources of knowledge arises from the fact that their writings are not linked with any material benefits or career advancements, but with their mere desire to communicate (since most of those who write in the Little Magazines are not formal academics nursing secret desires to become professors, but working as blue collar workers. Even for those formal academics, these publications do not further their career interest as these are not counted as valid publications in the universities. They are only driven by their urge to communicate what they feel and think. Another important factor is something very specific centrality of 'oracy' against the centrality of literacy in modern expressive traditions. In cultures that privilege oracy over literacy, utterance is also taken as an action in its own right. In other words, saying something 'terrible' is equivalent to doing something terrible. For example, when leaving home one is not supposed to say "I go," instead they should say "I go and come back." The former is taken to be dying and never returning.

Building from this understanding, the non-institutional intellectuals of Little Magazines claim that social research cannot be conducted for the sake of mere knowledge and intellectual advancement alone. Action is so inseparable from utterances. Hence, the demand for 'activist research': Here the activist research must be differentiated from the institutionalized action research in the western academia. Activist research[2] arises from two different but connected understandings of what is action or activism. One which has been briefly commented above bases itself on utterance as action perspective. The other considers activism as the validating force of utterances of a researcher. In other words, we can summarily characterize the two as follows: utterance resulting in action, action resulting utterances. This latter is very crucial here and needs elaboration. Normally in the western context action research means research as a process that generates actions and is simultaneously built on actions in the process of research being conducted. But the action research programme itself does not diverge from the scientific and objectivity paradigm. Here action nearly assumes a

---

[2] Here I recognize the prevalence of pleas for activist research in western academia. Although the one proposed here in this paper is still slightly different from that on the one hand and such instances of activist re-search is still a marginal tendency in the western contexts on the other hand. In this connection see the work of Fals Borda, Orlando, and Mo-hammad Anisur Rahman, (1991).

clear instrumental value, in that action is not sought as an end in itself, rather as, at worst, a means to the research output as end. In the best of the circumstances, action is seen as a co-end to the research output. Action research does not claim its validation on the sole basis of actions generated by it. In the activist research, on the other hand, the researcher is not qualified to pursue his or her research if such researcher has not got his/her hands dirty in the field with action of a transformative type—not just self-transformative for the researcher, but also for the co-researchers. The ridicule and scorn reserved for a so-called pure researcher by the Little Magazine champions is intense, as they do not regard such research findings arrived at by even theoretically strong researchers as "good research," though it may be inspiring and exciting to read. The legitimacy and validity of a good research is derived from the politically active engagement of the researcher in the subject he/she is writing her research paper on. Therefore, the researcher is exhorted to make his research valuable by paying by his life and his activism, rather than by adhering to the so called objectivity parameters or scientific standards. It is not the objective science that validates research but the subjective engagement and the transformation that happens both for the researcher and the researched.

Asif elaborates, "Social research is not only about human experiences and relationship of equality it presupposes between the research and co-researchers, but also an activist research. But in reality, by resorting to terminological feat and sleight of hand, such as 'preservation of objectivity', 'rigorous quantification' and 'vast coverage', much of the research endeavours characterize themselves as pure research. In the realm of human experience, no research can claim to pure information-gathering agenda without touching the lives of people it purports to study in the same breath as the one who undertakes the research. Even the most rigorously quantitative studies aiming only to collect observable data from the human persons, tend to generate expectations, promises and disappointments from the people it studies. In several other cases such studies tend to 'spoil the field' for the subsequent researchers, thanks to the badly established relationships with the people. These may all happen, despite the studied objectivity and detachment of the researchers" (Asif 2003: 14).

He further adds, "But in social research of the kind I propose, not only the co-researchers end up undergoing changes–changes of expectations, or self-awareness, but also the researchers, who give up the impossible objectivity for the sake of critical subjectivity. Quite apart from the mutual transformation that a qualitatively oriented social research causes in the primary actors of social research, such research need also to anticipate and eventually lead to a broader social change through expression of responsibility and solidarity between the researchers and co-researchers. It is in this sense, that I visualize the social research as an activist research." (ibid.: 14)

We further see, the claim for the formation of a research community which is so inclusive in nature. The in-divisibility of researcher from the researched is reflective of the nondualist nature of the reality not easily celebrated in modern world view. They welcome a research community of core-researchers and co-researchers. This community is characterized by its consistency of involvement across the length of study operates on shared-conscience basis. If the researchers are primarily triggered by the passion to positively touch the lives of the people they study, such passion must be passed on to and generated in the co-researchers too. This produces a heightened commitment and responsibility. It also creates moral accountability to each other. It goes without saying that there is no limit of the membership in this community of researchers who can agree to share the conscience of the others who are already citizens of the community.

The community of action researchers, as previously stated, should firmly believe that research is primarily a relationship exercises characterized by generation of right process, rather than by right questions. Thus, they aspire to involve in the life-worlds of the select people's lives and the community, and its moral universes as authentic individuals. Getting right answers can only happen as an outcome of attitudinal transformation and authentic immersion. Once an authentic relationship evolves through mutual transparency, then raw fact-gathering can happen more as a voluntary disclosure or even as an expression of trust.

However, in the process of entering into the moral universe of the co-researchers and their life-worlds, and listening to them, we may end up touching their lives. We make all efforts to touch their lives positively, as we wish to ensure that they touch our lives positively. Our authentic relationship and collective sensing of reality may help all of us—researchers and co-researchers—to change, modify and alter our conception of our 'selves' and our reality. We should be cautious enough to lead such transformation to affect critical self-awareness for empowerment, and conscientisation along mutual lines, and not as a one-way process.

Conclusion

Much of the above alternative practices and strategies have not yet become mainstream trends to give us cause for celebration in anticipation of alternative social sciences or their emergence as universalizing influences having the power to recast Western theories. There is so much confusion, contradictions and mutual animosities among their voices. Their plurality of voices is both a cause for optimism and concern too. There is so much freshness in their observations but the equally intense presence of mutual lionizing and assassinations that can reduce them to one-off eruptions and fleeing angsts of an angry mob.

Above all, we need to be conscious of the fact that all these attempts are occurring in a world historical condition in which the power and resources are unequally distributed. The Little Magazine intellectuals are operating with least power and meager resources. Their aspirations and language of resistance may get muted, if the knowledge power centres master and co-opt them in far more powerful and fluent manner. But that is a question for another day (or is it not?).

References

Arasu, V. (1999) Siru Pathirikayin Arasiyal (The Politics of Little Magazies). Chennai: Kangu Publications.

Asif, M. (2003) Listening to People Living in Poverty Project: Training Manual. Actionaid India, Mimeographed.

Das, V. (ed) (1990) Mirrors of Violence. New Delhi: Oxford University Press.

Fals Borda, O. and M. A. Rahman (1991) Action and Knowledge. Breaking the Monopoly with Participatory Action Research. New York: Apex Press.

Kannan, T. (2011) Arivu kuitha oru Paarvai (Knowledge: A Perspective), Thisaigal.

Laing, R.D. (1990) The Politics of Experience. London: Penguin Books Ltd.

Pandian, M. S. S. (2002). Social Sciences in South India: A Survey. Economic and Political Weekly (August 31). pp.3617–3627.

Pradeep, K. (2004) Idhayahal Oru Aayvu Seivom (Lets do research through Heart), A note on the training programme to Homeless Researchers. Actionaid India (Chennai Office), Mimeographed.

Ramakrishnan, S. (2005) S. RamakrishnaniN Ezhuthukagam (Ramakrishnan's World of Writing), an Interview Published in Atchram (Webzine). Retrieved fromhttp://www.tamiloviam.com/atcharam/page.asp?/ID=43&fldrID=1 (Last access on 23 November 2012).

Sivagurunthan, M. (2010) Thamilil SirupathirikkaigalinKaalam Mudinthu Poivittatha?, (Has the era of Little Magazines in Tamil ended?). Retrieved from http://panmai2010.blog.com/2010/07/10 (Last access on 20 November 2012).

Alternative Theories?

A Universal but "Nonhegemonic" Approach to Human Rights in International Politics: A Cosmopolitan Exploration for China

Sang-Jin Han
Guimei Bai
Lei Tang

The Aim of This Paper

Human rights as a global regime strongly implies universalism. Human rights as a global regime, however, can also be hegemonic. In this paper we would like to explore whether it is possible to conceive of human rights in terms of universal but nonhegemonic values, and whether the Chinese discourse of human rights will be able to evolve in that direction. We are well aware of the short-sightedness and ambiguities frequently found from the official and semiofficial positions taken by the Chinese government as well as the contexts of politicization of human rights in international politics. Yet when we interpret Chinese discourse, we are not so much interested in its obvious message at the surface level as in its potential significance, which remains only implicit. This requires a particular method of reading that makes the implicit explicit by dislocating a claim from the original context of its expression and by relocating it within a broader context of human rights discourses. In this way we would like to pay sympathetic attention to the potentially significant normative orientation underlying a claim that can be further developed.[1]

The idea of human rights as being universal but nonhegemonic presupposes a distinction between universal globalism and hegemonic globalism. Both are globally oriented but with diverging foci and attitudes. The term universal globalism was first used by the late president of South Korea, Kim Dae-jung (1998), as a key concept for his political philosophy and the policy packages he developed. This concept makes sense when we see it as contrasted to "hegemonic globalism" (Han 2011). According to Habermas (2006: 184) "hegemonic liberalism" assumes that formally independent states "would operate under the protection of a peace-securing superpower and obey the imperatives of a completely liberalized global market." Habermas argues that this assumption is not only empirically misleading but also normatively ill-grounded since the decision can be impartial and justified only when it is based on discursive procedures that "are inclusive (all affected parties can participate) and compel the participants to adopt each other's perspectives (a fair assessment of all affected interests is possible)." Hegemonic liberalism is problematic because "the unilateral undertaking by appeal to the presumptively universal values of one's own political culture must remain fundamentally biased" (Habermas 2006: 185), falling short of fully understanding and respecting diversities and differences involved. In short, hegemonic globalism

---

[1] This method can be called a deconstructive-reconstructive method used for cultural analysis (Han 1999)

represents a power system maintained by military force and globalized economy rather than based on consensus free of coercion.

Hinging on this insight, this paper attempts to explore (1) whether the idea of a universal but nonhegemonic approach to human rights is conceptually meaningful, and (2) how this can be implemented in international politics. As to the former, our position is that this approach is meaningful and can be better articulated by the concept of cosmopolitanism. This means that we can talk of a cosmopolitan approach to human rights. As to the second, our position is that cosmopolitan approach is characterized by the emphasis on the universality of human rights as well as the sensitivity to differences and diversities. A cosmopolitan approach can hardly go well along with an attempt to politicize human rights. One of the key issues in this regard is whether or not, and, if so, under which assumptions, the use of force (violence) can be justified in the name of human rights (Han 2011).

Cosmopolitan Imagination of Differences and Diversities

To begin with, the universal orientation in the discourse of human rights is clear enough (Falk 2009; Milne 1986). It means that human rights are the rights that all human beings are entitled to simply as a human being, regardless of religions, gender, ethnicities, nations, races, and social origins. Not only the rights holder but also the list and the content of human rights are universal. That is to say, all human beings should be equal in claiming for the list of rights, including civil, political, economic, social, and cultural rights. Furthermore, the provision of a specific right should be universally applied to everybody, as it is provided by the Universal Declaration of Human Rights. In short, human rights are natural rights and all human beings are equal (Bai 1997).

In contrast to this, the term hegemonic contains many different connotations. In ancient Greek, for instance, it meant that a big city state had the power to control small ones. In contemporary international relations, it refers to the phenomenon in which superpowers do not respect the state sovereignty of powerless countries and intervene into their internal affairs, or even attempt to control and rule these countries. Such intervention in the name of protecting human rights by force has often turned out to be problematic. No one can be sure if there is any single case of humanitarian intervention carried out for a purely humanitarian purpose. National interests of the powerful or hegemonic countries have always been behind the scene.

It is in this context that the cosmopolitan approach to human rights has attracted much attention (Beck 2006; Delanty 2009; Held 2010). The meanings of cosmopolitanism are diverse. We believe that the cosmopolitan approach to human rights has something to do with the question of how to live together with the so-called "radical others" whose actions and value presuppositions are very difficult to understand. We come up here with some questions. Simply put, what do we mean by differences and diversities? To what extent and how can we live together peacefully with radicalized others (Barash and Webel 2008; Nash 2005; Nazzari et al.

2005)? To what extent can we justify the sanctions applied to those who have failed to comply with the so-called universal values?

International politics tends to emphasize diversity on the surface, but in reality, impose the "universal" values originated from the West as principles behind the global integration. International politics is then fundamentally hegemonic in this sense. What is the status of human rights in this context? Is it natural for human rights to become embedded in this hegemonic international politics? Is it possible for human rights to get distanced from this system of global hegemony? How can we enhance diversities and differences within a universal framework of human rights? It is not easy to answer to these questions. But these questions should be asked when we explore the possibility of a universal but nonhegemonic approach to human rights.

Asian Value Debate and China

The debate about Asian values evolved under the premise that human rights have originated in the West and can hardly be guaranteed in Asia where the tradition of individualism is weak (Lee 1994). Our intention is not to examine this debate in detail (Kim 1994; Han 2011). Rather we want to move quickly to argue that it is wrong to identify the Chinese discourses of human rights as advocating a relativist view of human rights endorsed by Lee Kuan Yew, former prime minister of Singapore who initiated the Asian values debate. To be sure, there have been Chinese leaders and intellectuals who have argued in a similar way. But a forward-looking perspective can be obtained only when we go beyond this and pay attention to the Chinese efforts to embrace the universal value of human rights while keeping their own identity as Chinese or East Asians.

The Chinese discourses on human rights are complex (Angle 2002; De Bary and Tu 1998; Donnelly 1999). Human rights activists, such as Liu Xiaobo (2011), Nobel Peace Prize laureate in 2010, have demanded constitutional reform, liberal democracy, and protection of human rights in China from a Western perspective of the concept of human rights. They take the Western standard as universally valid. In contrast, the official position of the party-state of China attempts to defend its policy against the Western critiques (Information Office 2011; Human Rights in China n.d.), and many attempts have been made to reinterpret Confucian traditions as a new source of imagination for human rights (Chan 1999; De Bary 1998; Han 2010; Xu 2006).

The official discourse claims that the communist revolution has made possible real progress in human rights in China, particularly with respect to the economic and social rights, including the right to development and the right to subsistence (food, shelter, clothing, healthcare, education, and job) in a country with such a huge population that it composes 22 percentage of world population. The official discourse maintains a priority of state sovereignty over individual freedom. This owes something to the Chinese experience of modernization (Chen 2005; Dong 2012; Yan 1997; Zhang D.

1998) characterized by "striving inward for human rights and outward for state sovereignty"[2].

Deeply shocked by the result of the Opium War of 1840, modern Chinese intellectuals believed that strong nation-state is the basis for protecting individual human rights, and that the primary goal of modernization should therefore be nation-state building. The official discourse also claims that significant progress has been gradually made even with respect to citizens' civil rights and political participation, and that, due to domestic conditions such as the high rate of illiteracy, it will take time for China to move forward to a full political democracy in the Western sense.

There can be no doubt that China lags far behind the West in this respect, as evidenced by the existence of a systematic control over basic rights of citizens such as freedom of body, expression, assembly, press, religion, and so on. The future of Chinese politics is a matter of debate and speculation. In China, however, no one can convincingly justify the current state of affairs characterized by the lack of citizens' basic rights in terms of Asian values and other cultural equivalents. Universal values seem to have been tacitly assumed albeit with many confusions and ambiguities. China has often reacted against U.S. fingerpointing by insisting that human rights in the United States are inadequate as evidenced by racial discrimination, poverty, and violence. This mutual criticism does not mitigate the importance of universal values.

---

[2] Neizheng renquan, waizheng guoquan.

It should be noted that there has been a strong tendency in China to view human rights as socially and historically constructed rather than as given innately. Grounding human rights on natural rights may not be as convincing to Chinese as to the Westerners. Since we are living in the postmetaphysical age, nothing can be taken for granted in a transcendental manner. This means that the idea of the social construction of values in history has good point. However, this view is problematic in that it can reject the idea of universal values. On the contrary, it is still an open question as to whether or not the processes of social construction of human rights in different historical contexts may give rise to a common framework of universal values, albeit with different background assumptions. Social construction of human rights does not necessarily lead to relativism but, instead, offers a new insight into the possibility of an overlapping consensus.

Of particular significance in this regard is the Confucian approach to human rights which provides many possibilities for exploration. Confucianism can be interpreted as defending the idea of universal values, as professor of philosophy Tang Yijie at Beijing University has shown. The well-known historian William De Bary and his associates[3] have demonstrated that Confucian traditions, if read from a liberal perspective, can be linked to enriching human rights. In the West, the idea of natural laws was invented to justify human dignity and human rights in the fundamental sense. In

---

3 Articles included in De Bary and Tu (1998) deal with different aspects of Confucianism in its close relationship with human rights.

China Confucianism has worked out a distinctive worldview with universal values regulating the basic relationships among heaven, earth, and humanity.

> The system of human rights recognized by the West underscores individual life, private property and individual liberty (especially political freedoms). The first value in the rights system based on the individual is liberty, with equality coming to the second. Liberty and equality not only prevail over justice, but even alter what justice means in the first place. Modern theory often interprets justice in terms of liberty and equality, squeezing out the original meaning of justice and reducing it to a mere form of combination of liberty and equality. Thus justice ends up left out, giving rise to many self-destructive evils. Rights mean the space of sovereignty for the individual's free will. Where are the boundaries of this space? That is the question. Once justice is not regarded as the supreme criterion for judgment, no standards are available to determine these boundaries, and among different subjects there always remains room for dispute, as happens at all times in the international arena. (Zhao 2007: 19)

Zhao (2007: 25) draws attention to the "self-destructive logic of rights against rights." Far from being accidental, this requires a fundamental solution since this tendency makes the Western conception all the less mature as a universally valid theory of rights. "Due to the hegemony of Western discourse, the concept of human rights shaped by biased Western values now serves as the only framework in vogue for interpreting what human rights are all about." This is a serious intellectual problem for him since "even objections to Western criticisms concerning human rights have to be presented in the form of justificatory attempts within a Western-defined framework" (Zhao 2007: 14).

Zhao has made an ambitious attempt to counteract against this tendency. His suggestion is to ground human rights on the ontological condition of human life, that is, social relationship, and a concept of justice that can provide space for balancing or limiting individual-centered rights (Zhao 2007: 15). He argues that "what we call human rights is the space of liberty allowed by a relationship of justice, rather than the space of liberty claimed by the individual" (Zhao 2007: 20). Deeply concerned about the increasing collision of rights claims by legal subjects, destroying the moral fabric of the community, he is eager to find "a non-Western theory of universal human rights" by suggesting what he calls "credit human rights."

The sympathetic reading that we want to present is meaningful since it sensitizes our attention to the painful attempts by Chinese scholars (Huang 2009; Li et al. 2008; Wang and Zheng 2008; Xia 2004) to break away from their typical preoccupation with Chinese characteristics and explore the possible Chinese contribution to enriching human rights as universal values.[4]

---

[4] An example is the public lecture by Professor Tang Yijie on the topic of "Confucianism and Universal Value" on March 31, 2011, which attracted a wide attention from students of Beijing University. In addition, in a forum on Chinese human rights held at Seoul National University in May 2011, Professor Bai Guimei (2011), deputy director of Human Rights Center at Beijing University, explained how the institute had survived to manage human rights education

Because these discourses are new, still emerging, and challenge many assumptions hitherto taken for granted, care should be taken to catch the hidden assumption underlying these discourses.[5]

In this context, we want to argue that all these attempts can be interpreted as painful searches for the missing social ground of human rights community. From the point of view of intercultural dialogue, we can understand why Chinese scholars are reluctant to accept the Western focus of human rights on individual empowerment and why they want to pursue a new framework in which their cultural identity can be better expressed (Angle 2002). But they still seem to be far from comprehending the missing assumption, that is, the concept of a human rights community, as a potential key to their painful search.

Tianxiaism Reconsidered

It is now time to move one step further to examine the notion of "Tianxia"[6] or "Tianxiaism"[7] sympathetically as we have done so

---

    program at Beijing University despite unfavorable conditions for academic discourse for universal human rights.

[5] Chinese discourses can be made intelligible when properly placed in the context of this hidden assumption. This assumption can be grasped only when one gets out of the conventional framework of interpretation and adopts what we call a symptomatic reading.

far. Becoming salient among the Chinese scholars in the fields of humanities and social sciences, particularly international relations, this concept may help us understand the Chinese imagination about the possibility of a universal but nonhegemonic approach to human rights and its implementation in international politics. In a paper entitled "Globalization and Chinese Cultures," Li Shenzhi,[8] pointed out that ancient China developed the ideal picture of global order with the concept of "the world is for all"[9] and "all are brothers within the Four Seas."[10]

The key to this worldview, Li argued, lies in the concept of Tianxia, which is something to which China should return to become better able to address to global affairs after the age of nationalism. He conveyed a strong belief that Chinese traditional values such as

---

[6] Tianxia literally means all under Heaven (Tian), and refers to "nation," "China," and "all over the world" in different contexts. To know more about the notion of "Tiianxia" in Chinese tradition, see Li Mining (2011).

[7] Tianxia Zhuyi.

[8] Li Shenzhi (1923–2003) closely observed the responses of South Korea and Japan to globalization and became sensitive much earlier than other Chinese intellectuals. He argued before that Chinese nationalism of the late nineteenth century was the result of the invasion of western powers, the substance of which was national emancipation rather than national expansion. While he wrote the paper about Tianxiaism in 1994, he began to move in the direction of liberalism.

[9] Tianxia weigong.

[10] Sihai zhinei jiexiongdi.

"harmony between man and nature"[11] could contribute much to reevaluating the moral orders of the whole world (Li 1994).

In the new age of "a postnational constellation" (Habermas 2007), it may no longer be as suitable as in the past to understand global affairs as "international" relations and human rights as embodied in a framework of "nation-states world." The tension between human rights and national sovereignty remains unchanged even for the UN Security Council and other international organizations claiming responsibility to protect human rights (McClean 2011). Under such a background, there has arisen a new need for theoretical reflection to step out of the predicament before achieving the practical goal of achieving global governance.

It was within this context that some Chinese scholars began to put forward Tianxiaism as a new focus of academic discussion from the mid-1990s. Various intellectual expressions such as cultural conservatism, nationalism, and New leftism sprang out of the post-Tiananmen environment. One concern for them was to think about Chinese cultural values for China's future from a forward-looking perspective, as they had experienced the big change of world order and domestic political environment. They were looking for a creative response to new challenges inside and outside of China by reexcavating Chinese traditions (Xu 2006). In particular, with the concept of Tianxia, they were eager to reactivate the moral dimension of international politics while expressing an ambition to construct an alternative theoretical framework of

---

[11] Tian ren he yi.

world politics and relations. Consequently, Tianxiaism has begun to manifest itself in varieties of forms of discourses, out of different strategies and goals of interpretation.

For instance, Sheng Hong, an economist with sympathy to liberalism, suggested there are two ways of realizing Tianxiaist civilization in the world: a European way and Chinese way. The former just extends national boundaries into the world, while the latter can go beyond it (Sheng 1996) to open up the new principles of global order out of Confucian traditions (Sheng 2012). Li and Sheng were well aware of the crisis of Western civilization, such as the inevitable conflicts emerging from the expansion of nationalist drive (Sheng 1996), the "clashes of civilization" from market globalization, and the disorder of morality (Li 1994). Therefore they suggested Tianxiaism as a possible source of new ways of thinking about transcending Western hegemony.

Zhao Tingyang's Theory of the Tianxia System

Perhaps, the most influential figure in China in this regard is Zhao Tingyang,[12] a philosopher at the Chinese Academy of Social Science, who published The Tianxia System: *A Philosophy for the World* Institution (2005). He has built his "Tianxia system" on two

---

[12] Zhao Tingyang(1961–) is a professor of philoshophy at CASS(Chinese Academy of Social Science), who got his Ph.d from the graduate school of CASS, under the supervision of Li Zehou(1930–), one of the most Influ-ential philosophers in contemporary China.

theoretical reflections. First, he refers to the need for a theoretical concept for "world politics" that is more than "international politics." Nevertheless "the interpretations of world politics remain in the framework of internationality and thus the viewpoint of world-ness is still missing" (Zhao 2009). Hence, he has attempted to explore how "thinking from the perspective of the world" can be made possible today (Zhao 2005: 4). He believes that a nonhegemonic world order can be constructed only when the new worldview is properly formulated. Second, for shaping a new worldview, "rethinking about China" is necessary not only because China should become a responsible country in the world, but also because China should recover its own thinking ability (on the level of the world), which goes beyond just transplanting Western ideas and theories (Zhao 2005: 4–11).

Based on this, Zhao (2009) points out that "our supposed world is still a non-world, it has not yet become a world of oneness, but remains the chaos of a Hobbesian situation." He contrasts this by saying that "Chinese political philosophy defines a political order primarily from the perspective of the world, whereas the nation/state is primary in western philosophy" (Zhao 2009). He argues that the outlook of Tianxiaism should be made explicit and elaborated in order to raise cosmopolitan questions better. Specifically, Zhao argues that because of the lack of a theoretical basis of a world institution that is more encompassing than the "nation-state," the concept of apparent cosmopolitan human rights is interpreted and implemented by each country.[13]

Likewise, the principles of justice, democracy, equality are all in effect just within the nation-state, not universally grounded all over the world (Zhao 2005: 94–95).

Zhao speaks highly of the Chinese Confucian tradition of political philosophy emphasizing homogeneous construction of the family, state, and Tianxia, which guarantees the consistency and transitivity of effective governance at different levels of political units. To create an "effective world," a top-down transitivity of political governance should be forged first; the highest level is just the world or Tianxia, so the world institution should replace the nation-state institutions (Zhao 2005: 142–43; Zhao 2008). Furthermore, Zhao attempts to explain the "pure type" of the world institution whose legitimacy comes not from any ideology, but from the common will and universal humanity. In this regard, the Tianxia theory is a full-fledged theory clarifying the conditions of not only the efficiency of political governance but also its moral efficiency (Zhao 2005: 145–46).

Zhao's discussion of Tianxia system or Tianxia theory has evoked strong responses from historians as well as experts of international relations. Some of them have followed Zhao's approach to Tianxiaism to build a new and nonhegemonic world order (Li

---

[13] For example, about democracy, Zhao argues that it cannot necessarily and efficiently carry the voice of common feelings of people (minxin) according to Chinese context (Zhao 2005: 153).

2011; Jiang 2007). They admitted that Zhao's provocative arguments had suggested a new way of thinking about the world order by tracing back to pre-Qin thoughts, which had become popular in China. On the other hand, Zhao's argument has incurred a lot of criticism, within and out of China (Zhang S. 2006; Xu 2006; Zhou 2008; Wang 2010; Callahan 2008, 2012).For his critics, Zhao's normative approach to world institution involves double standards, remains poorly grounded and too utopian. The most severe criticism is as follows,

> Tianxiaism in essence plays the role as a "shadow" of the domestic absolutism and autocracy on foreign affairs, which totally neglects either ordinary citizen's basic human rights or the benefits of civilians in neighboring countries, only enhancing the privilege and the pride of the ruling class. . . . It is unwise to make Tianxiaism as the rising China's new vision of the world order or the substitute of the current mainstream international system based on national sovereignty. (Wang 2010)

From the point of view of Western scholars, Zhao's theoretical discourse on Tianxia system seems to be a kind of "Sino-speak," which "overwhelms nuanced notions of identity and politics to establish the new discursive world order of new orientalism" (Callahan 2012), and "the success of the Tianxia system shows that there is a thirst in China for 'Chinese solutions' to world problems, and a hunger for nationalist solutions to global issues, especially when they promote a patriotic form of cosmopolitanism" (Callahan 2008).

These fierce critics seem to miss the reasonable factors within Zhao's arguments. For example, Zhao (2005: 61) has argued that the concept of Tianxia does not represent a cultural barrier blocking openness to alien culture. On the contrary, it helps China absorb other cultures. Furthermore, given the problems of hegemonic globalism today, Zhao's deliberative approach to human rights as universal value and the Tianxia system as a cosmopolitan order demonstrates a painful attempt of Chinese scholars to seek for the philosophical ground for a new international order fully respecting human dignity as well as differences and diversities involved in international politics (Zheng 2009, 2010).

Chinese Nonhegemonic Approach to Human Rights

The above discussions are primarily concerned about the normative implication of Tianxiaism for international politics but not about the political reality of China. Therefore, we would like to turn attention now to the interaction between the Chinese government and Western countries concerning how to implement human rights policies in international relations. The typical response of the Chinese government has been either defensive or passive: defensive in the sense that it attempts to defend the Chinese position against the external critique; passive in the sense that it raises questions when the Western superpower intervenes into other countries in the name of human rights protection. In either case, the Chinese government has been in no position to make use of human rights for its own advantages. Apart from this, widespread worries have emerged about China and whether it is becoming another hegemonic power as it has grown in economic and military strength. Insofar as human rights policies are concerned, however, there seems to be no reason to see China from that perspective.

In fact, China has accepted global conventions of human rights such as the Universal Declaration of Human Rights, while heavily defending the right of each nation and country as an equal member of global community. China has also become a state party to about twenty-five human rights conventions, including seven out of the nine core UN human rights conventions.[14]

Furthermore, China signed the International Covenant of Civil and Political Rights in 1998, which means that China has accepted the text of the convention and is obliged to refrain from acts which would defeat the object and purpose of the convention.[15] When China signed or ratified those human rights conventions almost no reservations were made.[16]

This amounts to China's almost total acceptance of the universal human rights standards. The Chinese government has published

---

[14] See "The List of Human Rights Conventions Ratified by PRC," in Bai-Guimei (ed.), Human Rights Law, Beijing University Press, 1997, pp. 318–319.

[15] China is now preparing for ratification of the ICCPR. Reservations might be made on ratification.

[16] Except the dispute settlement clauses, in which arbitration or ICJ set-tlement are provided. Article 8 of the International Covenant of Economic, Social, and Cultural Rights was one of the very few articles over which China made reservations when the government ratified it.

American Human Rights Records against the United States annual "Country Reports on Human Rights" for twelve years. Comments and criticisms in these Chinese reports are ironically based on universal human rights standards.

However, when the alleged goal of human rights protection is enforced coercively by powerful foreign countries, China has expressed concerns or questions because it believes that each country has its own problems. Such differences and diversities cannot be resolved everywhere in the same way. Precisely at this level of implementation, China has been keeping distance from the tendency to use human rights as a political weapon. The China's official position has been that hegemonic power is the contemporary source of war. Assuming that Third World countries used to be exploited and oppressed by the imperialist countries, Deng Xiaoping, for instance, pointed out that "the origin of world upheaval is the hegemonic contention" and that "war is related to hegemonic world order"[17], this antihegemonic policy has been carried out by the Chinese political leaders so far.[18]

The reasons for this position are complex and rooted in history, culture, and politics. Historically, Chinese people suffered much from poverty and exploitation with a long history of semicolonization. Culturally, Confucian tradition has advocated that "harmony

---

[17] China Daily, 18 May 1981.

[18] Zhou Huijie, "The Continuation of the Chinese policy on Antihegemonism and Its Development" Journal of Qiqiha'er University 2 (2004).

is precious." Politically, China has been subject to many instances of external intervention.

The Chinese advocacy of a nonhegemonic approach to human rights can be exemplified by many examples, for instance, the recent crisis of Syria in which China opposed armed external intervention aiming at regime change. The use of force or threat by external powers for their own political advantages will not be helpful to the proper settlement of the issue. "China opposes external intervention under the pretext of humanitarianism"[19].

The key issue here is not the relationship between national sovereignty and human rights. We have no intention to say that sovereignty should prevail over individual rights. We only want to underscore the fact that the Chinese government has refused to follow the hegemonic approach to human rights.

Why does China keep a nonhegemonic approach to human rights? First of all, due to the particularity of international human rights law, the potential force of reciprocity among states does not work as well as it does in other fields of international law. When there are violations of human rights, international monitoring mechanism may work well. However, human rights implementation depends largely, if not totally, on domestic measures within

---

[19] The Chinese Statement by Ambassador Li Baodong at the Security Council Ministerial Meeting on the Middle East, From Chinese Mission to the United Nations, March 12, 2012. See the website of Ministry of Foreign Affairs of the People's Republic of China, http://www.fmprc.gov.cn/eng/wjb/zwjg/zwbd/t913341.htm visited on 2012-5-3.

the jurisdiction of each state. Due to the lack of juridical institutions in the world community to monitor and enforce international human rights law, powerful states take this advantage to act as the world police. They often politicize human rights by applying double standards in international politics. The extreme case of hegemonic approach is the use of military force against the target states where humanitarian crisis takes place. The lesser form is nonmilitary measures, such as blockade or economic sanction.

A universal but nonhegemonic approach to human rights can be well documented by the sunshine policy of the late former president of South Korea Kim Dae-jung toward North Korea (Han 2011). Advocating the cosmopolitan principle of reciprocal communication, he argued that the actions of the North Korean leaders should be understood not from the fixed assumptions of South Korea or the United States but from the points of view of North Korea, and that insofar as they continue to express intention to communicate, the first thing to do is to invite them to the table of dialogue rather than relying on the use of force and sanctions. Though he suffered from numerous accusations and misrecognitions, Kim was consistent in maintaining his cosmopolitan standpoint against hegemonic globalism while embracing differences and diversities within his policy framework of reconciliation and cooperation.

Kim firmly believed that the very conception of human dignity is rooted in every world religions. The conditions of human rights can then improve well when this cultural norm gives rise to social consciousness and action in support of human rights. This is why

Kim was cautious with the attempt to utilize human rights as a political means of external intervention. He believed that external involvement alone can hardly improve human rights records internally. The best option of human rights policies is to take wise steps designed to help nurture the domestic conditions for human rights movement and consciousness.

Contrasted to this, the hegemonic approach is aimed at implementing human rights to the target states from outside. More often than not, however, external threat makes the situation worse. As a result, confrontation takes place between the hegemonic superpower and the targeted states. Therefore, it is of crucial significance to put emphasis on the nonuse of force in human rights promotion and protection. The nonhegemonic approach rejects military means. Recently, responsibility to protect (RtoP) has been a hot topic resounding through the halls of the United Nations General Assembly (UNGA). But only the third pillar, that is the world community's responsibility to protect, is mostly emphasized. During the debate among the UN members many Third World countries expressed their serious concern that the concept of RtoP is very likely to be abused by the hegemonic countries to intervene with military means into small and weak countries. RtoP may be better supported when it is implemented by the UN Human Rights Council than the Security Council. In case that force has to be used as the last resort, it should be used strictly for humanitarian purposes rather than regime change (Sevastik 2011, 201).

Actually some progress has been made in that direction. The depoliticization of the charter-based bodies, particularly the replacement of the Human Rights Commission by the new Human Rights Council,[20] showed some hope for the UN. At the same time, the treaty bodies have made efforts at turning the reporting process required of the various states into a constructive dialogue instead of confrontation between the committees and the member states. Likewise, human rights implementation has turned out to be a long-term social engineering process. Building and keeping a rule of law community is important not only for a sovereign state but also for the international society. The nonhegemonic approach to human rights requires effective preventive measures in various human rights institutions at both the global and regional levels, including UN human rights organizations, international treaty bodies, and NGOs.

Cosmopolitan Exploration for China

This paper has suggested that China has defended a universal but nonhegemonic approach to human rights in international politics. Please note that this is limited to the issue of human rights only, nothing more than that. How China will develop its own vision for global order is an open question to be answered by the Chinese people. Yet we would like to draw out cosmopolitan implications from the Chinese tradition of Tianxiaism.

---

[20] See the resolution adopted by the UNGA, Res/60/251.

As Ge Zhaoguang (2011: 187) pointed out, "As a cultural resource, Tianxiaism with a deep historical origin may either be interpreted into cosmopolitanism that opens to universal gospels and values . . . or follows the tradition of exclusive nationalist mentality and develops into an ambition of reigning Tianxia through economic and military modernization." What attracts our attention is the first evolutionary trajectory of Tianxiaism. Wang Gungwu at the National University of Singapore offers a more benign thought for shaping a new vision of Tianxia. Although the Western empires and the Chinese Tianxia systems had broken down and been replaced by nation states, the experience of globalization, especially the experience of transnational organizations at different levels of world politics, suggests that we can develop fresh ideas about a new global order.

> TianxiaYitong, as the Chinese equivalent of empire, embodied the idea of universalism and a superior moral authority that guided behavior in a civilized world. In the secular world, it may refer to the authority, somewhat akin to "soft power" that might be employed to check or moderate political and military dominance; in religions, it highlights the underlying moral values behind acts of faith. (Wang 2006)

In other words, the ideal of Tianxia can find its expression in moral universalism as we do from the mainstream Western civilization. This ideal can then serve as the basis of soft power or moral power:

The benign image of empire would need a soft power that would spread universal values like freedom, human rights and democracy to benefit all humankind. If these ideals distilled out of Western experiences could be projected peacefully, they would remind Chinese elites of their ancient faith in the concept of tianxia. Though the tianxia ideal had been less activist and missionary, it nevertheless conveyed a similar wish to represent the highest universal values everywhere. If that wish is revived, the new Chinese elites may recognize that, beyond the nation-state, there are new, fresh and vibrant values of universal validity that could be accepted and used to support, restore and even enhance those that their ancestors had espoused (Wang 2006)[21].

The quest for a new global order by the Chinese scholars in line with the Chinese tradition of Tianxiaism may be characterized by an attempt to combine universal values and East Asian identity. It means neither a complete "wholesale Westernization"2222 Quanpan xihua, It refers to the trajectory of Western modern civilization and its supporting values such as freedom, equality, reason, and so on which indicate the exact direction of development that China should follow. nor coming back to traditionalism. Li Shenzhi (1994), for instance, argued that in order to establish a new world order China should be engaged in a double-edged inquiry of taking universal values of globalization as "substance (Ti)," on the one hand, and its own experience as "practical use" (Yong), on the other. Xu Jilin makes this point clear by suggesting that "for China,

---

[21] To know more about Gungwu Wang's thoughts about new Tianxiaism, see Zheng (2009, 2010) and Evans (2010).

nation-state building means forging a real modern nation-state by making use of all civilizations of human being. This is a form of nationalism of a higher order, which I prefer to call new Tianxiaism. Cosmopolitanism may be seen as anti-nationalist, but is, in fact, the most capacious nationalism in essence" (Xu 2012).

The cosmopolitan imagination in China can be traced back into two streams. One is to follow the track of "wholehearted cosmopolitanism" suggested by Hu Shih (1935), which takes the Western development as the model to duplicate. Another is to follow the ideal of Tianxiaism, which does not stop with modernization of China but goes beyond it to realize a world of Tianxia style. As Fairbank noted, the concept of Tianxia "is not only an idea, but a sentiment, a feeling habituated by millennia of conduct. It attaches the highest importance to Chinese civilization, which consists of all those people who live in a Chinese way" (Fairbank 1983: 461; Evans 2010). In this sense, the Chinese way of maintaining national and cosmopolitan identity in terms of culture may be "stronger than a mere Western-style nationalism." But this question is still open to further reasoning and elaboration (Zhao 2006). One of the key issues to be addressed in this regard is how to reconcile unity and differences, or how to embrace differences and diversities as much as possible within the goal of constructing a great harmonious world.

References

Angle, S. C. (2002) Human Rights and Chinese Thought. Cambridge: Cambridge University Press.

Bai G. et al. (1997) Human Rights in International Law. Beijing: Beijing University Press.

Barash, D. P. and Webel, C. P. (2008) Peace and Conflict Studies. Los Angeles, CA: Sage Publications.

Beck, U. (2006) The Cosmopolitan Outlook. Cambridge: Polity Press.

Callahan, W. A. (2008) Chinese Visions of World Order: Post-hegemonic or a New Hegemony?, in International Studies Review 10: 749–761.

——(2012) Sino-speak: Chinese Exceptionalism and the Politics of History, in Journal of Asian Studies 71, no. 1: 33–55.

Chan, J. (1999) A Confucian Perspective on Human Rights for Contemporary China, in Joanne Bauer and Daniel Bell (eds.), The East Asian Challenge for Human Rights. Cambridge: Cambridge University Press, 212–237.

Chen, Y. (2005) Kunjing zhongde zhongguo xiandai yishi [Modern Chinese Consciousness in Puzzledom]. Huadongshifan daxue chubanshe [East China Normal University Press].

De Bary, W. T. (1998) Asian Values and Human Rights: A Confucian Communitarian Perspective. Cambridge, MA: Harvard University Press.

De Bary, W. T. and Tu W. (eds.) (1998) Confucianism and Human Rights. New York: Columbia University.

Delanty, G. (2009) The Cosmopolitan Imagination: The Renewal of Critical Social Theory. Cambridge: Cambridge University Press.

Dong, Z. (2012) Jindai zhongguo renquan guannian de shanbian [Evolution of the Idea of Human Rights since Modern China], in Shixue Lilun Yanjiu [Historiography Quarterly] 2: 120–122.

Donnelly, J. (1999) Human Rights and Asian Values: A Defense of "Western" Universalism, in J. Bauer and D. Bell (eds.), The East Asian Challenge for Human Rights. Cambridge: Cambridge University Press, 60–87.

Evans, P. (2010) Historians and Chinese World Order: Fairbank, Wang, and the Matter of Indeterminate Relevance, in Zheng Yongnian (ed.), China and International Relations: The Chinese View and the Contribution of Wang Gungwu. London: Routledge, 42–57.

Falk, R. (2009) Achieving Human Rights, NY and London: Routledge, Taylor & Francis.

Fairbank, J. K. (1983) The United States and China. 4th ed. Cambridge MA: Harvard University Press.

Ge, Z. (2011) Zhaizi Zhongguo: chongjian youguan "Zhongguo" de lishi lunshu [Here in China I Dwell: Reconstructing the Historical Narratives of "China"], Beijing: Zhonghua Shuju [China Book Store].

Habermas, J. (2006) The Divided West. Cambridge: Polity Press.

——— (2007) Dispute on the Past and Future of International Law Transition from a National to a Postnational Constellation, in Ioanna Kuçuradi (ed.), Philosophy Facing World Problem. Proceedings of the Twenty-First World Congress of Philosophy, vol. 13, 31–39.

Han, S-J. (1999) Confucianism and Postcolonialism, in the East Asian Context of Development, in Review of Korean Studies 2, no. 1: 23–44.

―― (2010) Confucianism and Human Rights, in Wunsuk Chang and Leah Kalmanson (eds.), Confucianism in Context: Classic Philosophy and Contemporary Issues: East Asia and Beyond. Albany, NY: State University of New York Press, 121–144.

―― (2011) From the Asian Value Debate to Cosmopolitanism: An Active Interpretation of the Political Thought of Kim Dae-jung, in Korea Journal (autumn): 196–222.

Held, D. (2010) Cosmopolitanism: Ideals, Realities, and Deficits. Cambridge: Polity Press.

Hu, S.(1935) Chongfen Shijiehuayu Quanpanxihua [Whole Hearted Cosmopolitanization and Wholesale Westernization]. Retrieved from http://www.21c com.net/articles/lsjd/jwxd/article_2012010451400.html (Last access on 23 December 2012).

Huang, J. (2009) Where to Find the Non-occidental Universal Theory of Human Rights? A Query to Zhao Tingyang's Theory of Credit Human Rights, in Journal of National Prosecutors College 17, no.1.

Human Rights in China. (n.d.) Retrieved from http://news.xinhuanet.com/zili ao/2003-01/22/content_702907.htm (Last access on 23 December 2012).

Jiang, X. (2007) Cong tianxia zhuyidao hexie shijie: zhongguo waijiao zhexue jiqi shijian yiyi [From Tianxiaism to Harmonious World: Choice of Chinese Diplomatic Philosophy and Its Practical Meaning], in Contemporary Asia-Pacific Studies 12: 20–27.

Information Office of the State Council, PRC. (2011) White Paper on Peaceful Development, Retrieved from http://www.fmprc.gov.cn/eng/zxxx/t85632 5.htm (Last access on 23 December 2012).

Kim, D-j. (1994) Is Culture Destiny? The Myth of Asia's Anti-Democratic Values, in Foreign Affairs 73.6: 189–194.

——— (1998) Dawning Era of Universal Globalism, in Korea Times November 5.

Lee, K. Y. (1994) Culture is Destiny: A Conversation with Lee Kuan Yew, in Foreign Affairs 73, 2: 109–126.

Li, C., Thomas P. M. and Barnett et al. (2008) Debating China's Future, in China Security 4, no. 2–3 (spring): 3–26.

Li, M. (2011) Luntianxia sixiang zhongde zhengdao yu zhidao [The Political Way and Governed Way in Tian Xia Thoughts], in Shijie Zhengzhi yu Jingji [World Economics and Politics] 12: 109–125.

Li, S. (1994) Quanqiuhua yu zhongguo wenhua [Globalization and Chinese Culture], in Meiguo Yanjiu [American Studies] 4: 126–138.

Liu, X. (2011) Selected Writings, Tienchi Martian-Liao and Liu Xia (ed.) Frankfurt: Fischer Verlag.

McClean, E. (2011) The Dilemma of Intervention: Human Rights and the UN Security Council, in M. Odello and S. Cavandoli(eds.), Emerging Areas of Human Rights in the 21st Century: The Role of the Universal Declaration of Human Rights. London: Taylor & Francis, 24–44.

Milne, A. J. M. (1986) Human Rights and Human Diversity: An Essay in the Philosophy of Human Rights. Basingstoke, UK: Macmillan Press.

Nash, K. (2005) Human Rights Culture: Solidarity, Diversity, and the Right to Be Different, in Citizenship Studies 9, no. 4: 335–348.

Nazzari, V., P. McAdams and D. Roy (2005) Using Transformative Learning as a Model for Human Rights Education, in Intercultural Education 16, no. 2: 171–186.

Sevastik, P. (2011) Human Rights and the Development of International Law, Presented at Law Research Institute Foreign Authority Forum, Seoul National University, May 21.

Sheng, H. (1996) Cong minzizhuyi daotianxiazhuyi [From Nationalism to Tianxiaism], in Zhanlue yuGuanli [Strategy and Management] 1: 14–19.

——(2012) Tianxia wenming: lun rujia de guoji xianzheng yuanze [Tianxiaist Civilization: On Confucian principles of International Constitutionalism]. Retrieved from http://www.21ccom.net/articles/sxwh/shsc/article_20120 81065467.html (Last access on 23 December 2012).

Wang, G. (2006) Tianxia and Empire: External Chinese Perspectives, Inaugural Tsai Lecture. Retrieved from http://www.fas.harvard.edu/~asiactr/Archive %20Files/Tsai%20Lect.Harvard.05.06.doc (Last access on 23 Decemer 2012).

Wang, G. and Zheng Y. (eds.) (2008) China and the New International Order. London: Routledge.

Wang, P. (2010) The Poverty of Tianxiaism: From Archaeology of Knowledge to Philosophical Critics and Political Assessment, BACS annual conference held in September 2010. Retrieved from http://ishare.iask.sina.com.cn/f /14197906.html?retcode=0 (Last access on 23 December 2012).

Xia, Y. (2004) Minben yu minquan: zhongguo quanli huayu de lishi jichu [Minben and People's Rights: Historical Foundation of Chinese Discourses of Rights], in Social Sciences in China 5: 4–23.

Xu, J. (2007) Tianxia tixi yu shijiezhidu [Tianxia System and World Order—Remarks on ZhaoTingyang's The Tianxia System: A Philosophy for the World Institution], in Guoji Zhengzhi Kexue [Quarterly Journal of International Politics] 10: 113–142.

Xu, J. (2012) Te shu de wenhua haishi xintianxia zhuyi [Exceptive Culture or New Tianxiaism], Wenhua Zongheng[Culture Review] 2: 20–23.

Xu, X. M. (2006) Hexie quan: di si dai renquan [The Right to Harmony: The Fourth Generation of Human Rights], in Renquan [Human Rights] 2: 30–32.

Yan, X. (1997) Pushixing minzuzhuyiyu zhongguo de jueqi [Universal Nationalism and the Rising of China], in Taipingyang Xuebao [Pacific Journal] 2: 68–75.

Zhang, D. (1998) Sixiang yu Shehui[Thoughts and Society], first published by Shangwu Yinshuguan (Shanghai, 1946), reprinted by Liaoning jiaoyu chubanshe [Shenyang: Liaoning Education Publishing], 1998.

Zhang, S. (2006) Tianxia lilun he shijie zhidu [Tianxia theory and world institution: some questions for Zhaotingyang according the book of Tianxia tixi], in Zhenglai Deng (ed.), Zhongguo Shuping [China Book Review], vol. 5, Shanghai: Shanghai renmin chubanshe [Shanghai prople's publishing house].

Zhao, T. (2005) TianxiaTtixi: Shijie Zhidu Zhexue Daolun [The Tianxia System: A Philosophy for the World Institution], Nanjing: Jiangsu JiaoyuChubanshe [Jiangsu Education Publishing].

———(2006) Rethinking Empire from a Chinese Concept "All-under-Heaven" (Tian-xia), in Social Identities 12, no. 1: 29–41.

———(2007) Credit Human Rights: A Non-Western Theory of Universal Human Rights, in Social Sciences in China 1: 14–26.

———(2008) All under Heaven, in comment on "Debating China's Future," in Chinese Security 4, no. 2: 15.

———(2009) Cong guojia, guoji dao shijie: sanzhong zhengzhi de wenti bianhua [From States, the International to World: Changes of Three Kinds of Political Problems], in Zhexue Yanjiu [Philosophy Studies] 1: 89–95.

Zheng, Y. (2009) Zhongguo guojiajianguanxi de goujian: cong "tianxia" dao guoji zhixu [Organizing China's Inter-state Relations: From "Tianxia" (All-Under-Heaven) to the International Order], in Dangdai Yatai [Journal of Contemporary Asia-Pacific Studies] 5: 33–66.

——(ed.) (2010) China and International Relations: The Chinese View and the Contribution of Wang Gungwu. London: Routledge.

Zhou, F. (2008) Tianxia tixi shi zuihao de shijiezhidu me? [Is the Tianxia System the Best World Institution?], in Guoji ZhengzhiKexue [Quarterly Journal of International Politics] 14: 98–104.

Individualization and Community Networks in East Asia: How to Deal with Global Difference in Social Science Theories?

Young-Hee
Sang-Jin Han

Introduction

This study is aimed at investigating the concrete pathways to individualization in East Asia with a specific focus on the relationship between individuals and community networks. We argue that East Asia is distinctive by its cultural emphasis on the value of flourishing community, including the family, and therefore consider this relationship to be of paramount significance for understanding individualization. We begin by raising a question of whether the theory of individualization based on the Western tradition of individualism can be reasonably extended to East Asia. The aim of this research is then to demonstrate how individualization as a structural transformation tends to be combined with cultural traditions in multiple ways, making East Asia quite different from the West.

More specifically, this research will first compare the pathways to individualization in East Asia and the West and then examine variations within Korea by formulating a clear-cut analytic framework. The study will treat individualization as a structural process of transformation significantly affected by the relationship between modernity and tradition, on the one hand, and the interaction between the push and pull factors of individualization, on the other. The push factor means a structural force compelling large numbers of people in a society to change their patterns of behavior. More often than not, this is socioeconomic in nature, whereas the pull factor is deeply associated with the cultural and discursive process of social construction. We would like to argue that individualization as a structural transformation can be adequately understood only when both the push and pull factors and hence both socioeconomic and cultural-discursive dimensions are properly understood in close interactions.

In the West, among others, Beck (1992), Beck and Beck-Gernsheim (2002) have carried out pioneering research on the problems of individualization. However, we think that such a theory of individualization has, in fact, unfolded with the tacit historical assumption of the individualist tradition. Thus it is debatable whether we can take this as a self-evident reference and apply it to non-Western countries such as those in East Asia where the individual has been considered not as a socially isolated, atomized, independent subject, but rather as deeply interwoven with the community as a person is with his or her family. Thus it is important to pay full attention to the relationship between individuals and community and better understand significant variations and complexities involved. It is hoped that this investigation may lead us to understand better why and how East Asia differs from the

West while comprehending common characteristics of individualization.

The Western Theory of Individualization

Individualization is a complex process related to as diverse conditions as cultural changes, legal entitlement, political participation, and internet communication, among others. The concept of individualization indicates a categorical shift in relations between an individual and the society (Beck 1992: 127). First, it is related with cultural democracy. Individualization presupposes that individuals get liberated step by step from the taken-for-granted constraints exercised by collectives of various kinds. An outcome of this historical process is human rights or individual sovereignty. Second, individualization involves the emergence of an individual as subject of legal rights. It is an individual, not any collectivity that is legally entitled to make a claim for right. Third, individualization means the emergence of an individual citizen as the subject of political participation whose mode of action differs significantly from collective actors. Fourth, the process of individualization tends to be further facilitated by the development of the communication and digital revolution.

Another line of exploring the meaning of individualization today is how to manage risks and dangers that citizens may face in their life. In the Western countries, responsibility for risk management is shifting more and more to individuals. With respect to the economic life the concept of individualization assumes that individuals get unleashed from the previous frameworks of welfare financed by either the state or business firms or the family. In other words, individuals have to take care of their life by their own means, as seen in personal insurance packages.

According to Beck-Gernsheim (2008), Westerners left their traditional way of life, pushed not only by detraditionalization but also by legal development and the emergence of welfare state. Divorce, for example, which was extremely difficult for women, became possible through changes in social mores expressed through changes in the law and the emergence of the welfare state (Beck and Beck-Gernsheim 2002). The rise of the "post-familial family" (Beck and Beck-Gernsheim 2002; Shim 2011) is a case in point. Different from the nuclear family, the "post-familial family" refers to diversified forms of family: (1) based on confluent love, (2) characterized by gender equality, and neither assuming (3) heterosexual relationship only, nor (4) people from the same nation (Giddens 1992). Thus the family in the Western countries today is characterized by "marriage and divorce chains," "conjugal succession," "multi-parent families," "patchwork families," and "elective family relationship" (Beck and Beck-Gernsheim 2002: 96). It is a change from "living for others" to "a life of one's own" (Beck and Beck-Gernsheim 2002: 54), which is based not only on individualization, but also on individualism. It is a historical process that tends to break up people's traditional rhythm of life, that is, so-called "the standard biography," and to give way to "do-it-yourself" life history (Beck and Beck-Gernsheim 2002). The basic idea that everything depends on individual free choices we would like to call a "libertarian individualization" of the West.

An Overall Analytic Framework

The relationship of individuals and community in East Asia differs significantly from the salient characteristics of libertarian individualization. This can be shown clearly by examining individualization within the context of the family. The extent to which individuals in East Asia get unleashed from previous social bondages in industrial society, such as family, kinship, gender, and class and become responsible for their survival will be examined. An assumption of this research is that individualization, as a historical process of transformation, can work well as in the West when the action-oriented, cultural-discursive dimension of individualism is strong and effective. However, the cultural-discursive factor in East Asia is significantly different from the West. This is why we need to investigate the concrete pathways to individualization in East Asia which differ from the West.

For such an analysis of the process of individualization we will use the model we have developed (Shim and Han 2010) utilizing Beck (1992) and Beck and Beck-Gernsheim's (2002) theory of individualization. In order to better reveal the dynamic aspects of individualization as a three-dimensional process of "disembedding," "disenchantment," and "reembedding" (Beck 1992: 128)[1], we combined the structural-objective dimension and cultural-discursive dimension on the one hand, and push and pull factors of transformation on the other, to make the following model (Shim and Han 2010).

To clarify, the process of disembedding unfolds under the objective-structural conditions such as global risks, which, as a push factor, unleash individuals from traditional and modern welfare arrangements. This objective-structural tendency gives rise to the collective experience of fear, anxiety, and disillusionment, which

---

[1] Beck's original explanation of individualization shows the following three-dimensional process:

"[D]isembedding, removal from historically prescribed social forms and commitments in the sense of traditional contexts of dominance and sup-port (the "liberating dimension"); the loss of traditional security with respect to practical knowledge, faith and guiding norms (the "disen-chantment dimension"); and—here the meaning of the world is virtually turned into its opposite—re-embedding, a new type of social commitment (the "control" or "reintegration dimension")" (Beck 1992: 128; italics original).

The first axis of distinction refers to the two deep layers of reality with equally substantive consequences. The objective-structural layer is mostly, if not exclusively, about economic conditions on which institutions are formed. The cultural-discursive layer is about the practical field of actions in which "dispositive" and "habitus" manifests itself. Beck and Beck-Gernsheim seem to have paid more attention to the objec-tive-structural dimension, although they refer to the problem of reembedding.

originates from survival uncertainty. In other words, the cultural-discursive stream of disenchantment (Beck) works as a push factor. Reembedding, in turn, can be made possible in reality when a new institutional arrangement is formulated and backed up by public policies and laws. Yet the process of reembedding cannot stop here since it requires a forward-looking perspective or motivational support from cultures, ideologies, and collective aspiration. Otherwise, the process of reembedding may face serious misunderstanding, conflict, and tension. Therefore, individualization can move well only when the culture-based pull factors operate reasonably well leading individuals to accepting and, if needed, justifying a new institution offered (Shim and Han 2010). Seen from this conceptual framework, reembedding is as crucially important as disembedding for individualization.[2]

The relationship between individuals and community is an important factor that distinguishes East Asia from the West. With regard to this, this research attempts to show the difference between East Asia and the West by suggesting a typology. The difference is more about the function of the pull factor, that is, the cul-

---

[2] We see no problem with the issue of disembedding since it is exactly what is going on almost everywhere in the global risk regime today. The analyses of Japan (Suzuki et al. 2010), China (Yan 2010), and Korea (Chang and Song 2010) clearly demonstrate this. We have no intent to dispute about it. However, we perceive that this is only half of the story to be investigated. What remains to be seen is where and how reembedding is proceeding, and with what kinds of consequences.

tural-discursive factor, than the push factor. The push factor works as structural pressure toward individualization in all countries. The extent of pressure may vary depending on the circumstances of the given country. Yet the tendency of economic crisis and polarization yields structural pressures to discharge individuals from the given welfare institutional frameworks. What is decisive in this context is the pull factor. The concrete pathway of individualization is shaped by the cultural-discursive pull factor.

Individualization in East Asia: Japan

There is considerable research on individualization in Japan within the context of the family. Japan seems to be somewhat ahead of Korea and China in this field of study (Suzuki et al. 2010; Ishida et al. 2010). As to individualization as a structural transformation, Suzuki et al.'s (2010) work is representative. They argue that two mechanisms were responsible for risk management in the first modernity: first, Japanese management/company-centrism (private corporations that guaranteed long-term stability for employees and their families), and second, land development policies implemented under the guidance of bureaucrats. This means that company-centered society and the developmental state functioned as a buffer. However, from the 1990s these systems were fundamentally destroyed by globalization and neoliberal policies. Japanese company-centrism broke down, paving the road to individualization of employment. Since then individuals in Japan had to rely on themselves and find their own way. Now, individualization within the context of the family has advanced as the rate of unmarried people and the divorce rate have climbed.

Suzuki et al. (2010) have demonstrated the tendency of disconnecting individuals from the first-modern institutions and placing the burden of survival on the shoulders of individuals. In this neoliberal context, individuals are encouraged to be independent and autonomous. Yet individualization involves not only disembedding but also reembedding. However, their discussion remains largely tied to the role of the push factor and not well extended to the pull factor. Thus there is a further need for a research.

The relationship between individuals and community has been touched upon by Ochiai's (2004), Morita's (2009), and Yui's (2009) works. First of all, Ochiai's (2004) book is about the new family model of the twenty-first century from the feminist perspective. She criticizes the so-called "the crisis of the family" discourse, claiming that it is nothing but an official view of the Economic Planning Bureau of Japan. She also claims the model of woman as a house wife was a postwar ideology based on the change of industrial structure from agriculture to employee-centered society. As the characteristics of the family of the 1990s, she points out both independence of women and the reemergence of "ie," that is, the family. As a new type of the family, she discusses the "neighborhood network" and "single unit society" as salient characteristics of the Japanese pathway to individualization. She thinks the trend from the "family unit society" to "single unit society" will continue, but she does not consider it as the "collapse of the family."

Morita (2009) shows an interesting contrast between Japan and the West in terms of an ideal-typical self. In line with Charles Taylor, he contrasts the typical self in the West as "buffered" while the Japanese case is "porous." The "buffered" self has developed discipline and self-control and seen him/herself more and more as an independent and sovereign individual not subject to any external constraints. This idea emerged from the Western process of religious reform toward a transcendental existence of the individual in dialogue with god. While the Western modern self had to enclose its boundary completely, the self in Japan remains porous even after it is institutionally modernized, because in Japan where collective rituals are not considered negatively, the "porous" self did not feel it necessary to close itself against the world completely. Consequently, the Japanese self is more vulnerable to intervention from the outside world in the form of collective rituals.

Yui (2009) makes a similar argument, claiming that the history of Japan shows the world of "habitat segregation." Many different "religions" could coexist simultaneously, which is different from the West where the drama of an "all or nothing" type of alteration between orthodoxy and heterodoxy prevailed through a long history of cutthroat battles. Presenting Kafu (the name of a man in a novel who lived in two worlds of habitat segregation), who lived in two separated spaces and ran away to downtown to hide himself there temporarily, as an example of Japanese modern man, Yui argues that this type of separation/fragmentation of time and space accelerated so drastically that members of the young generations are now running away in the contemporary configuration of time and space in this world. Differentiating the "habitat segregation" of time and space into minute details has given rise to a "transitional" identity as a self (subject), forming "polygamic" networks with different places. The logic and the psychology of "habitat segregation" make it possible for instrumental rationality and irrational world of "free and easy going (let joy be unconfined)" to coexist side by side.

Ochiai's, Morita's, and Yui's accounts are insightful in revealing the characteristics of "run-away individualization in networks" in Japan. However, their arguments are basically conceptual. Thus there seems to be a need to be substantiated.

ndividualization and Community in China

There are a few studies on individualization in China (Yan 1996, 2003, 2009, 2010). Yan's work (2010) traces the origin of the individualization process to the Maoist era, arguing that some collectivist programs of social engineering and the socialist path of modernization under Maoism ironically resulted in a partial individualization of Chinese society. He examines profound social changes during the three decades of the post-Mao reforms, discussing the contours of individualization in various aspects, such as the privatization of labor and the economy, rural-urban migration of workers, rights awareness, politics of lifestyle, and the self and the subjective domain of individualization. As a conclusion, Yan argues that there are similarities with the individualization process in Western Europe, but also some important differences.

Yan (2010) offered a great image of the Chinese way to individualization. Individualization in China is characterized by the management of the party-state and the absence of cultural democracy, the absence of a welfare state regime, and the absence of classic individualism and political liberalism (Yan 2010). Unlike in Western Europe where individualization results from the radicalization of modernity itself, Chinese individualization remains a developmental strategy under the direction and management of the powerful party-state (Yan 2010). The Chinese individualization process remains at the stage of emancipation politics of first modernity.

Yan's argument is persuasive. However, Yan (2010) focuses on the disembedding, not the reembedding process of individualization. Recent studies on the relationship between individuals and community, which focus on love, marriage, and family of the new generation of migrant workers in China, deserves careful attention. Representing about a 100 million people, they show distinctive characteristics (Liu 2007). As "double out-comers" (Tan et al. 2003), they are inclined to enjoy freedom to choose a spouse by themselves (Wu 2011). However, on the other hand, they want to choose fellow-villagers as the first choice for their spouse because fellow villagers share common language and habits. What is more striking is that 19.2 percent think they would go back to their hometown to find spouses, and they have a willingness to provide a better life for their family, especially for their children (Wu 2011).

Yan's more recent work (2012) deals with not only disembedding but also the reembedding process of individualization in China. He argues that with the individualization process a new model of individual appeared in China, which he called "the striving individual." Through his interviews with a farmer in a Chinese village, he revealed that many people in China strive hard to make money for their children's education and success. The "striving individual" is characterized as having a materialist goal in value orientation and is different from the "enterprising individual" of the West who is more oriented to expressive and postmaterialist goal.

These recent studies, including those on Chinese people's way of choosing spouse and married lives and Yan's research on the striving individual, indicate both an individualizing and a family-oriented tendency. This characteristic has also been found from our research on the transnational marriages in Korea, particularly from the women who have come to Korea for marriage from Northeast China and Southeast Asia (Shim and Han 2010). This characteristic indicates a type of individualization which may be called "communitarian individualization."

Two Salient Modes of Individualization in Korea

In the literature on the change of the family type in Korea we find two potentially conflicting perspectives. The first perspective is called "family disorganization" discourse, which considers such family problems as the increase of divorce, the decrease of marriage, and lack of communication in the family as family disintegration or family disorganization (Pyo 2000; Choi 1997). This perspective considers that these problems emerge because the traditional family norms collapsed.

The second perspective is called "a variety of families" discourse, which considers the recent change of the family type as an adaptation of the family members to the recent social structural change (Kim 2008; Kim et al. 2004; Lee 2004; Byon and Cho 2003; Lee 2003; Chang et al. 2001; Lee 1999; Yim 1999). Thus the increase of divorce, the decrease of marriage, the increase of the singles, the increase of late marriages, and the decrease of the birth rate, are considered as a matter of individual's choice, and even the homosexual family is recognized in this perspective. This is a perspective of feminists or pluralists who explore a new family order going beyond patriarchy, positively accepting the increase of individuals' choice.

However, neither of these perspectives focuses on the gap between the family type and family norm. They also cannot explain the macroscopic meaning contained in the recent family change. Of crucial significance in this regard is research on family values (Eun 2006; Eo 1997) and the effect of socioeconomic changes on these values (Park 2003). Combining the concepts of compressed modernity and risk society, Chang (Chang 2009; Chang and Song 2010) considers the recent phenomenon of delaying marriage and low birth rates as risk-evasive individualization. His argument is that in this state of compressed modernity, the family, which used to be the welfare foundation for individual, has lost its functions as welfare resource or buffer zone, and that the family members have no choice but to be unleashed from the family and rely on one's own efforts and ability, even though they are not equipped with strong individualism as in the West. Thus he calls the individualization in Korea "individualization without individualism" (Chang and Song 2010). This is a very important observation.

However, Chang's discussion focuses mainly on the disembedding process of individualization, not on the reembedding process. In other words, he pays far more attention to the push factor than pull factor. Individualization referred to by "a variety of families" discourse above shows the consequences of adaptation to the changing reality of the neoliberal global economy. Adaptation differs from normative value. The "family disorganization" discourse reflects the breakdown of family norms taken for granted in the past. These two contrasting perspectives, though significant in many respects, fall short of grasping the reembedding process of individualization.

In this context we have attempted to deal with the reembedding process of individualization by paying attention to women marriage migrants (Shim and Han 2010). We have examined this because it shows both individualizing and family-oriented tendencies. More specifically, women marriage migrants are individualistic in the sense that they pursue their own course even taking the risk of being separated from their family, as a determined challenge to the survival uncertainty their family faces. They are "individualistic" because they came all the way from their home despite the various anticipated difficulties. On the other hand, they are also very family-oriented, that is, "familial," because they came for better living conditions of the family, and, with family responsibility, do their best for their new family and endure the difficulties for their families in the home country (Shim and Han 2010). This individualization was called "family-oriented individualization." Perhaps, a similar example is the so-called "wild goose families" (Lee and Koo 2006) frequently found in Korea. This case also illustrates well both individualization and family-oriented networks, not simply in a traditional way, but innovatively. This pattern of transformation is distinctive to Korea.

Another effort to integrate both the disembedding and reembedding process of individualization is seen in Han (2007). In a recent work on the so-called the "386 generation," that is, the postconventional generation, Han (2007) argued that the salient characteristics of individualization and the relationship between individuals and community in Korea can be described as "postconventional networking individualization." The term postconventional has specific implications for the process of disembedding as well as reembedding. To be more specific, postconventional means that one breaks away from the taken-for-granted authority, taboo, and customs, on the one hand, and reactivate flexible networks as a shared way of life, on the other. With this concept he argued that we can cover both individualization as a structural transformation and strengthening of networks including the family solidarity in an innovative way. Thus he tried to present how individualization and strengthening of the family network solidarity can go well along in Korea from the perspective of "the postconventional networking individualization" as an ideal type.

In order to grasp these two salient modes of individualization we want to pay attention to two constitutive factors of individualization, that is, the subjective factor and value orientation. The former is whether one's way of thinking is traditional or reflexive. The latter is whether the action is oriented toward collective interests or self-interests. Thus a typology made of these two dimensions will be useful in tracing not only the change of traditional versus reflexive ways of thinking/acting but also the change of the orientation toward collective interests versus self-interests. By crossing these two dimensions of individualization as two main axes, we constructed the following four types of individualization.

Type A is characterized by both strong collective interests and traditional way of thinking, thus it can be called "conventional types of collectivism." This type can be typically found among those who consider collective interests to be more important than self-interest in a traditional way. Type B is characterized by traditional way of thinking (for example, family-oriented), but the Type B person tries to pursue self-interests for survival. The self-interests here can be interpreted as private interests. Thus it can be called "family-oriented striving individualization." This type tends to be frequently found among those who strive hard to get out of poverty for the welfare of the family rather than an individual in question. The type we have called "family-oriented individualization" (Shim and Han 2010) can be classified as a category of this type. Type C is characterized by a reflexive way of thinking closely associated with the mode of action pursuing and advocating public interests. A typical example is civil movements based on individual decision to join through either online or off-line deliberation in order to pursue certain values of public significance. Thus it can be called "public-minded participatory individualization."Han's study on the so called the "386 generation," or the postconventional generation, reveal this type of individualization (Han 2007). Type D is characterized by both a reflexive way of thinking and a pursuit of self-centered individualizing tastes and preferences. This type can be typically found among the younger generations like the teenagers or those in their twenties. Libertarian individualization may develop fully when such conditions as cultural democracy, welfare state, and classical individualism are met (Beck 1992; Beck and Beck-Gernsheim 2002).

According to a survey research on individualization (Han and Shim 2012), all the types above are found in Korea. And the distribution of these four types of individualization is as follows: the proportion of the type A, that is, conventional collective arrangement, is 41.9 percent; that of type B, that is, family-oriented striving individualization, is 29.9 percent; that of type C, that is, public-minded participatory individualization, is 15.5 percent; and that of type D, that is, self-centered libertarian individualization, is 12.7 percent. And the age distribution shows that while the proportion of type B is high among the age group over fifty, that of type C is high among the age group of thirties and forties, and type D is found among the younger age group between ten years of age and into the twenties (Han and Shim 2012). Han's research (2007) shows the prevalence of type C among the thirties through forties age group, even though there are some variations in them. Shim's research (2012) shows the prevalence of type B among elderly people, even though there are some variations in them. In the following we will discuss Shim's research as an example of data resisting Western theory of individualization.

"Striving Individualization" among Korean Elderly Women

Shim (2012) conducted research based on in-depth interviews to seventeen elderly women to explore the types of individualization among elderly women in Korea. The people of this study underwent "family-oriented striving individualization" while trying to overcome the risks of poverty and family conflict they encountered. This type of individualization is characterized by traditional way of thinking but oriented to self-interests (not public-minded). The people interviewed for this study can be divided into two subtypes according to the risks they had encountered: the "poverty overcoming type" and the "family conflict overcoming type." The risk for each subtype was material risk and relational risk respectively. More specifically, the "striving individualization" can be found in the interviewees' life stories. Among the seventeen interviewees, six cases can be classified as "poverty overcoming type." They suffered from extreme poverty during their childhood, thus they did not have enough to eat and could not go to school. Thus more than half of them left the parents and home and came to Seoul during their teen ages, either with or without telling their parents, like many rural young girls who left villages to make money in Seoul. In Seoul, they made all their efforts to make their own living and to succeed, working as house-maids, factory workers, or as peddlers, even though they encountered various difficulties. When they reached marriage age, many of them managed to find spouses without the help of their parents, at a time when most of the marriages were arranged by the family. Most of them met a husband who either was very poor, an orphan, or in a similar situation. After marriage they made all their efforts together with their husband, performing all kinds of low-paying dirty works "in order not to pass down poverty to their children." Now they are better off materially, thanks not only to their industrious effort but also and mainly to the economic development of the country as a whole. They often go to the welfare center for the elderly to attend various educational courses and to enjoy life with new friends.

As can be seen in the foregoing stories, the social constraints these "poverty-overcoming types" were unleashed from are the hometown and the parents whom they left when they were young. Thus they managed to find spouses without the help of their parents. And most of them made efforts together with their husbands with a strong determination to overcome poverty and not to pass down poverty to their children.

On the other hand, the life stories of another six interviewees of "the family conflict overcoming types" were different. Most of them grew up in well-to-do families, did not suffer from poverty, and received good educations. When they got married, most of them followed their parents' opinions. They left their parents with the marriage. After marriage, most of them suffered from living with the in-laws, from a patriarchal husband who is violent and/or who has an affair with another woman, or a husband with no love. Most of them lived a life for others, for in-laws, husband, and/or children. Even though they suffered from the family conflict, they endured the husband's abuses due to various circumstances such as economic dependence, their parents, and children. As the relationship with the husband did not change even as time passed, many of them wanted to have a divorce but went only as far as "domestic divorce"[3], and only two ended up in a divorce. As for those who had a divorce, they got a divorce with the support of

---

[3] "Domestic divorce" became a buzzword after the publication of a novel Domestic Divorce (1985) by Ayashi Yigyu in Japan. This novel described the collapse of a couple and family relationship. Domestic divorce refers to a situation when a couple lives together and maintains the hus-band-wife relationship on the surface while the husband-wife relation-ship has in fact broken down. A couple in this state lives together in the same house, but eats and sleeps separately and does not talk to each other. The reason why people choose a "domestic divorce" is because they cannot separate due to economic reason, children, social stigma, even though they want a divorce (Yamada 2010: 30).

grown-up children, not with one's own decision alone. Even though they had a divorce with the husband, they maintained their relationship with the children and families. Now they go to the welfare center for the elderly to take courses and to enjoy life with new friends.

As can be seen in these life stories, the social constraints these "family conflict overcoming types" were unleashed from are the family, that is, the husband and the in-laws. However, their unleashing is rather late compared with the poverty overcoming type. Also their unleashing is rather limited in that most of them stayed in "domestic divorce." This can be called individualization, because they tried to get out of the existing settings of relationship, or standard biography and dreamed of a life of one's own.[4]

When we analyze the disembedding and reembedding process of individualization, we can see the characteristics of the individualization of Korean elderly women more clearly (Shim, 2012). The factors that influence the individualization turned out to be different according to the different subtypes. The women interviewees in the "poverty overcoming type" were forced to leave their home and parents due to poverty, and they were eager to get out of poverty

---

4   Some might question whether "domestic divorce" can be considered in-di-vidualization. However, it can be considered so, because it involves a couple living together in the same house, but eating and sleeping sepa-rately and not talking to each other. This can be considered as an un-leashing from the husband even though they cannot separate due to economic reason, children, and social stigma.

and discrimination. The emergence of new job opportunities pulled them to the cities; they had aspirations to learn, to make money and succeed for the family. Thus the risks or structural-objective push factors were the Korean War, the poverty of the time, and discrimination against daughters, while the cultural-discursive push factors were aspirations to get out of poverty and discrimination. And their structural pull factors were industrialization, urbanization, and the emergence of new job opportunities in the cities, while their cultural pull factors were aspiration to learn, to make money, and succeed.

Many of the women interviewees in the "family conflict overcoming type" suffered from living with in-laws and from violence and extramarital affairs of the husband. However, they endured it for a long time for their parents and children and also because of social stigma and economic dependence. Now they went out to the welfare centers to learn and to make new friends. They expressed and acted out their feelings only when they got old and when social changes such as emergence of diverse families and new welfare facilities occurred. The new opportunity and circumstances probably helped them think and decide for a life of one's own. But most of them did not get divorced, but stayed in "domestic divorce." Thus the structural push factors were stubborn patriarchy such as living with in-laws, violence, and extramarital affairs of husband, while the cultural push factors were cumulated distrust and disillusionment against the husband and in-laws. And the structural pull factors were the second modern transformation such as emergence of diverse families and change of household generation composition and emergence of new welfare facilities, while the cultural pull factors such as classical individualism were hard to find, almost nonexistent.

Despite the differences between these two types, they share a common theme that they strived hard in their life and they did it for their families. And this common theme can be called "family-oriented striving individualization."

Concluding Remark

The above discussion shows that the characteristics of the individualization of Korean elderly women are different from that of the West. They are different in three aspects (Shim 2012). First, the risks or structural push factors are complex in that they are not only from the radicalization of the modernity but also from deficiency of modernity, that is, the mixture of the first and second modernity (Han and Shim 2010). Second, the pull factors are also complex in that the structural ones are there, but cultural ones are almost nonexistent. That is, no classical individualism is found among Korean cases as in the West. Third, in terms of the relationship between the individual and the community, the cases show a strong family-orientation even though the targets are varied, with many of them oriented toward their children, some toward their husbands, and others toward their parents. Even though they have made new friends at the welfare centers, which can be considered to have characteristics of the second modernity, the family-relationship is central to them. Even in the cases where their relationship with their husband is not good, most of them do not leave the family, but remain in it, living in the state of "domestic divorce." The individualization of Korean elderly women is different from the self-centered libertarian individualization of the Western societies in these senses. In this sense it can be said that the Western theory of individualization has difficulty in explaining individualization in Korea and that a new theory better fitting to East Asian situation is needed to explain it.

References

Beck, U. (1992) Risk Society: Towards a New Modernity. Mark Ritter (Trans.) London: Sage.

Beck, U. and E. Beck-Gernsheim (2002) Individualization: Institutionalized Individualism and its Social and Political Consequences. London: Sage.

Beck-Gernsheim, E. (2008) Family Life Today: New Diversity, New Options, New Pressures, in Gender and Society 7(1): 11–32.

Beck, U. and E. Grande (2010) Varieties of Second Modernity: the Cosmopolitan Turn in Social and Political Theory and Research, in British Journal of Sociology 61(3): 409–443.

Byon, W. S. and Cho, E. H. (2003) Issues Related with the Emergence of a Variety of Families and the Direction for the Family-Related Laws (in Korean). Seoul: KWDI.

Chang, H. K. et al. (2001) Adaptation of the Remarried Families and their Support Measures (in Korean). Seoul: KWDI.

Chang, K-S. (2009) The Family, Lifecourse, Political Economy (in Korean). Seoul: Changbi.

Chang, K.-S. and Song M.-Y. (2010) The Stranded Individualizer under Compressed Modernity: South Korean Women in Individualization without Individualism, in British Journal of Sociology 61(3): 539–564.

Choi, S. M. (1997) Confucianism and Community Ethic., in Search of a New Community (in Korean). Seoul: Hanmaik.

Eo, S. Y. (1997) Value Change and Life Politics: Comparative Study of Four Countries, Korea, Japan, USA, and Mexico (in Korean). Seoul: Ewha Woman's University Press.

Eun, K. S. (2004) Family Values of the Koreans: Comparative Study of Five Countries (in Korean), in Korean Studies Quarterly 27(3): 137–182.

——(2006) An International Comparative Study on Family Values: Focusing on Hierarchy and Generation Different (in Korean), in Family and Culture 18(3): 1–31.

——(2009) A Comparative Study of "Asian Family Values" in East Asian Societies (in Korean), Annual Meeting of Korean Sociological Association, December.

Giddens, A. (1992) Structural Transformation of Intimacy: Sex, Love, and Eroticism in Modern Society. Stanford, CA: Stanford University Press.

Ham, I. H. (2002) The Crisis of the Korean Family: Is it a Disorganization or Restructuration? (in Korean), in Family and Culture, 14(3): 103–184.

Han, S.-J. (1995) The Rush to Industrialization and Its Pathological Consequences: The Theme of "Risk Society" in the Asian Context, Paper presented at the Sixth International Conference of Asian Sociology. Beijing, Nov. 2–5.

―――(1998) Korean Path to Modernization and Risk Society, in Korea Journal 38.1 (spring): 5–27.

―――(2007) The Formation and Differentiation of Postconventional Generations in Korea: A Search for the Agency of Social Change (in Korean), in Theory and Society 11: 4–48.

Han, S.-J. and Y.-H. Shim (2012) Articulation of Individualization and Community Networks in East Asia: Historical and Empirical Study (in Korean), Paper presented at the Annual Meeting of the Korean Society of Social Theory. Seoul, August 22–23.

―――(2010) Redefining Second Modernity for East Asia: A Critical Assessment, in British Journal of Sociology 61(3): 465–488.

Ishida, M. et al. (2010) The Individualization of Relationship in Japan, in Soziale Welt 61 (3/4): 217–235.

Kim, H. Y. (2008) Increase in a Variety of Families in Korea and Its Double Implications (in Korean), in Journal of Asian Women 47(2): 7–37.

Kim, S. K. et al. (2004) The Emergence of a Variety of Families and Measures for Social Support System (in Korean). Seoul: Korea Institute of Health and Social Affairs (KIHASA).

―――(2005) The Emergence of a Variety of Families with Social Change in Korea (in Korean), in Health and Welfare Forum 103, May, 5–23.

Lee, H. S. (2003) Individualization of Women and the Family Change: Focusing on the American Society (in Korean), in Family and Culture 15(3): 111–134.

Lee, J. K. (2004) Is the Korean Family in Crisis? A Feminist Criticism on "Healthy Family" Discourses (in Korean), in Journal of Korean Women's Studies 20(1): 229–244.

Lee, M. K. (1999) The Nuclear Family and "the Crisis of the Family" under the Backlash of Neoliberalism: Issues of Feminist Criticism (in Korean). Seoul: Gonggam.

Lee, Y. J. and H. Koo (2006) "Wild Geese Fathers" and a Globalized Family Strategy for Education in Korea, in IDPR 28(4): 533–553.

Liu, J. E. (ed.) (2007) Report on the Contemporary New Generation of Migrant Workers (in Chinese). Chinese Youth Publishing.

Liu, S. W. (2008) Fellow-Workers or Going Back Home for Spouse: A Research on the Love and Marriage of the New Generation of Migrant Workers (in Chinese), in Chinese Youth Research 2009(1).

Morita, A. (2009) Difference in the Conceptions of Self as Subject of Human Rights between the West and Japan: Can Confucian Self Be Strong Enough to Exercise the Positive Liberty in the Authoritarian Society?, Paper presented at the Twenty-fourth IVR World Congress. Beijing.

Ochiai, E. (2004) To the Family of the 21st Century—The Family and Society in Japan (in Japanese). Yu-hikaku sensyo.

Park, M. J. (2003) Gender Difference in the Meaning of Marriage: Focusing on University Students (in Korean), in Family and Culture 15(2): 3–32.

Pyo, G. S. (2000) Welfare for Children and Youth (in Korean). Seoul: Nanam.

Shim, Y.-H. (2011) Toward a Community-Oriented Family Model of the Twenty-First Century: From a Perspective of Second Modernity and Individualization Theory (in Korean), in Journal of Asian Women 50(2): 7–44.

———(2012) Striving for the Family: Individualization of Korean Elderly Women, Paper presented at East Asian Sociologists Network. Tokyo, November 22–23.

Shim, Y.-H., and S.-J. Han (2010) "Family-Oriented Individualization" and Second Modernity: An Analysis of Transnational Marriages in Korea, in Soziale Welt 61(3/4): 237–255.

Suzuki, M. et al. (2010) Individualizing Japan: Searching for its Origin in First Modernity, in British Journal of Sociology 61(3): 513–538.

Tan, L. et al. (2003) The Life of the "Double Out-comers": An Analysis of Life History of Women Marriage Migrants (in Chinese), in Sociological Research 2.

Wu, X. H. (2011) Between Tradition and Generation: Love and Marriage of the New Generation of Migrant Workers (in Chinese), in Chinese Youth Research 1.

Yamada, M. (2010) Restructuring of the Family, Shin-Yo-Sa (in Korean). Jang Whakyoung (Trans.) Seoul: Greenbi (original in 1999).

Yan, Y. (1996) The Flow of Gifts: Reciprocity and Social Networks in a Chinese Village. tanford, CA: Stanford University Press.

———(2003) Private Life under Socialism. Stanford, CA: Stanford University Press.

———(2009) The Individualization of Chinese Society. London: London School of Economics.

———(2010) The Chinese Path to Individualization, in British Journal of Sociology 61(3): 489–512.

———(2012) Of the Individual and Individualization: The Striving Individual in China and the Theoretical Implications., in Angelika Poferi et al. (eds.), Futures of Modernity. Bielefeld, Germany: forthcoming.

Yim, I. S. (1999) Debate on the Family Change in the American Research Associations (in Korean), in Family and Culture 11(1): 23–46.

Yui, K. (2009) Multiple Reflexive Modernities under Glocalization: Focusing on the Case of Japan, A paper presented at the Conference on "Second Modernity in East Asia," held in Berlin, Germany, October, 2009, and a translation of a Japanese article published in the special issue on "Globalization Reconsidered" in Japanese Sociological Review, December, 2009.

Yun, Z. W. (2010) An Analysis of the Marriage and Family Problems of the Second Generation of Migrant Workers (in Chinese), in Chinese Rural Observation 3.

Notes on the Contributors

Guimei Bai is an international law professor at Peking University Law School, Beijing, the People's Republic of China. Her general interests are on theories of international law, international human rights law, particularly on mechanisms of human rights protection. She is also interested in rights of women and rights of the child. At the same time she is devoted to human rights education in China. Her recent publications (in Chinese) include International Law, 2nd edition, Beijing: Peking University Press, (2010); Human Rights Law, Beijing: Peking University Press, (2011), Human Rights Handbook on the Rights of the Child, Hunan: Hunan University Press, (2012).
E-mail: baigmi@pku.edu.cn

Sang-Jin Han is Professor Emeritus at Seoul National University, Korea and Visiting Professor at Beijing University, China. He lectured at Columbia University in New York, Ecole des Hautes Etudes en Sciences Sociales in Paris, and University of Buenos Aires in Argentina. His current main interests are on second modern transformation in East Asia, middle class dynamics, human rights and transitional justice. His publications include Habermas and the Korean Debate (1998), Divided Nation and Transitional Justice (2012).
E-mail: hansjin@snu.ac.kr

Michael Kuhn is president of the World Social Sciences and Humanities Network and director of Knowwhy Global Research. His background is philosophy, political science and international economics. His research interests include philosophy of science, epistemological and infrastructural implications of internationalizing social sciences, economy and politics in the era of "globalisation". Recent publication: M. Kuhn and D. Weidemann. (eds.), (2010), Internationalization of the Social Sciences, Bielefeld: transcript.
E-mail: michaelkuhn@knowwhy.net; mkuhn@worldsshnet.org

Léon-Marie Nkolo Ndjodo is a philosopher at the Department of philosophy of the University of Maroua in Cameroon. His general interests are on contemporary esthetic, poststructuralism, postmodernism and African postcolonial studies. He is also interested in cultural challenges of globalization in developing countries contexts. His current publication includes 'Société civile, Etat et capitalisme postmoderne', (2012) Kalio, Revue pluridisciplinaire de l'Ecole normale supérieure de l'Universite de Maroua, Volume 5.
E-mail: leonnkolo@yahoo.fr

Kazumi Okamoto is Secretary General of the World Social Sciences and Humanities Network, Germany. She is currently pursuing her PhD study at Karlsruhe Institute of Technology, Germany on 'academic culture' in the Japanese social and human sciences. Her research interests are internationalization of social sciences and humanities (SSH), working cultures in SSH in the context of international collaborations, and internationalization of Higher Education. Her recent work includes Okamoto, K. (2010), 'Internationalization of Japanese Social Sciences: Importing and Exporting Social Science Knowledge' in M. Kuhn and D. Weidemann. (eds) Internationalization of the Social Sciences, Bielefeld: transcript.
E-mail: okamoto@worldsshnet.org

Sujata Patel is a sociologist at the University of Hyderabad. An historical sensibility and a combination of four perspectives-Marxism, feminism, spatial studies and post structuralism/post colonialism influences her work which covers diverse areas such as modernity and social theory, history of sociology/social sciences, city-formation, social movements, gender construction, reservation, quota politics and caste and class formations in India. She is also an active interlocutor of teaching and learning practices, and has written on the challenges that organise its reconstitution within classrooms, University structures. She is the author of more than sixty papers and is the Series Editor of Sage Studies in International Sociology (including Current Sociology Monographs (2010–2013), Oxford India Studies in Contemporary Society (Oxford, India). She is also the editor of The ISA

Handbook of Diverse Sociological Traditions, Sage London (2010). She has been associated in various capacities with the International Sociological Association and has been its first Vice President for National Associations (2002–2006).
E-mail: patel.sujata09@gmail.com

Kumaran Rajagopal, who regards himself as a 'Learners' Assistant', is a sociologist with the Department of Sociology at the Gandhigram Rural University, India. His research interest has been around the issues of alternative and 'other' sociologies and methodologies. He is specifically concerned about the ways formalized social knowledges are used up in the development context in India and, thus, regularly alternates between academics and development sector, as matter of career choice.
rkumara@gmail.com

Young-Hee Shim is a sociologist at the Law School, Hanyang University, Seoul, Korea. Her general interests are on social changes in East Asia compared with the West, particularly on second modern transformation and individualization, focusing on women and the family. She is also interested in the human rights of women and minority groups. Her publication includes Sexual Violence and Feminism in Korea (2004).
E-mail: yhshim@hanyang.ac.kr

Kwang-Yeong Shin is professor of the Department of Sociology at Chung-Ang University in Seoul, Korea. His research areas are class analysis and inequality, comparative social welfare regime, and philosophy of social sciences. Recent publications include 'The Dilemmas of Korea's New Democracy in an Age of Neoliberal Globalization'(Third World Quarterly. 33(2)) and 'Economic Crisis, Neoliberal Reforms, the Rise of Precarious Work in South Korea'(American Behavioral Scientist, December 2, 2012 online).
E-mail: kyshin@cau.ac.kr

Lei Tang is an associate research professor at the Institute of Information Studies of Chinese Academy of Social Sciences (CASS), Beijing. His general interests are on the sociology of knowledge and contemporary history of scholarship and social thoughts in China, digital humanities, sociology of Internet, and sociology of transition. He is also interested in the role of the intellectual and cultural tradition for social transition in contemporary Chinese contexts.
E-mail: buddytang@gmail.com

Hebe Vessuri is a social anthropologist at the Centre of Science Studies of the Venezuelan Institute of Scientific Research (IVIC), Caracas. Her general interests are on the sociology and contemporary history of science in Latin America, science policy, and sociology of technology. She is also interested in the challenges and dilemmas of expertise and democracy in developing country contexts. Among her most recent publications are Vessuri, H. (2011), Equality and Hierarchy in Antajé (in Spanish). IDES/_Editorial Al Margen, Buenos Aires. López, M.S. & H. Vessuri. (2012), 'Tensions and Resistances in the Political Alignment of Public Research within Venezuela's New Political Setup'. Science and Public Policy. vol. 39, issue 5, pp.602–612. October.

E-mail: hvessuri@gmail.com

Doris Weidemann is a cultural psychologist and professor of intercultural training with focus on the Greater China area at the University of Applied Sciences of Zwickau, Germany. Her research interests include intercultural science collaboration, indigenous psychologies, and methods of intercultural training. M. Kuhn and D. Weidemann. (eds.), (2010), Internationalization of the Social Sciences, Bielefeld: transcript

E-mail: Doris.Weidemann@fh-zwickau.de

Shujiro Yazawa is a professor of Sociology at Faculty of Social Innovation, Seijo University in Tokyo. Professor Yazawa's interest is Social Movement, Sociological Theory and Comparative sociology of information Society. His publications include 'Insurgents Against the Global Order' Berkeley Journal of Sociology, Vol.20, (1996), (with Manuel Castells and Anna Kiselyova), pp.21–59. 'Alberto Melucci e la Sociologia Japonese' in Luisa Leonini ed., Identita e Movementi Sociale in una Societa Planetaria, (2003), pp.184–194. 'Two Interpretations of Japanese Network Society' in Georgy Szell et al (ed.), European Social Integration—A Model for East Asia?' (2009), pp.239–252. He is a board member of British Journal of Sociology, Chinese Journal of Sociology and New Cultural Frontiers.

E-mail: syazawa@seijo.ac.jp

***ibidem*-Verlag**

Melchiorstr. 15

D-70439 Stuttgart

info@ibidem-verlag.de

www.ibidem-verlag.de
www.ibidem.eu
www.edition-noema.de
www.autorenbetreuung.de